Married and
How to Stay That Way

MARRIED
and How to
Stay That Way

by

Steve Carr

ACW Press
5501 N. 7th Ave. #502
Phoenix, AZ 85013

Married and How to Stay That Way
Copyright © 1998
Steve Carr
All rights reserved.

Cover design by Eric Walljasper
Page design by Steven R. Laube
Typeset using Electra 11pt. Designed in 1935 by William Addision Dwiggins, Electra has been a standard book typeface since its release because of its evenness of design and high legibility.

Unless otherwise noted, all Scripture verses are taken from the *Holy Bible,* New King James Version copyright © 1982 by Thomas Nelson Publishers. Used by permission.

Scripture quotations marked NIV are taken from the *Holy Bible,* New International Version, copyright © 1973, 1978, 1984 by International Bible Society. Used by permission of Zondervan Publishing House. All rights reserved.

Scripture quotations marked KJV are taken from the *Holy Bible,* King James Version.

Publisher's Cataloging-in-Publication
(Provided by Quality Books, Inc.)

Carr, Steve (Steven R.)
    Married and how to stay that way /by Steve Carr -- 1st ed.
    p. cm.
    ISBN 978-0-9656749-3-5

    1. Marriage. 2. Marital conflict. 3. Communication in marriage
    4. Marriage--Religious aspects.   I. Title

HQ734.C37 1998   646.7'8
                          QBI97-41372

Printed in the United States of America
Second printing, November 1998
Third printing, August 2001
Fourth printing, February 2004
Fifth Printing, March 2007

To obtain more copies please contact:
Steve Carr
PO Box 463
Arroyo Grande, CA 93421
(805) 489-9088
See the order form in the back of this book.

Dedication

I dedicate this book to my Lord and Savior Jesus Christ. The truths found within these pages are simply the application of His timeless truths. I also dedicate this book to all the couples who are struggling to find hope and practical direction for their marriage in the midst of a world that has so many conflicting messages.

About the Author

During the past twenty years Steve Carr has been the senior pastor of Calvary Chapel in Arroyo Grande, California. Before coming to his present ministry, he spent an additional eight years teaching Bible studies with Calvary Chapel of Costa Mesa, California under the ministry of Pastor Chuck Smith. Steve has been married for twenty-five years to his wife, Susan, and has raised two sons.

In addition, Steve writes a quarterly marriage publication, *Covenant Keepers*, that has an international circulation of over six hundred churches (translated into several languages and distributed in Central America, South America, Japan, India, and Africa). Back issues of these publications can be found on the internet at www.covenantkeepers.org.

Together Steve and Susan lead married couple retreats throughout the United States and abroad, bringing practical solutions to the problems couples struggle with as well as providing workshops to enhance their marital relationship.

Table of Contents

SECTION ONE
ESTABLISHING A FOUNDATION TO BUILD UPON

CHAPTER ONE: ARE YOU WILLING TO TAKE ACTION? 13
CHAPTER TWO: THE PURPOSE AND GOAL OF YOUR MARRIAGE 25
CHAPTER THREE: THE KEY TO REAL COMPANIONSHIP 37
CHAPTER FOUR: WHAT IS YOUR STANDARD OF TRUTH? 49
CHAPTER FIVE: UNDERSTANDING HOW TO LOVE 57

SECTION TWO
WHAT HINDERS YOU FROM BUILDING
COMPANIONSHIP & ONENESS WITH YOUR SPOUSE?

CHAPTER SIX: DON'T MISS THE ROOT OF THE PROBLEM 77
CHAPTER SEVEN: DO YOU HAVE REALISTIC EXPECTATIONS? 87
CHAPTER EIGHT: WHAT DO YOU NEED TO KNOW ABOUT CONFLICTS? ... 99
CHAPTER NINE: PRACTICAL STEPS TO RESOLVING CONFLICTS 109
CHAPTER TEN: HOW TO FULLY SOLVE A CONFLICT 129
CHAPTER ELEVEN: DEALING WITH A HARD HEART 143
CHAPTER TWELVE: FORGIVENESS THAT LASTS 153

SECTION THREE
KEYS TO BUILDING YOUR RELATIONSHIP

CHAPTER THIRTEEN: BUILDING SECURITY THROUGH TOTAL
   COMMITMENT 167
CHAPTER FOURTEEN: BUILDING YOUR RELATIONSHIP GOD'S WAY 175
CHAPTER FIFTEEN: BUILDING UNDERSTANDING, HONOR, AND RESPECT. 195
CHAPTER SIXTEEN: BUILDING YOUR COMMUNICATION 207
CHAPTER SEVENTEEN: BUILDING ROMANCE 225
CHAPTER EIGHTEEN: BUILDING YOUR SEXUAL RELATIONSHIP 237
CHAPTER NINETEEN: BUILDING SELF-DISCIPLINE 251
CHAPTER TWENTY: LOVE REKINDLED 263

APPENDIX A: WHAT IF YOUR SPOUSE REFUSES TO COOPERATE? 271
APPENDIX B: WHAT IF YOUR SPOUSE IS OUT OF CONTROL? 283

Acknowledgments

I would like to thank my wife, Susan, for the many afternoons and evenings she unselfishly gave up that I might pound my keyboard. She was as committed as I was to putting these truths into book form. I would have nothing to share with anyone without you. Thanks, Honey!

My sincere and heartfelt gratitude goes to Daylene Marshall for the many hours of editing that went into this manuscript. You have blessed my life incredibly. I could not have accomplished this without your assistance.

Preface

The book you are about to journey through was written out of an intense desire to help the many couples I have counseled over the years. I often felt that the short amount of time I had face-to-face with two hurting people was insufficient and I wanted to develop some biblical tools to send with them that would help to heal and strengthen their marriage relationship. So I began in a small way, writing my own worksheets for couples to take home and complete, seeking to help them identify the real problems and teaching them to apply the practical solutions found in God's Word. Over the years, *Married and How to Stay That Way* was developed from real life circumstances and from real people who struggle in their relationship. People like you and me.

A successful marriage is a tough job to accomplish. Yet, within God's Word you will see how to resolve those areas that tear you apart. He is our great Counselor; I only bring to you His truths and help you to understand His answers. This book addresses almost every aspect of marriage in detail. Within these pages you will come to understand God's plan and purpose for your marriage as well as discover His enabling power.

There is hope for your marriage. You will be able to say of one another, "This is my beloved, and this is my friend" (Song of Solomon 5:16). With all of my heart I pray that this book will strengthen and enhance your marriage.

Steve Carr
Arroyo Grande, CA

Due to the dual gender complexities inherent in the marriage relationship, the publisher chooses to avoid additional tedium to the reader by the prolonged use of "he or she" and "his or her." The publisher has therefore decided, where appropriate, to use the plural pronoun "they" or "their" to refer to a singular individual even though in some style manuals it is not considered grammatically correct.

ESTABLISHING A FOUNDATION TO BUILD UPON

When a contractor begins to build a house, he must first lay a solid foundation upon which to construct his building. The foundation is critical to the sturdiness and strength of the structure. Will the building stand the test of time and the storms that will come against that house, or will it fall? The entire house depends upon the structural integrity of this foundation.

I want to deal with five basic building blocks that are necessary to establish your marriage on a solid foundation. This critical groundwork will enable you to effectively handle all of the problems and trials that test your most important relationship. The storms of life will come and the winds of adversity will blow and beat on your home, but it will stand because your marriage relationship has been built on a sound foundation.

1

ARE YOU WILLING TO TAKE ACTION?

"If you are willing and obedient..." Is. 1:19

As you begin reading this book, your marriage is in one of two phases. The first category is typified by times in your relationship when the situation seems as though it will never change. Feelings of hopelessness and despair have become your companions, and you find yourself involved in a marriage relationship that is far from what you expected when you first recited your wedding vows. Everyday living with your spouse has become one of the most difficult things you have ever faced. Is there hope for your marriage? Can these feelings of despair and hopelessness be eliminated? Is there a way that both you and your spouse can come to agreement on the issues that plague you? Yes, there is! I invite you to begin one of the most important journeys you will ever take. By God's power and the life-giving principles in His Word, change is possible and you are about to discover how to do it.

There are others reading this book, however, who are merely looking to strengthen and enhance their marriage relationship. Their desire is a worthy pursuit because there is always a deeper and more intimate relationship waiting for the couple who diligently searches it out. As you understand more completely God's plan for your marriage, you will grow and build your relationship together.

In these first chapters, we will consider the primary goal as well as some of the foundational principles for marriage that are indispensable to building a lasting relationship. A clear understanding of these concepts will ignite a hope in your heart and provide the necessary tools to build your relationship. The illustration of building is appropriate because it is one that we can all relate to. Each of you has seen a house being built and can understand this analogy. A contractor who decides to build a house will always first take special consideration in laying a solid foundation. He does this to ensure that the building will stand all the internal pressures and external stresses that will come against the structure. If the walls of your marriage are crumbling at this moment under some difficult problems, you need to strengthen your foundation. If you have no significant problems and you simply want a closer relationship with your spouse, the principles you will learn will be like adding steel reinforcements to the already strong foundation of your marriage.

You may ask, "Where do I begin? What should I do to strengthen the foundation of my marriage? How do I begin to eliminate the despair and hopelessness facing me today?" Let me relate a story to you of a couple I once counseled. To protect their anonymity, I will call them Gary and Susan. Their story will illustrate one of the most fundamental building blocks for any marriage to grow. The principle conveyed in this chapter is critical to every other principle in this book. In fact, I'm reasonably sure that a similar conversation to some degree and at some time has occurred in your own marriage.

When I entered my office, Gary and Susan were sitting as far apart as space would allow within the room. They were both looking in opposite directions as I sat down at my desk. They hardly even looked at me. The obvious tension of silence told me there was serious trouble between them. This was Gary and Susan's first counseling appointment, so I asked them to begin by explaining their situation to me. Susan immediately began to cry as she started to speak. "I had so many hopes and dreams of what it would be like when I got married, but it has turned out so different. When we first married we had such a love between us. Now it seems all we do is fight and bicker over everything. I thought we had so many things in common when we started out, but all those things are gone. We are growing further and further apart every day, and we don't know what to do. What's wrong with us?"

I turned to Gary and asked him, "Do you see your relationship the same way?"

Gary began to nod his head in agreement and said, "Yes, that's about the size of it. We aren't real happy right now, but I don't think it's as bad as she says. We have some problems, but I believe we can work them out."

"Well then," Susan interrupted, "why haven't we worked them out? All you say to me is, 'We will work them out,' but nothing happens! Talk, talk, talk, that's all I hear. I'm sick of talk. I didn't even want to come today because I knew all we were going to do is talk some more."

I could see that Susan had a lot of pent-up anger and frustration over these long-term problems, so I stopped the conversation and assured them that I would require each of them to do much more than talk. I explained to Gary and Susan that talking was only the first step to real change, but the follow-through of action was even more important. I then asked them a question that I ask every first time couple who comes for counseling. "How would you rate yourself from 1 to 10 as to your willingness to take real practical action to change this marriage? A 10 would mean you are ready to do anything and everything that God requires of you to change your relationship. To rate yourself a 5 would mean you are somewhat willing, but you're very skeptical about the possibilities for change. To rate yourself a 1 would mean that you simply want out of the marriage, and you don't even want to be here today."

The answer to this question was quite revealing. They both rated themselves at an 8 to 9 on my scale. Even though they were experiencing great frustration, skepticism, and anger, this told me that they were both willing to take real action to change their relationship. I then began to explain why this attitude of willingness to take action was so important.

As you begin to read this book, I want to ask you the same question. How willing are you to make the practical changes necessary to build a strong relationship with your spouse? How would you rate yourself on a scale of 1 to 10? Your answer to this question is the key to how effective this book will be in bringing about real change in your marriage. Let me explain exactly why your willingness to take real practical action is so important.

WILLINGNESS IS THE KEY TO ALL CHANGE

For the last twenty-five years I have counseled many couples through their marital struggles, and I have come to realize that an attitude of willingness to take real action is essential. Partners must be willing to first sit down and talk, and then be willing to take practical action to reconcile the conflicts between them once and for all. Later, I will explain in great detail how to do this, but for now, understand that your willingness to take action is fundamental to beginning the work of building your relationship.

For years I have seen various couples with many different circumstances. For example, one couple came for counseling who had minor problems that could have been easily resolved, and yet, the marriage ended in separation and divorce. One time another couple with very serious problems came and I thought, *It will be a miracle if this marriage survives.* I then saw this couple have a dramatic change of heart and turn from their stubbornness, becoming willing to make the changes necessary to turn their marriage around. Their relationship went through a glorious transformation and the marriage was saved. For years as a young pastor, I struggled to understand why this would happen. Then one day it dawned on me that there was one dramatic difference; one couple was willing to talk and then act, and the other was not.

Ultimately I came to believe, that God can fix any marriage if He just has two willing hearts. This is what He looks for in a marriage, and when He finds it, He works miracles. It's not a question of God's willingness to do His work in your marriage, but of your willingness to let Him. It is much like the leper who came to Jesus and asked, *"Lord, if you are willing, You can make me clean. Then Jesus put out His hand and touched him, saying, 'I am willing; be cleansed' "* (Matt. 8:2, 3). Jesus demonstrated that He was more than willing to solve the problems of this leper. He is still ready, willing, and able to do His mighty works today. Are you willing to bring your marriage to Him and ask for help as this leper did, or will you hide your problems and resist taking action? Don't do as so many I have seen, who wait until they are ready to leave their spouse before finally deciding to take action. If you want to see His miracle-working power in your relationship, you must be willing, at all costs, to do whatever it takes as quickly as you can. The issues that are hindering the intimacy and friendship between you and your spouse will not go away by themselves. You must take action to deal with these issues.

Is this where your heart is right now? It must be if you want to see any real and lasting change in your relationship. This is the first step to building the life and marriage you long for. The Bible is absolutely clear on this point. Let's look at some further examples of how important willingness is to affecting real change:

1. Willingness determines the greatest change of all. Jesus ministered the truth of His Word to many in His day, but to no avail. They would not change and, as a result, could not experience the abundant life He desired to give them. They refused the greatest change of all—salvation and eternal life. Jesus put His finger directly on what caused them to turn His offer away. He said, *"You are not willing to come to Me that you might have life"* (John 5:40).

Jesus didn't talk about meaningless issues that had nothing to do with the problems of man. He went right to the heart of the matter. It was the unwillingness of men to simply come to Him that excluded them from the life and blessing He wanted to give. They were more willing to disobey Him and reject His Word than to come and humbly fall at His feet. Jesus could not do anything about this because it was the free choice of man exercised against His will.

This is what happened in the beginning when Adam and Eve willfully chose to rebel against God. God refused to force them to obey Him. He allowed them to make the choice to accept or reject Him and His commands. In the same manner today, God requires men and women to make a willful choice to surrender to Him. He would not force Adam and Eve to stay in fellowship with Him, nor force them to return to Him.

Likewise, He will not force anyone to do His will today. Every individual must willingly choose to come into fellowship with the Father. God makes this clear even in the last call made to man in the Bible. *"And the Spirit and the bride say, Come! And let him who hears say, Come! And let him who thirsts come. And whoever desires, let him take the water of life freely"* (Rev. 22:17).

Don't exclude yourself from the blessings of God because of a hard and unwilling heart. The Father wants to bestow His blessings upon you and your marriage today! Ask Him for a willing heart to take the action necessary to change your marital relationship. This is where you must begin.

2. Willingness was the key to God's provision for the children of Israel. The Old Testament reveals the many problems and trials of the Jewish people. God spoke through the prophets in an attempt to change His people and to communicate the means of how this work could be done. The prophet Isaiah spoke directly of the essential ingredient necessary for real change. He declared what the people had to do to see God's blessing and provision for their nation: *"If you are willing and obedient, you shall eat the good of the land; but if you refuse and rebel, you shall be devoured by the sword, for the mouth of the Lord has spoken"* (Is. 1:19, 20).

Isaiah gave the Jewish people a simple and direct way to be successful and build their nation. If they would just be *willing and obedient,* they would be divinely protected and enjoy the fruits of the land. Again, God put His finger squarely on the most important issue. This willingness of heart to take action and obey God's Word was the key. In fact, this attitude, along with their obedient action, was the catalyst that would enable growth as well as blessing to continue. God is also just as clear about the alternative. If they refused and rebelled, certain destruction would result.

This is God's word to anyone who desires His blessing and aid in life. Be willing and obedient! If you desire God's blessing in your marriage, you must follow His plan and His commands. Scripture is clear on this issue. Wherever you will obey and honor Him, there will be peace. But where you disobey and rebel, there will be tribulation and anguish. God declares that He will render *"eternal life to those who by patient continuance in doing good seek for glory, honor, and immortality; but to those who are self-seeking and do not obey the truth, but obey unrighteousness — indignation and wrath, tribulation and anguish, on every soul of man who does evil, of the Jew first and also of the Greek; but glory, honor, and peace to everyone who works what is good"* (Rom. 2:7-10).

Remember when Jesus stood and wept over the city of Jerusalem? He longed to bless His people, even though He knew they were about to reject Him! Remember what He said to them? *"O Jerusalem, Jerusalem, the one who kills the prophets and stones those who are sent to her! How often I wanted to gather your children together, as a hen gathers her chicks under her wings, but you were not willing"* (Matt. 23:37). He was so willing to give to His people, but they were not willing to receive. God's heart was breaking because of the rebellious attitude He saw in their hearts of stone. Their unwillingness caused them to lose out on all He wanted to give them. Do you see how critical this attitude is to a person, a nation, or even a marriage? Your attitude will either open wide the door to God's storehouse of blessings or slam it shut.

3. Willingness is the key to keeping your marriage together. When the apostle Paul sought to answer the questions of the Corinthian church about marriage and divorce, notice what he identified as the key to staying together with even a non-Christian spouse. He said, *"If any brother has a wife who does not believe, and she is willing to live with him, let him not divorce her. And a woman who has a husband who does not believe, if he is willing to live with her, let her not divorce him"* (1 Cor. 7:12, 13).

Again, we see that willingness is the key, and in this case, within the context of marriage. The apostle knew this attitude was the key to solving any problem, no matter how difficult; even if the marriage partner was not a Christian (because a non-Christian would probably disagree over many more issues than a Christian spouse would). Yet, if the non-Christian partner is willing to remain in the marriage, even that couple could live together peaceably.

If you have a Christian spouse, my question to you is no different. Are you willing to live with your spouse, and if so, are you seeking peace with him or her? Are you willing to resolve the conflicts with your mate and build a new and better relationship? Are you willing to be obedient and take the action needed to make the necessary changes? Or do you just want to talk?

Your spouse longs to see this attitude in your life; to see and hear that you are willing to live in peace. You also want to see this attitude in your partner, which is a very natural desire. However, don't wait for your loved one to demonstrate this willingness. Why don't *you* take the first step to start the process?

What is Your First Step?

The first step will always entail action. To have a willing heart is important, but it is not enough to change anything. You must *do* something if you are truly willing to see change in your relationship, and taking action is proof of that. For each couple this will be a little different. Let me illustrate.

It was necessary for Gary and Susan to do more than rehash the problems over and over again. They needed to take very practical and specific actions in order to resolve their conflicts. Susan would not have been satisfied with anything less than this on that first day of counseling. Yet, for another couple who doesn't talk at all about their conflicts, the first step would be to verbally admit to each other that there is a problem. For the couple that is separated, the first step might be for one to write a letter or make a phone call to communicate their desire for reconciliation.

Your first step will always be action of some kind. Action is the other half of Isaiah's command. *"If you are willing and obedient,"* you must do something! Don't wait for the other person, you take the initiative. Humble yourself and ask for his or her forgiveness. Take that hard first step and admit your faults. Make the phone call or write the letter.

Scripture constantly encourages each of us to do this. No matter what the issue, each of us must, at some point, take action on what we know is right. James says, *"Be doers of the word, and not hearers only, deceiving yourselves"* (James 1:22). Self-deception will cause you to talk or listen to your mate, and then do nothing. Don't be the person who fails to act, and therefore hinders the change that's needed in your marriage.

Remember, Jesus told the parable of the two builders. One man built his house on the sand, and the other built his house on the rock, and *"the rain descended, the floods came, and the winds blew and beat"* on both of these houses; one house stood and the other fell (Matt. 7:24-27). Jesus explained why this occurred. He was illustrating the fundamental difference in the way people respond to what He teaches. He said, *"Whoever hears these sayings of Mine, and does them, I will liken him to a wise man who built his house on the rock"* (Matt. 7:24). One took action and obeyed what He taught, and the other man did not. Which man's example will you follow? Will you only hear and take no action, or will you wisely do what you know is right? This will determine whether your marriage is built on a sound foundation, or whether it will fail to stand against the elements that seek to destroy it.

If you want to build a lasting marriage, then take your first step. Declare to your spouse today that you are willing to work at your marriage and begin to do whatever God requires to reconcile your differences. Tell your spouse that you want to begin to build your relationship again. Often, this first step of verbalizing your intent to change is what begins to soften your mate's heart and initiates a similar response.

Then take action against the things you see wrong in your life. This will demonstrate to your spouse that you really mean business. Your spouse needs to see you dealing with your faults instead of only trying to point the finger. What faults am I referring to? In each chapter, I will attempt to deal with the key issues that build or destroy a marriage. Take these truths and apply them to your life.

What happens when you make the choice to become willing to obey God? A dramatic change will begin to take place in your personal life and in your relationship with God. The closer you draw to Him as a person, the more you will experience His abundant life, and His love will begin to motivate you to further action. This is a blessing God will bestow upon you no matter what your spouse does. Take this opportunity to go forward and grow in your relationship with Christ, because doing so will give you the strength and the peace to deal with all that lies ahead. Your personal growth will also be a tremendous positive influence on your mate.

I must say, however, that *your* willingness to take action will not be enough to solve all the problems in your relationship. Realistically speaking, it does take *two willing people* to completely change a marriage. Your willing heart and your action can only do so much. You can't change someone who willfully refuses to work at the marriage. It is only when two people wholeheartedly begin to deal with the problems that changes begin to occur. This is the key that determines the success or failure of any marriage. Even in a stable marriage, *willingness to take action* will determine whether or not the marriage relationship stagnates or flows.

Therefore, let me ask you some questions:

1. Are you willing to come to Him, fully surrender, and receive His abundant life?
2. Are you willing to let the Word of God teach you how to respond correctly to your spouse?
3. Are you willing to do more than talk?
4. Are you willing to do what God requires of you?
5. Are you willing to deal with yourself and your own faults first?

If you have answered *no* to any of these questions, it will impede your progress toward any changes you want to see in your relationship. Reluctance in any area is like putting up one more road block to change. Will you stop right now and ask God for the change of heart needed regarding any of the above questions? You may be very angry and hard at the moment, not even sure if you want to try to work at building your marriage. So let's look for a moment at how you get a willing heart if you don't have one.

How to Obtain a Willing Heart

You may have to start by first asking God to give you a willingness to be made willing. He can do that too. Ask Him to persuade you and convince you by His Holy Spirit that it is possible to reconcile and build your marriage. Remember, He is able to do anything if you are willing to let Him work in your heart! Paul said, *"Now to Him who is able to do exceedingly abundantly above all that we ask or think, according to the power that works in us"* (Eph. 3:20). Ask Him to begin to work in you, to soften your heart, and to make you willing to act.

This prayer is an act of surrender to the Lord in which you give yourself up to Him to do His work in you. As you give yourself to Him, He breathes a willingness into you to do all that He requires. In the early church when the believers in Jerusalem were in financial need, the apostle Paul asked all the churches to contribute financially. Many of those churches that gave were hurting financially themselves and were suffering greatly. What caused these churches to give so sacrificially? Paul attributed the source of their willingness to God's unmerited favor: *"Moreover, brethren, we make known to you the grace of God bestowed on the churches of Macedonia: that in a great trial of affliction the abundance of their joy and their deep poverty abounded in the riches of their liberality. For I bear witness that according to their ability, yes, and beyond their ability, they were freely willing, imploring us with much urgency that we would receive the gift and the fellowship of the ministering to the saints. And...not as we had hoped, but first gave themselves to the Lord, and then to us by the will of God"* (2 Cor. 8:1-5).

Their sacrificial giving began when the grace of God began working in their hearts after they first gave themselves to the Lord. When you surrender and give yourself to Him, God can and will work in your heart that which is *"well pleasing in His sight"* (Heb. 13:21). *"For it is God who works in you both to will and to do of His good pleasure"* (Phil. 2:13). Literally, anything is possible for a big God. If you surrender yourself to Him, He will give you the desire to do what is right, and then bestow the ability to do it. What more could you ask?

Is Change Really Possible?

What God has promised, He is also able to perform. God has always been in the business of restoration. He loves to fix broken people, nations, and yes, marriages. Take the nation Israel, for example. When the nation refused Isaiah's promise and warning, it turned away from God. The result was just as Isaiah had predicted; great destruction came upon the land, the people were overrun by their enemies, and finally they were taken into captivity. Their crops were eaten by locusts and caterpillars, and their cities were reduced to ashes. Everything seemed to go wrong for them. Yet the prophets of God told them that if they would return to the Lord, He would restore the years that the locust and caterpillar had eaten. He promised to give them beauty to replace the ashes all around them (Joel 2:25; Is. 61:3). The people did return to their God, and just as He promised, He performed His Word. He brought them back into their fertile land and restored them to their rightful place.

You may be looking at your marriage today and see nothing but a destroyed relationship lying in ashes. Or maybe it's not that bad, and you just need your marriage tuned-up a little to renew the spark of excitement. God is able to restore you and your marriage according to His promise. If He did it for a nation of thousands of people, is He not able to do it with just two? Isaiah declared, *"Surely the arm of the Lord is not too short to save"* (Is. 59:1). He is surely able!

God is described in Scripture as the *"builder of all things"* (Heb. 3:4). The church is characterized as His building or temple (Matt. 16:18; 1 Peter 2:5). Your individual life is also referred to as His building or temple (1 Cor. 6:19). Your home and family are described as a structure that can be built up or pulled down (Prov. 14:1). God is the master architect, and He has a plan for constructing a successful marriage for you and your spouse. He desires to richly build your life, your home, and your marriage to be a glorious testimony of His power and grace. Therefore, as I use this analogy of building as it relates to your marriage, always remember that *"unless the Lord builds the house, they labor in vain who build it"* (Ps. 127:1). Let's continue to lay the foundation so that we can get to building!

WILLINGNESS TO ACT

As I said earlier, don't wait for your spouse to take action. You take the first step to work on your own life. This is the only thing that will bring the happiness you long for. Jesus explained that obedience to the truth you know always brings about happiness. He made this clear when He spoke to His disciples that last night before His crucifixion. He said, *"If you know these things, happy are you if you do them"* (John 13:17).

If you long for real happiness in your relationship, then take the actions that you know are right. Begin with these:

Actions To Take

1. Ask God to bring you into a closer relationship with Him.
2. Ask God for a willing heart to receive His counsel and commands.
3. Ask God for a willingness to hear what your spouse has to say to you.
4. Ask God to help you begin working on your own faults.
5. Ask God to begin working in your spouse to develop this same willingness.
6. Take the first step that is appropriate in your particular relationship.

Now let's go on to the next part of the foundation of your relationship. It will give you an overall picture of your marriage and will enable you to see the goal for your entire relationship.

Group Discussion Questions

1. How did your unwillingness of heart hinder you from coming to Christ?
2. Without giving any names or information that would identify the couple, give an example of a marriage you have seen destroyed because one or both partners were unwilling to change.
3. Describe where you have been unwilling and stubborn and how this attitude has affected your marriage relationship.

2

THE PURPOSE AND GOAL OF YOUR MARRIAGE

"She is your companion..." Mal. 2:14

Lisa was a very intelligent woman who worked for a large company as head trainer for all new employees. She was a capable woman with excellent verbal skills and an inviting personality that radiated excitement and energy. Her husband, Mike, was also at the top of his profession, but was a very quiet and reserved man who had trouble expressing his love for his wife. The two had only been married for a few months when I first began to counsel them. After our initial greeting, I inquired as to why they had come for counseling.

"Steve," Lisa said abruptly, "I'm a person who likes to get to the bottom line quickly. The problem is that Mike wants a housekeeper, a baby-sitter, a second income, and a mistress, but he doesn't want a wife or a companion. And he especially doesn't want me to have any personal opinions of my own. In fact, I think Mike would like me to be there for him when he wants me to do something for him, and then disappear the rest of the time."

I turned to look at Mike only to see his eyes glaring at Lisa with anger and disgust. He answered quickly, "Well, isn't that what a wife is supposed to do? Isn't that your job, to take care of all of those things around the house? Aren't you supposed to be my help-mate? That's what the Bible says, Steve."

Lisa interrupted, "Yeah, but I'm not your little servant girl to jump when you say jump. I'm supposed to be your friend and lover, and I'm neither. Mike, do you realize that we rarely communicate or do things together like we did when we first dated? That's why I keep telling you I feel so alone in this marriage."

It was obvious there were some very serious misconceptions in their relationship. Therefore, I proceeded to ask Mike and Lisa if they were willing to do whatever God required in order to change their relationship. They both responded positively, so I began to ask them some further questions. "Do you know what the purpose of marriage is? Do you know why God created marriage in the first place, and what His ultimate goal is for your relationship?" They both looked at me and shook their heads no. I told them that this was where we had to begin because it was the most obvious misconception I could see from our conversation.

Have you ever stopped to wonder why you are married to your spouse? What is God's ultimate design and purpose for you being together? Why did you marry the person you are living with, and what was the goal you had in mind at that time? These are important questions you must answer if you sincerely want to build a lasting marriage. If you fail to understand the purpose for which marriage was created, you will be aiming at the wrong target and you will surely miss the bull's-eye. It was obvious that Mike and Lisa didn't know what the target was or how to hit it. Mike especially had missed the point of why he was even married. He saw marriage as more of a contract between them, where he got to order his wife around instead of having love, partnership, and a meaningful relationship with her.

I believe that failing to understand the purpose of marriage is the most fundamental reason why couples are so unsatisfied in their relationship. Many couples simply don't have a daily target to shoot for and therefore become confused as to what the essential priorities should be in the time they spend together. They can't see the overall goal as to why they are married. Without this goal clearly in mind, a couple will not detect the actions that ultimately and slowly ruin their relationship.

I have found that people get married for many different reasons, some good and some bad. Some people have told me that they were so anxious to get out from under the control of their parents that the first person to show interest and love was the person he or she married. One woman told me she simply didn't want to work anymore. She was tired of struggling to provide for her children as a single parent. A man made a similar disclosure to me that he married his wife because he just wanted someone to take care of his children. Yes, each loved and cared about the person he or she married, but these other reasons sometimes took precedence. Others have told me they married because they sincerely loved the person. Even though love is a great motive for marriage, it's not the purpose of your marriage. It's only the means to achieving God's purpose for a couple. Let's look at what God says is the purpose and goal that He desires for your relationship. This is the second foundation stone of a marriage built to last.

What is the Purpose of Your Marriage?

What I am about to explain concerning the purpose of marriage is by no means the only purpose for marriage, but it is the most fundamental one. Without this purpose all others will fail to be achieved. Therefore, let's start by looking at the purpose God had in mind when He created Adam and Eve.

In the beginning, after God had created Adam, He said, *"It is not good that man should be alone; I will make him a helper comparable to him"* (Gen. 2:18). So He created a comparable companion for him that could be his helper. The word *comparable* means one who is a counterpart or the other side of a matched pair. The woman was created to be the perfect complement to her husband, like two matched gloves, one the counterpart of the other.

It is also important to note that if God created a helper, this must have meant that Adam needed help. But this is also true of woman. It is not good for her to be alone either. Each of us can attest to the truth that it is not good to live alone and that we need help in many areas of our life. Your spouse is to be a companion to help you in the weak areas of your life; one who knows you better than anybody else, a counterpart that matches your needs in a very special way. Your mate is to be a person who can minister to and encourage you like no other person can because he or she knows you and is committed to you in love.

God went on to state the goal of this marital union between Adam and Eve. He said, *"Therefore a man shall leave his father and mother and be joined to his wife, and they shall become one flesh"* (Gen. 2:24). Oneness, then, was God's purpose and plan for them, and He fully desired to bring this about in their lives. He wanted them to find a special and unique oneness spiritually, emotionally, intellectually, and physically. This oneness was to be found only between them and would completely fulfill God's purpose for them and their relationship. This one-flesh relationship was also the result of a process; they would become one flesh.

Likewise, when Jesus was asked by the Pharisees if it was lawful to divorce, He brought them back to this same fundamental truth concerning marriage. He said, *"Have you not read that He who made them at the beginning 'made them male and female.' For this reason a man shall leave his father and mother and be joined to his wife, and the two shall become one flesh. So then, they are no longer two but one flesh. Therefore what God has joined together, let not man separate"* (Matt. 19:4-6). This was an obvious reproof to those men that they had not been reading the Scripture, nor had they sought to determine their actions based upon these teachings. Jesus took them back to God's original desire for all married couples based on His clearly stated purpose. He had created marriage to bring about oneness between two people, not division and divorce.

Paul the apostle also quoted this same passage in his great teaching on marriage in the New Testament. After explaining the responsibilities of the husband and wife, he reminded each party of this fundamental purpose, that they are to be *"joined...and the two shall become one flesh"* (Eph. 5:31).

It stands to reason that if this passage is repeated so often in Scripture that it is God's ultimate purpose for marriage. It is clear that He wants to take two people who have committed themselves to each other, join them together, and make them one. Oneness is, therefore, His ultimate purpose for marriage.

God further defined oneness by a word that explains the means of how this unity will be accomplished: *companionship*. Notice how God uses this word when He speaks about marriage and His hatred of divorce, which destroys His ultimate goal for two people. He said through the prophet Malachi, *"the Lord has been witness between you and the wife of your youth, with whom you have dealt treacherously; yet she is your companion and your wife by covenant"* (Mal. 2:14). God declares the wife to be a loving companion who should be dealt with in a respectful manner. Solomon similarly referred to a marriage partner as a companion when he warned his son about an adulterous woman. He told his son that wisdom would deliver him from the immoral woman, *"from the seductress who flatters with her words, who forsakes the companion of her youth, and forgets the covenant of her God"* (Prov. 2:16, 17). The word *companion* means one whom you are knit or bound together with; it describes oneness. The Bible explains that this process of knitting together should take place when two believers love each other. Paul prayed for the Colossian church *"that their hearts may be encouraged being knit together in love..."* (Col. 2:2). If this can take place between any two believers, how much more should it occur between a man and wife who have given and pledged themselves to companionship with each other? This is what marriage is all about. God taking a man and a woman and knitting their hearts together in the most intimate companionship that could possibly exist between two people.

Even as God has called you into fellowship and companionship with himself, He desires you to find this same oneness with your spouse. This is the great mystery Paul spoke of when he related the marriage relationship to the relationship between Christ and the church (Eph. 5:32). Don't miss the work of this mystery worked out in your marriage!

If this is truly God's purpose for your marriage, you need to look honestly at your entire relationship and determine where you are growing more together in your oneness and companionship and where you are growing apart. Determine what things you are doing that are promoting God's purpose for you and what things are destroying it. The worst that can happen to a couple is to be married for years and not find the oneness, companionship, and intimacy that God intends. Yet this is the condition in which so many couples find their marriages today. They are joined as one flesh but they are isolated, separated, and lonely after spending years together. This ought not to be! If this is the state of your relationship at the moment, here is where to begin.

Start by taking an inventory of your relationship by considering the various actions you take toward your spouse. These actions reveal what your real priorities are and whether or not companionship is truly your goal. Taking this inventory will also show you where you need to get to work in your relationship; that is, what changes need to be made. You must consider your entire relationship from your spiritual relationship, to your sexual relationship, and everything in between, and judge how it relates to your oneness and companionship. Let's take an inventory right now. After each of the actions that are listed, rate yourself from 1 to 10 (10 meaning very satisfied):

1. Spiritual issues.
   - Do you pray with your spouse about the personal issues in your life?
   - Do you pray with your spouse about your marriage on a regular basis?
   - Do you go to church and sit with each other on a weekly basis?
   - Do you talk about the things you have learned from the sermon later that day?
   - Do you talk over the things you are learning in your personal reading of Scripture or from a book about the Bible?
   - Do you serve others together? As Sunday School teachers? Edifying others? Giving of your time to help others in practical ways?

2. Communication issues.
   - Do you talk over your day with each other when you gather together in the evening?
   - Do you freely share your opinions and ideas with your spouse?
   - Do you regularly give encouragement, and can you also receive it from your spouse?
   - Do you make future plans together and can you make decisions together?
   - Do you share your hopes, fears, hurts, and goals with each other?
   - Do you have any mutual recreation that you do together in which you communicate? Walking, biking, working out at a gym, etc.
   - Do you go shopping together and enjoy just being together?
   - Do you have a weekly date night?
   - Do you daily verbalize your love to your spouse?

♦ Do you do chores around the house together?
♦ Do you write cards or love notes to each other?

3. <u>Emotional issues</u>.
   ♦ Do you share your deepest emotions with each other?
   ♦ Do you give and receive emotional support to and from each other?
   ♦ Do you have the freedom to laugh and cry with each other?
   ♦ Do you accept your emotional differences?

4. <u>Physical and sexual issues</u>.
   ♦ Do you give thoughtful gifts periodically to your spouse just to say "I love you"?
   ♦ Do you take thoughtful actions just to say "I love you"?
   ♦ Do you serve your mate when your help is requested?
   ♦ Do you, in a non-sexual way, touch and hold each other on a daily basis?
   ♦ Do you approach each other regularly for sexual relations, and are your advances received favorably?
   ♦ Do you express real affection while engaged in sexual relations, or is it just a physical act with little emotion?

Each of these actions is a means by which you can promote oneness and companionship. If you are unwilling or unresponsive in any of these issues, you will be missing an important sphere of companionship with your spouse. This inventory is not intended to discourage you, but to help you determine where you need to take action. As you do, you will naturally be drawn more and more into companionship, friendship, and the relationship you desire.

How Does Companionship Occur?

Let me give you an analogy that will help to illustrate how companionship occurs in your relationship. Remember I explained earlier that the Hebrew word for *companionship* literally means to be knit together with another person? Companionship within marriage is, therefore, like knitting a beautiful sweater as you choose to daily intertwine your lives together. Every time you make the choice to take one of the actions in the inventory above, it will be like knitting one stitch in your sweater. As you daily choose companionship over independence and selfishness, a beautiful design will begin to appear in your relationship. But knitting requires careful attention and a willingness to devote lots of time and work to accomplish the task set before you. You must make companionship the priority of your daily life together. This will ensure that the beautiful design God has intended for your marriage will be fully realized.

Likewise, every time you choose independence and selfishness toward your spouse, it's like undoing a stitch in your sweater. This is why a couple can spend many years of their life together and then confess to me in counseling they have nothing of the relationship they once had together. They are strangers living independent lives, simply existing in the same house. The reason for their lonely existence is that they have not been choosing to knit their lives together and have completely missed the ultimate purpose for their marriage. Don't make this same mistake!

Which of these two actions are occurring in your marriage? Are you choosing by the priorities you have established to make oneness and companionship your ultimate goal? Are you knitting your lives together every day by the choices you are making to be together? Or, are you unraveling any progress you have made by living independently from each other? Only you know, and only you can change it. Make the choice for companionship today.

What Keeps You From Companionship?

This is an important question to consider because it is essential for you to understand what is hindering your companionship. The reasons why couples fail to build companionship with each other are simply the same reasons why we as individuals refuse companionship with God. Remember, Paul made a direct comparison between the marriage relationship and our union with Christ (Eph. 5:32). You don't have to look far to understand why couples fail in this endeavor of companionship. Let me give you three of the most important reasons:

1. Some individuals willfully choose to be independent and aloof. Jesus said this was the reason that the Pharisees refused companionship with Him. *"You are not willing to come to Me that you may have life"* (John 5:40). Likewise, I have found that some individuals just don't care to be a friend and companion to their spouse. They only want their spouse around when it suits them or when they selfishly want something. This is a sad situation that can only be changed by the independent partner.

2. Some individuals choose to be critical and combative. As you read the Gospels, it is obvious that the Pharisees always wanted to pick a fight with Jesus. They constantly criticized everything He did or said. Their attitudes and actions clearly destroyed any opportunity for friendship and companionship to occur between them and Jesus. Yet Jesus sought them out. He went to some of their houses to eat, but in their

hearts they were at war with Him. In my experience as a counselor, I have observed many individuals who have the same attitude toward their marriage partner. The constant verbal combat and criticism that is hurled back and forth daily only succeeds in driving a couple far from intimacy and companionship.

3. Some individuals simply choose other priorities. The Bible teaches that when you don't aim at correct priorities, you are sure to miss the mark. Paul taught this principle when he wrote to Timothy about the most important concern of the Christian life: *"The purpose of the commandment is love from a pure heart...from which some, having strayed, have turned aside to idle talk"* (1 Tim. 1:5, 6). The word *strayed* in this verse means to not aim at or to miss the mark. Paul was teaching that if anyone fails to aim at the purpose of God's commandment, which is love, this individual is missing the mark and God's ultimate design for the Christian life. In other words, love should be the foremost priority of your heart. It should naturally motivate you to obey God's commands. If this is not the case, we are not aiming at what is most important and this will eventually turn our Christian walk into idle talk, mere lip service.

The same is true for your marriage. Loving companionship with your spouse must be the highest priority of your relationship or your words of love are meaningless. If you fail to aim at companionship as your number one priority and the ultimate purpose of your marriage, you are sure to miss the mark of God's best for your marriage. Let me give you an illustration to further explain.

Imagine with me for a moment that your marriage is a big target. The purpose of having a bull's-eye on the target is so you will know where to set your aim. Companionship, which results in oneness, is the bull's-eye. Your aim is determined by the priorities you set and the actions that you take to fulfill them. If you get side-tracked and allow other priorities to take first place, you will fail at achieving oneness and your marriage will suffer.

What other priorities am I referring to? Your job, your children, your material possessions, or your personal pursuits are just a few. These are important priorities too, but they can never take precedence over God's ultimate purpose of companionship with your spouse. If you are wondering what is missing in your marriage relationship, look no further; companionship is the most important thing missing. Other things have taken priority, and your love relationship with each other has been sacrificed. Determine what these other priorities are right now and move with your spouse back to the bull's eye. Don't miss the mark of God's ultimate purpose for your relationship.

To hit the mark you must keep your eye on it. Companionship must remain your focus. You must also regularly check to see if you are hitting the bull's-eye. The companionship issues I listed earlier are a good way to see if you are hitting the target and how often.

I remember one couple that received this checklist. After looking at it for a moment they announced, "We only do one thing on this list together. Is there any hope for us?" A sudden fear came over them both and they immediately wanted to know what was going to keep them together until they could begin to build companionship into their lives. It was a very good question. What does keep you together while you attempt to build the oneness and the companionship that your marriage needs? Many times both partners are not always ready at the same time to make a radical change toward companionship, and therefore, the transition occurs very slowly. What holds you together during this transition period?

THE COVENANT

In both of the passages I have referred to, God uses the word *covenant* in direct association with companionship. *"She is your companion and your wife by covenant"* (Mal. 2:14). Proverbs 2:17 refers to the immoral woman as one *"who forsakes the companion of her youth, and forgets the covenant of her God."*

The covenant you have made before God is what holds you together and gives you the necessary time to work out the differences and build companionship. Without this commitment many couples would give up and bail out of their marriage before the changes could even take place. As I mentioned earlier, sometimes both parties in a marriage are not ready to change, or one person is rather slow to change. The commitment of the covenant acts as a cement to hold a couple together until other spiritual, emotional, and physical bonding can be established.

Remember the vows you said to each other on your wedding day? You made a promise, a covenant before God to be your mate's companion so long as you both should live. God expects you to keep this covenant because you made it before Him. He expects you to see its binding nature and work to fulfill your end of that commitment.

Why? Because it pleases Him that you would sincerely purpose in your heart to keep your commitment to your spouse. The motivation to honor your vows is what will enable you to do what it takes to build the companionship and relationship necessary to prosper in your marriage.

The motivation to please God is a much higher one than simply to please your mate. You need this higher motivation because when things are not going well in your marriage, you usually have little motivation to please or give to your spouse. A person is usually dominated by feelings in circumstances like this and retreats from his or her mate; ultimately choosing to only please self. Sometimes people seek to please themselves so much, they choose to just get out of the marriage. Yet, when you surrender to Christ, and when you choose to please Him first, He enables you to work at your marriage with real steadfastness and zeal. The covenant you have made before God, the covenant of companionship, is the binding force in your heart that keeps you there long enough to see the changes you desire.

Did you know that a biblical covenant is the most binding agreement known to man? In Old Testament times a covenant was made by taking a calf and cutting it into two pieces and walking between the parts while stating verbally the covenant or pledge. The death of the animal signified that the covenant was a commitment to be kept under the penalty of death. You can see how binding a covenant was in a biblical context by reading Jeremiah 34:8-22. God said, "[Those who have] *transgressed My covenant, who have not performed the words of the covenant which they made before Me...I will give them into the hand of their enemies...Their dead bodies shall be for meat for the birds of heaven and the beasts of the earth*" (vv. 18, 20).

God always intended the marriage covenant to be binding until the natural death of one of the partners. Jesus said, "*What God has joined together, let not man separate*" (Matt. 19:6). He made it this way so that people would not seek a way out of their marriages or explore some loophole in the agreement, but would instead seek a solution to the conflicts that divide them. The covenant you have made before God is the best reason to stay committed to your marriage and will provide the time necessary to work out the conflicts. Make a personal commitment in your own heart today not to seek a way out of your marriage, and commit yourself to resolving the conflicts between you. Commit yourself to being a companion to your spouse by the grace of God.

But what happens if your spouse doesn't respond, or continues to use or abuse you? Are there exceptions to this total commitment? Yes, but I will cover those questions in some of the last chapters of the book. But for now, give yourself totally to being the loving companion you have pledged to be. Give your spouse the time needed to respond to your love and new actions. Begin to take action using the inventory list (page

29) and see what happens. Don't wait for your spouse to be a companion to you. Remember, you pledged *your* companionship when you took your marriage vows. Therefore, you start taking the action God requires. Then see if there is not a new look of wonder or delight in your mate's eye.

I have seen many couples make radical changes once they have realized that God has called them to this covenant of companionship. They have acknowledged where they were failing, turned around, and have walked in the opposite direction. They had the power, motivation, and understanding to make this radical turnaround. Do you have this same power and motivation, or are you wondering at this moment if you can really change this dramatically? As you read the next chapter, you will understand why I believe anyone can be a companion and have an exciting marriage in which your spouse is truly your companion. You have the same opportunity to have this kind of marriage as anyone else. If this is what you want, begin with these actions.

Actions To Take

1. Ask God to show you where you are living independently and selfishly in your marriage right now.
2. Examine the inventory list and determine where you need to get to work.
3. Take at least one of the actions today.
4. Is there anyone you have more companionship with other than your spouse? Is there any family member, friend, or pursuit that has taken the priority over your spouse? Choose now to put your spouse first again.

Group Discussion Questions

1. Discuss and give examples of situations where you have not understood the design and purpose of some appliance or tool. How did this make you feel? Did you become frustrated in this circumstance? If you now realize after reading this chapter that you were unclear as to God's purpose and design for your marriage, can you see how this misunderstanding could frustrate your relationship? Discuss this with the group.
2. What do you believe are the biggest hindrances to a couple finding real companionship? What are the biggest hindrances in your relationship?
3. Discuss how the life commitment and covenant made with your spouse has been a strength to your marriage.

3

THE KEY TO REAL COMPANIONSHIP

"The fruit of the Spirit is love..." Gal. 5:22

It was the first time Calvin and Diane had ever come for counseling in their entire Christian walk. They never had a need for counseling before because they had always dealt with their problems quickly, but recently they had both begun to accumulate a number of issues that had now built up between them. They were quick to point the finger at each other as the principle cause of their marital problems.

"Something has changed between us," Calvin said. "We used to deal easily with these conflicts, but now we are at each other's throats constantly. She jumps on me for some little thing, and I snap right back at her. We both feel spiritually dead inside. All the motivation to work things out seems to be gone. It's like I have no power or love to even do what I know is right. Something is wrong, but I don't know what it is."

When Calvin finished speaking, all I could think about was his statement that they both sensed such a deadness in their lives. I thought to myself that this was an appropriate place to begin. I proceeded to ask if either of them had any devotional time studying the Scriptures or a personal time of prayer. Calvin looked past me and said, "Well, not much."

"What does that mean?" I asked. "Once a week, once a month, or none at all?" Calvin began to squirm in his chair a little.

"Well, it means none at all. I haven't had any time to really sit down to read my Bible in quite a while, and as for prayer...well, we pray at dinner."

At that moment Diane spoke up. "Yeah, but we don't do that much anymore either. He used to pray with me almost every morning before he went off to work, but we've been fighting so much we just don't feel like it. Steve, we're so distant. Something is wrong with us."

I then asked, "How often do you go to church?"

Calvin groaned again. "Not very often lately."

I asked Diane the same questions and received very similar answers.

I stopped my interview and said, "I can tell you the first thing that needs to change before anything else will, and that's your personal relationship with the Lord. This is the first and most obvious problem I see hindering your relationship. You both need to return to your first love before the love in your marriage has a chance to be rekindled. You need to right your relationship with Him first, and then you'll be able to deal correctly in your relationship with each other."

The problem with Calvin and Diane is very common. They both had strayed from their personal relationship with Christ, and the results were obvious and down-right heartbreaking. Both lacked the love and motivation to reconcile the conflicts between them, and neither was doing anything to build their relationship at all. They were simply existing with each other, living under the same roof with a relationship that had shriveled up. Theirs was not a marriage that was being built to last, but one that was destined for greater problems. Before they could love each other again, they needed to be filled with the love of Christ and the life that only He can give. This is where the *motivation* to change comes from and the desire to put something into the marriage, instead of just taking from each other and seeking our own rights. To have a marriage that is growing and increasing in love, you personally must be growing and increasing in your love relationship with Christ.

The natural result of drawing closer to Christ is that you will naturally draw closer to each other. The intimacy of your love relationship with Christ will of necessity overflow into your marriage simply because you are filled with the Holy Spirit. *"The fruit of the Spirit is love, joy, peace, longsuffering, kindness, goodness, faithfulness, gentleness, self-control"* (Gal. 5:22, 23). Aren't these the qualities needed for the marriage you long for? Being under the control of His Spirit is the means to attain the love, goodness, and kindness, the restraint of longsuffering and self-control, and the faithfulness to keep your commitment while your marriage grows through difficult times. As you seek the power of His Spirit and His rulership over your life, you come into intimacy and oneness with Him, which naturally results in oneness with each other.

For years in my earlier counseling ministry, I misunderstood and failed to grasp the importance of a couple's personal spiritual life. Many times I would spend weeks and months working with couples, giving them all the important principles and mechanics regarding how to have a good marriage. I would explain the different methods for implementing these principles, only to see them fail to put them into practice. I was dumbfounded as to why they couldn't seem to do what I told them. Then one day the light came on for me. I was involved in a counseling session much like the one with Calvin and Diane. I realized that day that the couple to whom I was speaking simply didn't have the ability to make the changes required to repair their marriage. I have today come to understand that many were willing to make the changes necessary, but they did not have the power to change because of little or no personal relationship with the Lord. It was as if I were giving these couples an electric appliance and telling them to use it *without plugging it into a wall socket.* Without power the appliance was completely ineffective and useless. Likewise, when an individual breaks his or her connection to Christ through independence, there is an immediate lack of power, motivation, and love in the marriage.

Since I came to this understanding, I now ask couples during our first counseling session to describe for me their personal devotional time and how they are applying the Word of God to their lives. I have found the response in most cases to be the same as it was with Calvin and Diane. They usually say they have little, if any, personal relationship and little personal devotional time in prayer or in studying the Word of God.

What about those who do spend time in prayer, study the Scriptures, and even regularly attend church but still have little companionship? Is this an exception? No, because it is necessary, even vital, to *apply* the Word of God to our personal lives. A personal relationship with Christ is built on two important things, hearing and *doing* the things God commands you. We are called to not only be hearers of the Word but also doers. Many couples know exactly what to do because they have heard it over and over again in church every week. However, they choose not to apply what they hear because of simple unbelief, unwillingness, pride, resentment, or selfishness.

If you sense something missing in your marriage, that things are not quite right, don't look at your mate first. Stop and look a little closer to home. The void is in you! Are you truly experiencing a personal walk that demonstrates the transforming power of God? Are you in love with the Lord and filled with His Holy Spirit? Are you taking what you are learning in your personal study of God's Word and applying it to your life? If you are, this will dramatically affect your entire life and marriage. You can't be a doer of the Word and not find the companionship you are looking for in your marriage. Yet many times as I teach this to people, they think I'm being too religious and pastoral. They tell me their connection with God can't be that important. What about you? What do you think? Let me explain *why* your personal relationship with Christ will profoundly affect your marriage, and why it is the key to having the power, motivation, and understanding to becoming the companion God has called you to be.

WHY IS YOUR RELATIONSHIP WITH CHRIST SO IMPORTANT?

Your personal relationship with Christ is vital because He is the power that changes and transforms you. One truth I have come to realize in marriage counseling is that *every marital problem is really a spiritual problem*. If you are struggling with unforgiveness, resentment, lying, or uncontrolled anger, be aware that these are all personal spiritual problems. They are sinful behaviors that should reveal to you that Christ is not controlling your life. Self reigns. Unforgiveness reigns. Anger reigns. The only solution is that Christ must reign in your life instead. How can you find companionship and oneness in your relationship when you are living and responding in a fleshly manner? The answer is, you can't!

Now stop and think through this point with me for a moment. Where did all of man's interpersonal relationship problems begin? Didn't they all start in the garden when Adam and Eve decided to live and act independently from God and disobey His revealed Word? The first thing they did after the Fall was to start blaming each other. Then envy, resentment, and ultimately, murder sprang up from their children. All their family and marriage problems began with their spiritual problem of independence and disobedience to God.

It is foundational, in resolving any marital problem, to first deal with the spiritual problem in your own life. The key to finding the companionship that Adam and Eve possessed before the Fall will be found in your returning to the intimate relationship they had with their Creator. If you want a Christian marriage, then you need Christ in the middle of your marriage. Paul said, *"Husbands, love your wives, just as Christ also loved the church and gave Himself for it"* (Eph. 5:25). Wives are encouraged *"to love their husbands"* and *"to love their children"* (Titus 2:4). But where do you get the love of Christ to actually do this? There is only one place to get God's love. It's from God! You need to ask and receive it from Him every day.

When the Philippian church had conflicts in their assembly, Paul told them they needed fellowship with the Spirit of God. He knew this would produce the love of Christ that would enable them to humble themselves and experience the oneness in their interpersonal relationships needed to reconcile all their differences (Phil. 2:1-4). As you grow in love with the Lord, you will naturally grow in your love relationship with your spouse. John says, *"He who loves God must love his brother also"* (1 John 4:21). If you don't love your brother, or in this case your spouse, you have to question the reality of your love for God. To truly love your spouse the way God intended, you need to fall in love with the Lord all over again. The love of God is all the motivation you need to be the companion your spouse is looking for.

Your relationship with Christ is also where you receive the power to walk contrary to your fleshly desires. Paul said, *"Walk in the Spirit and you shall not fulfill the lust of the flesh"* (Gal. 5:16). If there is one thing that destroys the love and giving in a marriage, it is your fleshly selfish nature. To live selfishly is very natural for all of us, but it takes a supernatural power to live contrary to our selfish desires. Without the power of God in your heart, there is no way you will be able to sacrificially love your spouse. Jesus said, *"Without me, you can do nothing"* (John 15:5). This means that you desperately need Him. Christ is the only person who can give you the power to love as He requires. If nothing is happening in your marriage as you originally intended, it may be because you are trying to do it without Him.

Furthermore, your one-on-one interaction with the living God is where you begin to understand how to be a true companion to your spouse. As you seek to know Him through the study of Scripture, you begin to see what Jesus did and how He acted toward others. As you are instructed and convicted, all of a sudden you begin to *want* to do what Jesus did. With His love and power at work in you, you begin to *do* what Jesus did. He was the perfect example of what a companion actually does. He was an effective communicator, sharing His heart with whoever would listen. He was a man who was not ashamed to show His emotions; from controlled anger to openly weeping over the city of Jerusalem. He served others to the point of even washing His disciples' feet, the job of a common slave. He accepted leadership responsibilities and would always step forward to resolve conflicts, ultimately resolving the greatest conflict: the sin of all mankind that stood in the way of our fellowship with the Father.

If you need understanding and God's perspective regarding your spouse, stay in the Word and study it daily. Jesus is the example you are looking for in your life. But Christ is more than just an example on the pages of the Bible. He will also come today in the power of His Spirit to enable you to live His example if you will but ask Him to come and fill your heart. He is the One who will give you the power to be the man or woman you want to be and the companion your spouse is looking for. Won't you ask Him to begin His work in you right now?

HOW CAN YOU BEGIN A RELATIONSHIP WITH HIM?

You may never have considered yourself as a person who needed a relationship with God. You may think you've come this far without God, and you probably figure you can make it the rest of the way without Him, too. However, when you look at the present needs and struggles in your marriage, you know that something has to change. You know you need a deeper love and a more committed relationship between you and your spouse, and you realize there is little real companionship between you. You may see your need for forgiveness and reconciliation or a host of other needs, but do you have the ability to handle all these things within yourself? If you did, you would have done so by now, wouldn't you? But you don't have the relationship you want, which means something is missing in the way you have been trying to fix your problems. Let me explain a little more as to why only Christ can give you the power to live and love the way God requires.

In the English language there is only one word for love that is used to cover everything. We use the same word to express our love for our wife as for our dog. Yet, in the Greek language, there are many different words used for love. The Greek word *eros* is used to describe sexual love. This is the root word from which we get our English word *erotic*. Eros love apart from Christ's lordship is usually a very self-oriented kind of love. Another word in Greek for love is *phileo*, which describes a brotherly love or a friendship. Brotherly love is a very reciprocal kind of love, so when someone loves you with this kind of love, you usually respond in like manner. We have the saying, *"You scratch my back and I'll scratch yours."* This is *phileo* love.

Yet the most important word for love in Greek is *agape*. This is the word used in the Bible when Jesus said, *"For God so loved* (agape) *the world that He gave His only begotten Son, that whoever would believe in Him should not perish but have everlasting life"* (John 3:16). This is a love that gives even when nothing is coming back. It's a love that is totally unselfish and reaches out to the one being loved even when there is hatred in return. God's love has and will continue to reach out to you, even if you never respond to Him. This is the kind of love the world needs. This is the kind of love your marriage needs.

Without God's agape love, you will never have the ability to really love your spouse unselfishly because human nature is always seeking something in return. When your spouse doesn't respond or give the way you want, then it's natural for you to choose to not give either. You will reciprocate in like manner. Instead, you need the power of God's love that gives even when that love is not returned.

This is why you need a personal relationship with Christ. He is the only one who can give you this kind of love. Yet there is something that separates and hinders you from receiving God's love: your independence from Him, which God calls sin. All sinful actions and selfishness are a direct result of your independent attitude toward God. That attitude that says, *I can do it without Him.*

The Bible also teaches that the real "you" is a spirit that is housed in your body. You also possess a mind, emotions, and a personality that make you a unique person. However, the Bible says that your spirit (that inner part of you) is dead because of sin (Eph. 2:1-3), separating you from God. This separation from God is what causes you to feel empty inside and gives you that sense that something is missing. Jesus is the answer to this problem. He came to breathe into your dead spirit new life; not just regular life, but an *abundant* life that satisfies this emptiness (John 10:10). His newness of life enables and empowers us to live the way God intended and is extremely satisfying. It is truly an adventure to be able to love one another, forgive one another, and live in harmony as He desires.

Christ died to take the penalty for man's sin once and for all. The Father only asks that you acknowledge your sin to Him in prayer, ask for forgiveness, and be willing to turn completely from your sinful habits and lifestyle. If this is something you know you need to do, then take these steps now.

1. If you believe God exists, then go to Him in prayer now. Talk to Him just like you would a friend. You don't need to use big spiritual words because He already knows every thought and every need you have. He just wants you to humble yourself before Him and ask. Jesus said, *"Ask, and it will be given to you; seek, and you will find; knock, and it will be opened. For everyone who asks receives, and he who seeks finds, and to him who knocks it will be opened"* (Matt. 7:7, 8).

2. If you believe you have sinned against God and broken His law and you truly want to turn from this way of life, then ask for His forgiveness and mercy. The Bible says, *"If we confess our sins, He is faithful and just to forgive us our sins and to cleanse us from all unrighteousness"* (1 John 1:9).

3. If you believe in Christ, invite Him right now to come in and take complete control of your life. The Bible promises that to *"as many as received Him (Jesus), to them He gave the right to become children of God, to those who believe in His Name"* (John 1:12).

4. Ask God to fill you with the power of His Holy Spirit to enable you to love and serve others, especially your spouse. Jesus said, *"If you know how to give good gifts to your children, how much more will your heavenly Father give the Holy Spirit to those who ask Him"* (Luke 11:13). Let His Spirit rule your life.

5. Now confess the commitment you've just made to someone else. This is important because Jesus said, *"Whoever confesses Me before men, him I will also confess before My Father who is in heaven. But whoever*

denies Me before men, him I will also deny before My Father who is in heaven" (Matt. 10:32, 33). This is the first step in denying yourself to follow Him. See the context of this statement in Matthew 10:38. Jesus declared that denying self is essential to becoming His disciple.

HOW CAN YOU RESTORE YOUR RELATIONSHIP?

What should you do if you have had a relationship with Christ in the past, yet you sense that you have left your first love? This is one of the central issues that greatly hindered Calvin and Diane's marriage. I gave them the same counsel that Jesus gave the Church of Ephesus. *"Nevertheless I have this against you, that you have left your first love. Remember therefore from where you have fallen; repent and do the first works..."* (Rev. 2:4, 5). If this is what you have done, here is what you need to do to restore that first love.

1. First, you need to do some remembering. What was it like when you were close to the Lord? Do you remember the love, joy, and the life you experienced as you walked with Him? Do you remember the days when you could hardly wait to open your Bible and spend quality time learning of Him? When worship opportunities arrived on Wednesday and Sunday, you were there with a hunger to grow because you loved to gather and fellowship with God's people. When requests were made for people to help serve others, you willingly offered your talents. You lived and acted then totally different than you do now. Remember how it was? The apostle Peter said that remembrance would have this affect: it would stir a person to action (2 Peter 1:13). If you will stop now for a moment to remember the relationship you used to have with Christ, it will also stir you to take the next step.

2. Repent! The word *repent* means to change your mind and to reverse direction. To bring about a change in your relationship with the Lord, repentance is essential. One of the functions of the Holy Spirit is to convict us of sin which enables this reversal of direction. True repentance is not possible without His assistance. Therefore, let Him begin to convict you; open your heart wide to Him. Allow Him to speak to you regarding your thought patterns or your behavior. Have you blamed God for your marital problems? Do you see Him as "out to get you" or indifferent? Have you been holding resentment in your heart? Have you been rebelling against Him or indifferent toward spending time with Him in the Word and prayer? As He reveals the dark areas of your heart, confess your need for Him and ask His forgiveness. Realize afresh that God is *"full of compassion, and gracious, longsuffering and abundant in mercy*

and truth" (Ps. 86:15). He wants to forgive and is able to restore you today. Let His goodness *"lead you to repentance"* (Rom. 2:4).

3. Do the first works. What does that mean? It means to go back and begin to seek God and walk with Him the way you did when you first came to faith. Ask God for a craving for the Word and devote yourself to studying it daily with all your heart. Take time apart each day to talk to Him in prayer because you long for fellowship with the One who has taken you out of darkness into His light. Let good works eagerly come from your heart and your hands as a demonstration of your love for all He's done. Submit yourself in every area of your life as an offering of dedication for the sacrifice He has made for you. These are the first works you did when He was the first priority of your heart. Paul gave this same counsel to the Colossian Church. *"As you have therefore* (first) *received Christ Jesus the Lord, so walk in Him"* (Col. 2:6). Go back and begin to walk with Him the way you did at the beginning, and the love of God will flood your soul again. Being filled with His love is the supreme evidence that you have renewed your relationship with Christ (Gal. 5:22). Jesus said, *"By this all will know that you are My disciples, if you have love for one another"* (John 13:35).

Once you have returned to your first love, you will begin to experience the power of God's love motivating you to change in your marriage relationship. This change will come naturally in all that you say and do. Be assured that God's love in you will enable you to love your mate and to be a faithful and life-long companion as never before. Don't settle for unforgiveness, resentment, indifference, or independence. He has much more for you! Let Christ control your thoughts and emotions; the actions will follow.

HOW WILL CHRIST MAKE YOU A BETTER COMPANION?

God wants to make you a companion who will lovingly meet the needs of your spouse. God is the only one who can make you become this kind of partner. The marriage you want is a work of God from beginning to end. Remember, Jesus said, *"What God has joined together, let not man separate"* (Matt. 19:6). It's God's work to join two people together, not yours. In fact, by your own efforts and in your own strength, you can't be a companion to anyone. He is the only one who can make two individuals become one flesh because marriage is a *work of God*. All your self-effort will be in vain if you fail to understand and implement this truth.

If your marriage is to work the way it's supposed to, you must allow Him to be at work in your life every day. Bear in mind *"it is God who works in you both to will and to do for His good pleasure"* (Phil. 2:13). He desires to make you a great companion, a man or woman filled with the fruit of His Spirit. This is why you must walk as close to Him as possible, allowing Him to work His work in you.

As you surrender yourself to Christ, you will become a changed person day by day. You will be *"transformed into the same image from glory to glory, just as by the Spirit of the Lord"* (2 Cor. 3:18). *Surrender* is how God does this powerful work of changing you, enabling you to live in a totally new way. The Spirit of God will work inside of you and cause you to walk in love toward your spouse. It is significant to note that this is the context in Ephesians chapter five. As a preface to explaining how a marriage is to function, Paul declared, *"do not be drunk with wine...but be filled with the Spirit..."* (Eph. 5:18). He then goes on to teach husbands and wives how to treat each other in their marriage relationship. Paul understood that the Spirit of God was the key to our ability to love each other as he stated in another place, *"the fruit of the Spirit is love..."* (Gal. 5:22).

When you are filled with the Spirit of God, He subdues selfishness, pride, anger, and all the other things that destroy the relationship between two people. You will *want* to deny yourself, which will make you a great companion to your spouse. Your mate longs to have this type of companion. It is so simple to become this man or woman; just give yourself to Christ and be transformed into His image, and your spouse will be totally satisfied with the person he or she married. Remember, Jesus possesses all the character traits your spouse is looking for. He was loving, a great communicator, a leader, submissive to His Father, and giving. I know what you are thinking right now. *How can I do all that? I'm not Jesus.* That's right! In your own strength you can't. As you *yield* to Him, you can become this person. I am absolutely sure that it's possible because I have seen this transformation take place many times in the lives of those I have counseled. I can be confident because Paul said, *"I can do all things through Christ who strengthens me"* (Phil. 4:13). You can do all God requires of you, too, if you will believe His promise and surrender to Him today. He will make you the lover, the leader, the communicator that you need to be because of His strength inside you. If you will apply these truths to your life and fall on your face before the Lord, you are in for a real adventure. You will become the companion your spouse has always longed for because you will be changed day by day into His image.

A CHECKLIST FOR YOUR DAILY LIFE

1. Do you daily read and study the Scriptures for your own personal growth and encouragement? This is what the Christians at Berea did. They *"searched the Scriptures daily..."* (Acts 17:11). Solomon taught that we should be listening to and receiving from the Lord every day. *"Blessed is the man who listens to me, watching daily at my gates, waiting at the posts of my doors"* (Prov. 8:34).

2. Do you look to the Lord daily for a personal inward renewal by the Spirit of God? This is what Paul said occurred in his life. *"Therefore we do not lose heart. Even though our outward man is perishing, yet the inward man is being renewed day by day"* (2 Cor. 4:16).

3. Do you daily ask the Lord in prayer to provide for your needs and the needs of your spouse and family? This was the example of David, a man after God's heart. He said, *"Lord, I have called daily upon you; I have stretched out my hands to you"* (Ps. 88:9). Jesus also taught the disciples to pray in this manner: *"Give us this day our daily bread"* (Matt. 6:11).

4. Do you daily perform the vows and commitments you have made before God and your spouse? David said this was his daily commitment. *"Oh, prepare mercy and truth...So will I sing praise to Your name forever, that I may daily perform my vows"* (Ps. 61:7, 8). This would include your marriage vows: promises to love, honor, and cherish (or any promise you have made to your spouse).

5. Do you daily seek to take what God has taught you and use it to encourage your spouse and family? We are to *"exhort one another daily..."* (Heb. 3:13). This would include nourishing your spouse or children with the Word of God (Eph. 5:29). It would also include verbal encouragement when members of your family are discouraged or deserve praise for a job well done. David described what he did with his son Solomon, *"Prayer also will be made for him continually, and daily he shall he praised"* (Ps. 72:15). It's easy to tell your spouse what he or she is doing wrong, but how about giving a little praise and encouragement? When is the last time you actually spoke words of praise and encouragement to your loved one?

6. Do you daily seek to deny yourself and live unselfishly toward those around you? This is the call of God upon every disciple of

Christ. Jesus said, *"If anyone desires to come after Me, let him deny himself, and take up his cross daily, and follow Me"* (Luke 9:23).

This is the kind of personal relationship with Christ that each of us needs to cultivate. It will take a daily action on your part to bring this about in your life. He is waiting for you to hear His voice and come to Him today. Jesus said, *"Behold, I stand at the door and knock. If anyone hears My voice and opens the door, I will come in to him and dine with him, and he with Me"* (Rev. 3:20).

Group Discussion Questions

1. Discuss what your life was like when you did not walk close to the Lord. How did your lack of relationship with God influence your other relationships?
2. Discuss what brought you back to a closer walk with Christ?
3. Discuss how God's work in your heart has made you a better husband or wife. How has He changed you to fulfill your responsibilities?

4

WHAT IS YOUR STANDARD OF TRUTH?

"My people are destroyed for lack of knowledge" Hosea 4:6

It was my second counseling appointment with Jerry and his wife, Joan. They had been married for little less than a year, yet there were already major disagreements between them. This was Jerry's third marriage and Joan's first. Jerry began describing the many arguments of the past week and summed it up by saying, "We just can't seem to agree on anything, Steve. She thinks her way is right, but I feel the Lord has shown me something different."

Joan exploded, "Yeah I know. The Lord showed you! Those are nice convenient spiritual words to cover yourself so you can do just what you want. It doesn't make any difference to you what the Bible says. You just do what you please and blame it on God. I show him verses of Scripture that are simple direct commands that don't take a brain surgeon to understand, and he just shrugs them off and says he doesn't feel that's what God is telling him to do. Steve, I'm so sick of this! I wish you could live with us so you could tell us what is right and wrong."

I looked at them both and said, "I hope you are both sick of this. I hope you're sick enough to look for a remedy. First of all, you need to decide what your standard of truth should be. When you disagree on what your ultimate authority is, how can you determine what is right in any circumstance? It can't be me who makes this determination because I can't live with you. It can't be your feelings or some perceived message from God because these will constantly change. Nor can it be the standard or example from your own family upbringing." I then proceeded to explain the absolute necessity of having the ultimate standard of God's Word as the authority over their lives and marriage.

After much discussion with them, I ultimately realized that the majority of the problem did reside with Jerry. Although he knew plenty of Scriptures, he would pick and choose how and when he wanted to apply them to his marriage. At first, all he had to say was "the Lord showed me" to gain his wife's agreement. However, it wasn't long before she figured out that this was his way of manipulating her to do what he wanted. She then began to point out where Scripture contradicted his action. He didn't like her rebuffs very much and the problems began to pile up.

Determining our standard of truth is one of the greatest and most fundamental problems in Christian marriages today and must be resolved at the very beginning. How do you determine what your responsibilities are and what actions you should take? Is Scripture really your standard of truth, or is it your feelings or what someone has told you? If Scripture is your ultimate standard of truth, are you diligently seeking wisdom from God about your personal problems? Are you then applying God's Word to these problems by obeying His commands? When His Word is your ultimate standard, His commands will be the actions you will take.

In every marriage I have ever counseled, one of two problems exists. The first is that a couple will have no real standard of truth simply because both partners have little or no understanding of what the Bible requires of them. Sometimes this is because one or both within the marriage are not Christians or are very young Christians who determine their actions and responsibilities by their own personal standard. This standard can be the result of various elements of their personal experience. Some use the standard of their own parents, while others use the example of a friend's marriage. Still others live by what feels good at the time or whatever their spouse will allow, basing their relationships on the shifting sands of the feelings and opinions of men.

On the other hand, there are couples who have a good understanding of God's Word and its requirements, yet simply choose to disregard it. They know what they should be doing, but their wants and desires take center stage. Everything seems to be going great until a conflict arises. Then the question is, *whose opinion is right?* It is at this point that people come to see me, wanting me, as Joan did, to give "the word" and solve the conflict. But my word is not the final say on any subject; only Scripture has that right and position. It's not what I think that's important or what anyone thinks. It's what Scripture declares that must be the final standard. This is what Jerry and Joan needed to see in the midst of their conflicts. In the end, it is only when a couple will obey what the Scriptures declare that they will experience the blessings promised in His Word.

In both cases the problem is clear. The reason for the unresolved conflicts is that there is no standard of truth that both will agree upon and obey. They are both basically doing that which seems right in their own eyes. If a couple cannot resolve their conflicts, they surely won't be able to build their marriage to last. Having a standard of truth is another fundamental building block that your marriage needs to grow and mature into the relationship you want and need.

WHY IS A STANDARD OF TRUTH NECESSARY?

1. Without the Scripture as your standard, you are at the mercy of human philosophy. Does man know how to make a marriage work apart from the teachings of Scripture? Have the human philosophies being espoused today made marriages more successful than in years past? The answer is an emphatic *no!*

Today our country is experiencing its highest divorce rate since statistics have been kept, with an incredible seven out of every ten marriages ending in divorce. The number of two-parent homes in America is now at an all-time low. Single parent families are now the norm instead of the exception. What does this reveal about our values? It is clear that men and women have lost their way in the confusion of man's philosophy and opinion. The statistics are the fruit that declares this to be fact. Jesus said, *"A good tree cannot bear bad fruit, nor can a bad tree bear good fruit"* (Matt. 7:18). The fruit of rampant divorce reveals that the standards and philosophies by which we, as marriage partners, make decisions are bad.

Let me give you an example of the confusion and contradiction of human philosophies today. Man's views concerning marriage have a constantly shifting standard of what is morally right and wrong. One book will tell you that you must first "find yourself" to be truly happy in your marriage. Another book advocates having an open marriage in which you can have sexual relations with as many partners as you like. This, they say, will keep the excitement in your marriage. Still another book declares that an open marriage is the wrong philosophy, but sings the praises of a trial marriage, in which we try each other out before we tie the knot, *then* vow to be faithful to each other. Who is right? Whose counsel should you follow? With each new year comes another new and contradictory philosophy of how you can be happy if you would just follow So–and—So's plan for a successful marriage.

Should you follow them? Let me give you an analogy. Let's say you were about to purchase a car at your local dealership. The salesman promised that it was the best car on the lot, and if you followed his every instruction, this car would run perfectly for you. Then he mentioned there was one slight problem. The car wouldn't start on seven out of ten mornings. What would you think? Would you believe you were getting the best car on the lot? Would his instruction be worth anything if, in the end, the car wouldn't start most of the time? Of course not! Would you buy the car? I would hope not!

Yet this is exactly what people do when they listen to and believe the philosophies of men concerning their marriage. Their counsel only works for three out of ten couples. It proves that our society does not know how to have a successful marriage. Yet the marriage gurus continue to sell their wares and people continue to buy.

I will grant these gurus one thing. They do espouse *some* truth. Not all they have to say is bad, but it's not the whole truth. Because there is some truth revealed in these works, people continue to read them. Some of the instruction will work, but you are only getting a percentage of the message you need for a successful marriage. My advice to you is this: with every book you read on marriage or any subject, do this one thing. Page through the book and see who is quoted. Is the Word of God quoted, or some expert in the field? Perhaps there are no quotes at all because the writer is himself the expert. I believe God is the expert on you and your marriage, and He is the one we should quote.

If there is anyone who knows how to make a successful marriage, it is the one who originally created marriage. He has given you the blueprint to enable you to construct a home that will stand all the pressures that come against it. He has given you an instruction manual to fix whatever breaks down along the way: the Word of God.

If you believe your marriage is broken, or you just need some maintenance, why don't you take a fresh look at the owner's manual? Ask Him to show you what needs to be removed or adjusted in your life.

Jesus said, *"Therefore whoever hears these sayings of Mine, and does them, I will liken him to a wise man who built his house on the rock: and the rain descended, the floods came, and the winds blew and beat on that house; and it did not fall, for it was founded on the rock. Now everyone who hears these sayings of Mine, and does not do them, will be like a foolish man who built his house on the sand: and the rain descended, the floods came, and the winds blew and beat on that house; and it fell. And great was its fall"* (Matt. 7:24-27).

The wise man hears and obeys the words of Christ. The foolish man hears and has other priorities. Which will you be? Are you a hearer but not a doer of the Word? Please understand, only obedience to His Word will bring the stability you desire for your home and marriage. God knows how to change you and your spouse if you will give Him a chance. A wise man will allow Him to do it!

The prophet Hosea revealed one of the reasons why the nation Israel fell and was ultimately destroyed. How similar this is with many marriages today. Hosea declared, *"My people are destroyed for lack of knowledge"* (Hosea 4:6). The people of Israel had rejected the knowledge of God as their standard of truth and looked to man for the answers. They *"willingly walked by human precept"* (5:11). As a result, God declared that the social fabric of the nation became *"like rottenness"* (5:12). When a person rejects the knowledge of God as his standard of truth, all that is left are human precepts. Many think that human precepts are of no harm and that it is all right to mix them with God's truth, but in reality, they become rottenness to the stability of the lives of those who trust and rely upon them. Therefore, take the example of the children of Israel and beware of human philosophies that have crept in. Ask God to reveal to you from His Word exactly which precepts to cling to, and then ask Him for the willingness to let the others go.

2. <u>Without the Bible as your standard, you will not know what practical changes to make and how to make them</u>. There are two great problems in the Christian life that relate in a similar way to the problems of marriage. Most new Christians ask the question, "What does God want me to do?" This is a very natural question, for they have found new life in Christ and desire to follow Him in every aspect of their lives. The next question is very similar. "*How* do I do what God requires of me?" This naturally follows the first question because a new Christian immediately realizes that he does not have the practical understanding regarding how to walk with the Lord.

The marriage relationship is very similar. Many couples get married with little or no premarital counseling. They have spent months preparing for the ceremony, ordering flowers and a cake, planning the reception, and honeymoon, but they have never been married before, and therefore do not know what to expect. Both spouses have a general idea of what they want from the marriage. They both have many goals and expectations, but many times these expectations are directly contrary to their mate's.

If there is no standard of truth that both partners can agree upon, then they will immediately be at odds with each other when the first problem occurs. Who is right? What's best? What should your attitude be? What action should you take? How will you do it? All these questions must be answered to the mutual satisfaction of both partners in order to maintain harmony.

The Word of God provides the answers to all of these questions. His Word, as King David said, is *"a lamp to my feet and a light to my path"* (Ps. 119:105). As you study His Word and how it relates to your life and marriage, you will be enlightened. However, God requires *both* husband and wife to take the specific path (attitude as well as action) required in Scripture. God lights the path for you by giving you understanding of

His will, and His Spirit empowers you to do it. When both partners are submitted to Christ, then both have the conviction that neither is forcing the other, and each partner is willing to yield to the commands of Scripture.

All Christian couples eventually experience division in their marriage simply because individual opinions and wills occasionally clash. It may take a while, but the problems will occur. Every couple needs the standard of God's Word to keep them accountable. *"Whatever a man sows, that he will also reap"* (Gal. 6:7). Also, *"There is no wisdom or understanding or counsel against the Lord"* (Prov. 21:30). If you are sowing your own ideas or the philosophies of men in your marriage, you will reap a miserable harvest. There is no wisdom in this course of action.

When Jesus battled with the Sadducees over their many questions, He pointed out that they had made one fatal error. He said, *"You are mistaken, not knowing the Scriptures nor the power of God"* (Matt. 22:29). Please don't make this same error. We can all be mistaken about the truth and what is right or wrong simply because we do not know what the Scriptures teach on a particular subject. However, you don't have to continue to make this error. Instead, begin to search His Word for the answers you need. If you fail to do so, you will also miss out on His power to do what He promises. The Scriptures reveal His truth, but they also produce faith in the heart to receive His power to implement that truth. Without His Word and His power motivating a couple to a godly lifestyle, the relationship will become an external one with little reality even as the Sadducees experienced.

Let me encourage you that there are answers to your specific situation. You can turn your marriage around and build the kind of relationship you want. It's never too late! You don't have to remain as two people going through the external motions of a marriage devoid of His life and power. To change it, first determine where you are violating the principles of God's Word and living by your own standard. Then resolve these issues by the means and methods that God reveals in His Word. Finally, you must follow the directions given in Scripture for all your future actions. These actions will build the relationship you desire. The specific principles in this book are designed to help you to do just that.

3. Without the Word as your standard, how will you be transformed? It is of the utmost importance that *you* be changed if you desire to see your marriage change. As explained in the previous chapter, every marital problem always begins as a spiritual problem in one or both partners in a marriage. The transformation of your life, then, is essential. What is the means of this transformation?

God's Word is the primary way that transformation takes place in your life. I will cover in greater detail exactly how this occurs in a later chapter. Let me simply say here that the Word of God, planted in your heart and obeyed in your life, is the seed that will produce the good tree and the good fruit you desire. How does this happen?

Jesus told His disciples that His Word was the key to becoming a disciple because it has the power to transform lives. He said, *"If you abide in My Word, you are My disciples indeed. And you shall know the truth, and the truth shall make you free"* (John 8:31, 32). Abiding in and obeying His truth is a fundamental key to following Christ as His disciple. No one can follow Him without denying himself and his own well thought-out ideas and philosophies. The blessing in this relinquishing action is that when you know, believe, and obey His truth, it makes you free. This is where the transformation process begins.

As you learn the Scriptures, they naturally produce faith in your heart. Paul said, *"Faith comes by hearing...the Word of God"* (Rom. 10:17). The seed of God's Word germinates and produces this new little shoot of faith springing out of the ground of your heart. As you feed this shoot of faith with more of the Word, it grows into a strong tree with roots that grow deep and with fruit that is sweet because faith naturally produces action. The apostle James said that *"faith without works is dead"* (James 2:20). Real faith will always produce works and actions that are in accordance with what you believe.

Is it not the action of love that changes a marriage relationship? This love comes as a result of the Word of God being believed and received as the standard of truth in your life. His truth is what sets you free and enables you to believe and act in harmony with His commands. This new godly perspective will encourage you to resolve conflicts and build something new and better between you and your spouse.

The Word of God is *"living and powerful,"* and it can accomplish amazing things in your life if you will accept it as your standard of truth (Heb. 4:12). Search the Scriptures daily and apply them to your thinking, to the way you see things, to what you value as important, and fruit will naturally begin to sprout in your marriage. Let the Word convict you and turn your heart around, and your actions will change. I know this is what you want or you would not be reading this book. This is how you can build your marriage to last. Why not begin right now? Put the book down for a moment and ask the Holy Spirit to reveal to you those attitudes and actions that are not in harmony with Scripture. Then ask Him to give you a more *biblical* and *eternal* perspective.

Group Discussion Questions

1. Without giving too much detail, describe a time when you did that which was right in your own eyes. What was the fruit?

2. Discuss a circumstance when you were confused about the teachings of Scripture and made a decision based on some human philosophy. What was the result?

3. Discuss a circumstance when you made a decision you were sure was based on the Word of God. What was the result?

4. How has the truth of God's Word transformed your life?

UNDERSTANDING HOW TO LOVE

"If you love Me, keep my commandments" John 14:15

M ike protested,"But I *do* love her! You just don't understand, Steve. I would never have married her if I didn't love her, and I sure wouldn't have stayed married if I didn't care about our relationship."

Mike shook his head in disgust with me because I had suggested that he wasn't loving his wife, Mary. The tension continued to build in the counseling session as I continued to question him. "Mike, why then, doesn't your wife see and sense this love you have for her? If you were truly expressing your love, don't you think she would be considering herself a loved woman? Is she totally missing something here?"

"Yes she is!" Mike responded angrily.

I proceeded to take a more indirect approach to calm Mike down a bit. "Tell me how you would define love, and what would you do to demonstrate it to your wife?"

He thought for a moment, and said, "That's silly, Steve. Everyone knows what love is!"

So I gave them both a piece of paper and asked each of them to write out as many two-or-three word phrases as possible to define how they should be demonstrating their love for each other.

The response was very enlightening. Mike listed only two definitions of love, and Mary had ten. I immediately understood that Mike had little understanding of how to practically demonstrate real love for his wife. Mary, on the other hand, had a very good understanding of how she should love her husband.

Then to be fair, I asked Mary, "How many of these things are you actually doing that you've listed here?"

Tears welled up in her eyes as she said sheepishly, "Not many."

Mary knew exactly what I was getting at. She recognized the fact that she wasn't even doing what she knew was right. She knew how to love but simply chose not to.

Mike and Mary offer a perfect example of another fundamental for a solid marriage: the need to understand and define what real love is, and then act on it. Most couples whose marriages are stale or troubled have one or both of these problems. Either one spouse or the other does not understand what real love acts like, or simply chooses not to take the loving action needed.

The first problem is only a lack of information and understanding. This would, of course, frustrate one's taking the action of love. Yet most people have plenty of knowledge as to what and how they should love their mate. Their problem is a refusal in the realm of the will. They choose not to act on their knowledge, and this is either because of resentment toward their spouse or basic selfishness.

Can you define what real love is? Can you describe in practical terms what you should be doing to demonstrate love to your mate? If you can, are you doing these things on a regular basis? Are you doing them even when your spouse is not showing much love toward you? These are the critical questions you must answer if you hope to restore your relationship.

Society has complicated this issue today in the way it has redefined what real love is and how it behaves. The biblical definition of love has been warped by Hollywood and modern psychology in a process that has taken place so slowly most people are not even aware that it has occurred. Let me give you some examples.

In the vast majority of films and television programs that Hollywood has produced in recent years, love has been depicted as the drive of simple lust or sexual exploitation. The overwhelming message we hear is, "If you really love me, you will sleep with me." It doesn't make any difference whether or not you are single or married to someone else. If you are really in love, then you should just take whoever you desire, no matter what the consequences. With the subtle barrage of substandard examples on television every night, many begin to see a monogamous and faithful view of love as simply old fashioned and not much fun. Love, according to Hollywood, is based more on what feels good than on truth.

Likewise, modern psychology, much of which preaches the philosophy of self-fulfillment, is equally at fault. Carl Rogers, a very influential psychologist, believed that we have failed to reach our full human potential by not doing what *we* value most. According to Rogers, we have failed to grasp our personal worth and therefore have little or no self-esteem. He proclaims that we must do what is good for ourselves first, esteeming our own life as the one to be valued. Only then can we give to others in any meaningful way. This is a me-first kind of love, which in reality is only selfishness dressed up in good-sounding rationales.

These and other current philosophies have undermined the biblical definition of what real love is. Such erroneous ideas of love only cause two people to become polarized and more self-oriented in their love. If these concepts of love are accepted, they will ultimately drive a couple apart.

Whose standard of love will you use to determine the actions you should take toward your spouse? If you had to make a list as Mike and Mary did, what would you write down on your paper? Determining what real love acts like is critical to building your marriage to last a lifetime. Your standard must follow the example of Jesus Christ as revealed in the Word of God. Yet, as I have said before, this love will only come to a man or woman who willingly surrenders to the Father and loves Him above all others. As you love the Lord with all your heart and love your mate in the same manner, true companionship and oneness result. If you want to experience the purpose God has ordained for your marriage, you must know how He defines love and then act on it.

WHAT IS THE BIBLICAL DEFINITION OF LOVE?

What do you mean when you say "I love you" to your spouse? What will you *do* if you really mean it? Is your definition of love in harmony with the ultimate standard of truth, the Bible? When you vowed to love your mate every day of your life, did you realize what that meant? Probably not. You were more than likely swept up in the emotion of the moment, never thinking that there would ever be any trouble performing that vow. Yet today you understand that love is more than just words easily spoken. As you read through this next section, compare your view of love with God's definition. By doing this you will begin to allow the searchlight of His Word to convict and encourage you to actually take the actions He desires. How will the love of God behave if it truly resides in your heart?

1. <u>Love causes you to work</u>. This first definition may seem strange, but it strikes at the root of one of the great misconceptions about love. Love is not some warm and fuzzy feeling that miraculously appears out of nowhere. Love is much more than a feeling. It is an emotion that results from hard work between two people. We quickly forget how hard we worked at our relationship when we first dated. We worked on our appearance so that we looked and smelled just right. We made sure we were on time to meet our date. We strove to take our prospective mate to a nice place for dinner. While we were there, we labored to converse over

the things that he or she enjoyed, making sure not to argue over insignificant things. At other times we brought special presents or flowers or made that special dinner. Now think for a minute. Why did we do all that? Because we were in love with each other!

However, after you got married, did you continue to work at your relationship with the same effort? Probably not for very long. Why? Because you began to take your spouse and his or her love for granted. You assumed that you didn't have to do as much, not understanding that real love is work and keeps on working.

This is the definition that Paul gave when he described love. In writing to the Thessalonian Church he said that he remembered their *"work of faith, labor of love and patience of hope..."* (1 Thess. 1:3, underline added). In the book of Hebrews the writer reminds the church that *"God is not unjust to forget your work and labor of love which you have shown toward His name..."* (Heb. 6:10 underline added) In both passages love is described as a labor that a person performs toward someone else. This is because biblical love is defined as something that you do, long before it is felt. When you work at loving your spouse just as you did when you first met, the feeling of love will continue to grow deeper day by day.

The best example of this kind of love is found in Jesus himself. It's important to realize that He did not sit in heaven and yell down to us, "I sure love you down there!" No, He came to show us the love of the Father through the actions He took and the words He spoke. He worked very hard at revealing and demonstrating God's love to us. *"God demonstrates His own love toward us, in that while we were still sinners, Christ died for us"* (Rom. 5:8). His whole life was a labor of love toward every one of us. He often preached, traveled, and healed others to the point of physical exhaustion. He said, *"I must work the works of Him that sent me..."* (John 9:4) The work of the cross was the ultimate demonstration that the love of God is love in action.

Did you know that God is still laboring over your life to bring about His purposes in you? Paul said, *"For it is God who works in you both to will and to do for His good pleasure"* (Phil. 2:13, underline added). His love is still working! He is working now to change your concept of what real love is so that He might work a dramatic change in your marriage. He wants to work a new desire in you to love and to work at your relationship with your spouse. I am confident with Paul that *"He who has begun a good work in you will complete it..."* (Phil. 1:6).

Is this your definition of real love? If so, you must labor daily to show your love by the actions you take and the words you speak. Ask Him right now to show you exactly what you can do to start demonstrating your love for your mate.

2. <u>Love causes you to give sacrificially</u>. A true godly love not only works, but it works sacrificially toward those it cares about. In other words, the kind of love I am describing here will personally cost you dearly. To love in this manner is definitely not the easy way. It will require giving to your spouse when you don't feel like it, when you would rather not get up from your easy chair. Love is action that requires you to leave your comfort zone and do things that are not comfortable at times.

Love is much more than a feeling. This is the very reason many fail to walk in love. They have reduced it to a mere feeling. This is especially true of today's generation. However, having contrary feelings didn't stop Jesus from His sacrificial giving. Remember His words just prior to offering His life upon the cross. *"Now My soul is troubled, and what shall I say? 'Father, save Me from this hour'? But for this purpose I came to this hour"* (John 12:27). Jesus didn't need emotions to demonstrate His love. On the contrary, He was *troubled*. He knew of the inevitable separation from His Father that was soon to occur, but He chose to leave His comfort zone for us.

Self-sacrificial love strikes at the root of conflict in every human heart–selfishness versus giving. At the root of all marital conflict is the struggle of whom I love more, myself or my mate? It entails the question of what I am willing to sacrifice. The problem is that we usually love ourselves much more than we love our spouse. We are more concerned about how our needs will be met rather than our partner's. This is why Jesus equated the two: *"You shall love your neighbor as yourself"* (Matt. 22:39). Jesus acknowledged the truth that we all love ourselves quite well. We are sensitive to our every need and take great care to make sure these needs are met every day. This self-oriented view of life is what causes the conflict of wills between two people. However, Jesus encouraged us to take a different action, that of showing the same care for others that we do for ourselves. He meant it as a general encouragement to all, and yet, isn't your spouse your closest neighbor?

Paul makes this same point to husbands in his letter to the Ephesians. He made the comparison between how we love ourselves and how we should love our wives. *"So husbands ought to love their own wives <u>as their own bodies</u>; he who loves his wife loves himself. For no one ever hated his own flesh, but nourishes and cherishes it, just as the Lord does the church"* (Eph. 5:28, 29, underline added). Don't you take great pains to nourish and cherish your body every day? You cleanse it, apply deodorant and cologne, dress it to look just right, and feed it to satisfy its every desire.

You may even exercise your body to tone and shape it, sacrificing other things in order to accomplish each of these activities. Paul is declaring that this is how you *"ought"* to love your spouse. Real love sacrifices, nourishes, and cherishes.

Note one further example of the sacrificial nature of love. When Jesus taught His disciples about loving their enemies, He said, *"For if you love those who love you, what reward have you? Do not even the tax collectors do the same? And if you greet your brethren only, what do you do more than others? Do not the even the tax collectors do so?"* (Matt. 5:46, 47). Jesus saw love as action that is *more than* just the normal response you would give to those you like. He saw love as something definitely out of the ordinary. Obviously, you must do way more than is normal to love your enemies. It's no big deal if you love those who love you, even non-Christians can do that. What if your enemy at the moment is your spouse? What are you doing to show love toward him or her that would prove your words of love? Jesus is calling you to go the extra mile and asking you, *"What do you do more than others?"*

This is how Jesus has loved you. He has given much more than required to demonstrate the love the Father has toward you in many powerful and wonderful ways. He has created all things, especially this beautiful and awesome planet for you to live upon. He then came to earth himself to allow all men to see Him face-to-face so they could see what He was really like. But there's more. He gave His life as the final sacrifice. He created you and brought you into this world, giving you life and the abilities you have. He sought you out in order to communicate His love and willingness to have fellowship with you. He sent people to you to share the good news of His love and sacrifice upon the cross, and since you've received Him, it has been the *"Father's good pleasure to give you the kingdom"* (Luke 12:32). His intense desire to give enables you to experience the fullness of His kingdom. This is real love! A love that does *"more than others."* He is your example of the way you are to love your mate. Love sacrificially!

3. <u>Love causes you to initiate giving</u>. Many times a person will ask me in counseling, "Why should I do this or stop doing that? What good would it do if my spouse isn't showing me the same love or concern?" My answer to these questions is this: Biblical love takes the opportunity to initiate. To truly love your spouse, you must learn to initiate, thereby proving your love. You will respond to those specific requests that your mate has mentioned to you. For example, "Honey, could you talk to me before you volunteer to coach another little league team?" Or, "Could you help me out with the yard work once in a while?" There are many

such requests made in every marriage weekly. Because of love you should respond of your own accord without having to be asked again. When your spouse mentions a desire for you to initiate conversation, initiate a date night, initiate family devotions, initiate prayer, or initiate sex, he or she expects you to remember this request. Your loved one is hoping you will think of taking action on your own and just do it! This is what love does. Specific responses and attention to detail are great ways to demonstrate your love toward your partner, and let me tell you, your spouse won't forget it! When you initiate loving action in this manner, it assures your partner that it's a real love from your heart. It means more than you can imagine.

You may be saying to yourself, *That's not me, Steve. I don't like to do those kinds of things. Do I really have to?* This is where you need to combine sacrificial love with initiating. If your partner's request is biblical and reasonable, then it is a great opportunity to demonstrate your love. In most cases, your mate's request won't be asking for the moon. So remember the request and surprise your spouse with a love that initiates.

The best example of loving initiation is, again, Jesus Christ. He initiated relationship with you. He initiated serving you sacrificially by laying down His life for you. Jesus could have said, "That's just not me. I don't want to lay my life down for them." But, thank God, it *was* Him; His very nature is love. Remember, God has given you His own divine nature to make you like himself, so it *is you* to love the way He does. "*As His divine power has given to us all things that pertain to life and godliness...by which have been given to us exceedingly great and precious promises, that through these you may be partakers of the divine nature...*" (2 Peter 1:3, 4). Peter declares that God's divine power and nature are available to you today to enable you to live with your mate and love in a godly way. You can love your spouse the way God intends if you will believe His promise and give yourself sacrificially to your relationship.

What is the result of initiating love toward your spouse in this manner? He or she will naturally be inspired to love you back in like manner. This is what happened in your relationship with Christ. Scripture declares that "*we love Him because He first loved us*" (1 John 4:19). Because God initiated, we have responded. Do you see why this initiating kind of love is so important? From the couples I counsel, however, I see how this type of love is sorely lacking in many marriages today. Each person is waiting for the other to show love first. We have forgotten the Golden Rule that says, "*Therefore, whatever you want men to do to you, do also to them...*" (Matt. 7:12). This passage clearly teaches us to initiate love toward others if we ever want to see love returned.

Where do you need to initiate some loving action toward your spouse? Can you remember your mate's last request? This is what it takes to begin to turn your marriage around and build a lasting marriage.

4. Love causes you to restrain certain actions. Are there certain things you do that drive your mate crazy and are always a source of aggravation? When you continue to do these things, your spouse perceives it as intentional, not unlike scraping your fingernails down a blackboard. You know what these actions are because you have had many fights over each one of them. Why? Simply because you have not restrained yourself from doing them. Consider some examples: Has your spouse asked you not to use foul language because it is offensive? To restrain your sarcastic criticism? To stop your angry outbursts? These and other requests are made often by your spouse, but do you remember them and restrain yourself?

Each time you fail to remember and restrain yourself, your spouse begins to question your love. People say to me continually in counseling, "If he really cared, why doesn't he remember what I asked him to do?" A spouse is right to draw this conclusion, because love restrains itself. If you love and care about your partner, you must remember the requests made to you and restrain yourself.

Jesus said to His disciples, *"If you love Me, keep my commandments"* (John 14:15). To keep His commandments would require two things. First, the disciples would have to remember and restrain themselves from that which they knew was offensive to Christ. Second, they would have to remember to initiate action they knew would please Him because they loved Him. This is the definition Jesus gave for what He considered to be real love. How many times has your spouse given you his or her "commandment" over certain things? Here is where you can start to demonstrate your love.

God is love, and He has demonstrated this love by restraining His actions too. He has revealed His restraining love by holding back His judgment upon mankind. He has done this because He *"delights in mercy"* and not judgment (Micah 7:18). God displayed this restraining love again to the children of Israel when He said, *"For My name's sake I will defer My anger, and for My praise I will restrain it from you, so that I do not cut you off"* (Is. 48:9). Even God restrains himself because of His great love. Aren't we glad that He does? Our entire relationship with Him is a revelation of His restraint. His long-suffering, patience, and endurance clearly demonstrate this fact.

What has your spouse told you is offensive to them? What do you forget to do that drives your mate crazy, causing them to question your love? If you desire to demonstrate your love, certain offensive habits must be restrained. If you are being conformed into the image of Christ, then you will act as He acted. Yes, this is work, but that is what love is all about.

5. <u>Love causes you to put your own will and desires aside and put your spouse first</u>. An attitude of serving is another essential characteristic of biblical love. Jesus was very straightforward with His disciples about midway through their relationship with Him. He told them that if they *"desired to be first,"* they had missed the whole point of His message and example. He made it clear that to be His disciple one must be the servant of all. *"For even the Son of Man did not come to be served, but to serve, and to give His life a ransom for many"* (Mark 10:44, 45).

The life of Christ was a continuous example of putting others first. His entire mission to save us put our needs above His own; He didn't come here to have people minister to His needs. He put His own will aside and put ours first in order to fulfill the will of His Father. *"For I have come down from heaven, not to do My own will, but the will of Him who sent Me"* (John 6:38). Jesus exemplified what it means to deny yourself. That "me first" attitude must die. As Christ surrendered himself, He demonstrated His love for the Father and for you.

Are you demonstrating your love in the same manner? Your spouse should be the first person you consider here on this earth when making any decision or taking any action. Paul explains this priority when he said that we are to *"first learn to show piety at home"* (1 Tim. 5:4). The word *piety* means "godliness or respect." The first priority of your Christian walk should be to show godliness and respect for the people who live in your home. You must put aside your own personal desires and put each family member's needs first, particularly those of your spouse. Does your wife hold this place and priority in your heart? Can your husband see you putting your will and desires aside simply because you love him?

As Paul writes to the Philippian church, he reaffirms that esteeming others first is the proof and fruit of the love of God ruling in our lives. He says, *"Fulfill my joy by being like-minded, having the same love, being of one accord, of one mind. Let nothing be done through selfish ambition or conceit, but in lowliness of mind let each esteem others better than himself. Let each of you look out not only for his own interests, but also for the interests of others"* (Phil. 2:2-4).

Are you practicing this kind of love in your home? Are you considering the interests of your husband or wife first? Are you, with humility of mind, esteeming your partner's needs more than your own? The words *"better than"* in verse three could be translated *"more than"* or *"more important than"* and are rendered this way in the New American Standard version. To love your mate more than yourself is truly the opposite of selfishness or a "me-first" mentality. God wants you to love your spouse this way day by day. What would it be like in your home if you began loving like this? More important, what would your home be like if you both treated each other like this? Would it not be a joy to be married?

6. <u>Love causes you to communicate</u>. There are three ways you communicate love: by your attitude, by your words, and by your deeds. All three must be present for your spouse to see and believe that you love him or her. You can say the right words, yet if your attitude is wrong, it nullifies every statement you've made. Words without deeds to follow them are completely worthless and, ultimately, will only anger your spouse because he or she has seen nothing to back those words up. Even actions of love without the words to define and explain them are confusing and insufficient. Your spouse needs to hear your love, see your love, and sense your heart behind all that you say and do.

When Jesus expressed love He utilized all of the above means. His attitude was humble and gentle (Matt. 11:29), which made Him approachable. Children, harlots, and lepers felt very comfortable coming to Him (Matt. 19:13-15); (Luke 7:36-50); (Luke 17:12-19). In those days these types of people did not feel at liberty to approach an important person. However, they sensed they could approach Jesus because His attitude indicated that He cared. His emotions revealed this attitude of love when He wept or rejoiced with people (John 11:35); (Luke 10:21). When people approached Him, they could instantly perceive that He cared and would be receptive to their needs.

He wasn't afraid to verbally express His love either. Jesus said to the disciples: *"As the Father loved Me, I also have loved you..."* (John 15:9). *"This is My commandment, that you love one another as I have loved you"* (John 15:12). He could call His disciples His *friends* (John 15:13-15). Jesus was very comfortable freely expressing His love with words toward those whom He cared about. What people sensed in His attitude, they also heard in the words that He spoke.

The deeds of Christ were the ultimate proof of His love. He came to earth to reveal how much the Father actually does love us. In every attitude and word expressed and with every action He took, He unveiled the visible proof of God's love. Ultimately, His death on the cross was the supreme demonstration of this love. Jesus pointed our eyes to this display of love when He said, *"Greater love has no one than this, than to lay down one's life for his friends"* (John 15:13). The life of Christ demonstrated once and for all God's commitment of love even to the point of giving the life of His own Son.

Are you loving like this? Does your spouse see all three of these aspects of love in you? Does he or she sense your love, hear your love, and see your love? All three are vital if you expect your mate to believe in the reality of your love.

There is one more essential point in the communication of love. Notice that Jesus also communicated how He wanted to be loved in return. He was very specific with His disciples when He said, *"If you love Me, keep my commandments"* (John 14:15) *"If anyone desires to come after Me let him deny himself, and take up his cross, and follow Me"* (Matt. 16:24). Jesus asked them to simply love Him in the same manner as He had loved them. He told them exactly how to do this, by denying themselves to obey Him. Our sacrificial love for Him is our response to His love for us.

Every relationship that lasts communicates how it desires to be loved. Think for a moment about a relationship you have with a friend. You have probably, at some time, told your friend about something that you did or did not like, and he or she responded by giving or restraining from doing what you requested. If your friend refused to respond, then the relationship would become strained and distant or possibly even end. When you communicate how you desire to be loved, you naturally expect your friend to at least try to respond favorably if they cared about you at all.

A marriage is no different. Has your wife asked you recently to sit and talk with her, to take the leadership in spiritual things in the home, or to be more appreciative of her efforts? Has your husband asked you recently to keep the house picked up when he comes home from work, to be more affectionate, or to refrain from overspending when shopping? It is perfectly acceptable for your spouse to ask you to love him or her in a specific manner. It is real love that communicates and attempts to comply with such requests. Sometimes it is easy, and sometimes it is a sacrifice, but love is always what motivates you.

If you love and care for your spouse, don't sit quietly, patiently hoping they will figure out how you desire to be loved. You should let your mate know how your relationship can be better and more intimate by giving the insight into what you consider love to be. When Jesus loved the world, He didn't sit around waiting for us to figure it out. We were blinded to His love, so He came to tell us and show us. You must do the same.

Yet many couples have great difficulty communicating with each other. They hold in the disappointments and the unfulfilled desires and rarely express them. Then in a moment of anger and frustration it all comes out in a barrage of accusations and charges. An angry tirade is the wrong way to communicate how you want to be loved. Your partner won't hear it now because you are only hurling accusations and insults, and it will only frustrate the situation more.

Instead, you must lovingly communicate how each other's desires to be loved and then to respond to these requests. (I am not referring to requests for you to sin or to take an unethical or nonbiblical action. These are, of course, to be refused.) Love will work very hard to fulfill reasonable, fair, and normal requests. Love will sacrificially work at these requests by initiating or restraining its actions as it puts the other person's needs first.

Are you communicating with your spouse how you desire to be loved? You must if you are to build your relationship. Are you responding to these requests? You must if you desire to see your relationship grow. This is what biblical love will do.

7. Love causes you to always seek compromise and reconciliation. This again was the example of how Christ has loved us. Because of His love, He has sought reconciliation with the whole world because He was *"not willing that any should perish but that all should come to repentance"* (2 Peter 3:9). The work of the cross was God's offer of reconciliation to everyone. It was His compromise instead of judgment. *"God demonstrates His own love toward us, in that while we were still sinners, Christ died for us...For if when we were enemies we were reconciled to God through the death of His Son, much more, having been reconciled, we shall be saved by His life"* (Rom. 5:8, 10).

What a demonstration of love to seek reconciliation with each of us! The love of God always seeks to save that which is lost. The only way to do this is to find a solution to the problem of that which separates God and man. Our sin has separated us from the Father, and the death of His Son reconciled this issue once and for all. He could have looked upon us in our sin and said, "That's too bad, guys. You have a serious problem here. I sure wish I could help, but you made your bed, now lie in it." He could have left us in our sin and separation, but He didn't. He solved the problem and then offered us the compromise of His grace and forgiveness in Christ if we would turn from our sin and trust Him.

Now some of you may have a problem with the word *compromise*, so let me explain. God did not compromise or concede any of His standards of righteousness or holiness; He satisfied them completely by the work of the cross. He devised a compromise to judgment by giving His Son in our place so that we are spared eternal separation in the lake of fire. *"For God so loved the world that He gave His only begotten Son, that whoever believes in Him should not perish but have everlasting life"* (John 3:16).

You must do the same in your marriage. To pursue love toward your spouse, you must give of yourself sacrificially, seeking compromise and reconciliation in all the issues that divide you. Love will seek to find a solution and compromise to every one of your problems. Love will not turn its back and say, "You made your bed, now lie in it."

If you are in the midst of major conflict at this moment, you may be thinking, *Wait a minute, Steve. You don't know how much I have sought compromise and reconciliation. But my mate is the unwilling party.* Yes, that may be true. And I agree there are situations where a spouse will frustrate and resist every attempt to reconcile. Just be sure that you are the one who is willing and is seeking to find a compromise in every issue. I will cover in more detail how to deal with this situation in a later chapter. For now, continue to seek God for understanding regarding how to resolve these issues that separate you. You want to be ready if your spouse decides in the future to change their mind and wants to reconcile. You need to have the right attitude and all the tools necessary to accomplish it. Remember, God's love in you will always seek to reconcile conflicts. This is the heart of the Father.

8. Love causes you to stop keeping score. The Scripture teaches that love *"thinks no evil"* (1 Cor. 13:5). The word *thinks* in this passage means to take an inventory in your mind, to number or keep a record of the evil done to you. In other words, to truly love your spouse means you can't be keeping a score card in your mind of all your mate's failures and faults. If you do, a loving relationship will be impossible.

Some of you may be thinking to yourselves right now that this is impossible. When I encourage couples to take this action, I am amazed by the number of Christians who look at me with raised eyebrows and tell me they think this is an unattainable goal. Is it possible? If it is, how do you practically do it?

First, you must fully and completely forgive your spouse for whatever evil has been committed against you. Forgiveness is a fundamental key to releasing the inventory in your mind of your mate's failures. As a Christian you are commanded to *"forgive men their trespasses"* (Matt. 6:14). As Jesus was on the cross loving you and me, His choice was to pray, *"Father, forgive them..."* (Luke 23:34). Sacrificial love forgives and cancels the debt completely. Your spouse's sins must first be blotted out in order to be removed from the record.

Second, to relinquish the score card you must control your thought life with considerable diligence. The real battle rages in the mind, and you must overcome it there. This is where Cain went wrong. In Genesis chapter 4 God pointedly asked him why he persisted in his anger toward his brother Abel and offered to him some profound insight into the nature of sin and the nursing of a grudge in particular. He said, *"But if you do not do what is right, sin is crouching at your door; it desires to have you, but you must master it"* (v. 7, NIV). God's counsel to Cain was simple. If he would have quickly dealt with his resentful thoughts and done what was right, this sin would not have overcome him. However, as we read the rest of the story we see that Cain rejected God's Word. He continued to think evil in his heart which ultimately led to the murder of his brother. See to it that you win this battle in your mind.

Isn't it easy to sit and reflect over some past sin against you and then begin to get angry all over again? However, when God forgives He promises, *"Their sins and their lawless deeds I will remember no more"* (Heb. 8:12). The word *remember* in this passage means "to hold in a mental grasp or to recollect." This is a wonderful promise and an example we should all follow for every offense that occurs in our relationship. God is not saying here that He forgets our sins, only that He chooses not to remember them against us. He is not holding a grudge against us, because this is what real forgiveness is all about. When He forgives, He blots the infraction out completely, never to bring it up again. I will cover this subject in greater detail in a later chapter devoted entirely to forgiveness.

Don't let your record-keeping of each other's sins destroy your love relationship. Forgive each other and demonstrate your love by not dwelling on past issues in your mind. The next time a past offense comes up in your mind, choose to forgive again and refuse to sit and meditate on it anymore. The mind is a powerful tool; therefore use it for good. As Paul said, *"Finally, brethren, whatever things are true, whatever things are noble, whatever things are just, whatever things are pure, whatever things are lovely, whatever things are of good report, if there is any virtue and if there is anything praiseworthy; meditate on these things...and the God of peace will be with you"* (Phil 4:8, 9). These are the things you should be dwelling on in your mind! If you do, the God of peace will be with you.

9. Love causes you to trust. Trust is one of the most fundamental ingredients to any successful and lasting relationship. Paul declared that love *"believes all things,"* revealing the necessity of trust in any loving relationship (1 Cor. 13:7). To grow in love, trust must be verbally expressed, and your every action must confirm it. On the other hand, to grow in your trust for each other, you must also be actively loving each other at the same time. Love inspires trust, and trust motivates love. One will always beget the other.

However, when couples come for counseling and their relationship has degenerated to suspicion and jealousy, the problem is always rooted in a lack of love. Sometimes suspicion is the result of a lack of expression of one's love, which creates the natural question in your mate's mind, *does this person still love me?* Sometimes jealously is a personal problem that is rooted in deep insecurities that cause an individual to be unwilling to receive the love expressed by another. At other times there has been a breach of trust because of one spouse committing adultery, repeatedly lying, or drug use. All these will destroy the depth of love and trust between two people. However, don't misunderstand me here. If this breaching behavior blatantly continues, God does not require us to trust. Scripture commands us not to believe someone when we see hatred and deceit exhibited. Solomon warned us, *"He who hates, disguises it with his lips, and lays up deceit within himself; when he speaks kindly, do not believe him…"* (Prov. 26:24, 25).

How does love break through this seemingly insurmountable barrier and build trust again? Only by putting into practice each of the previous actions of love I have referred to in this chapter. Love will initiate a time to communicate about this lack of trust so that you might find reconciliation and restoration in your relationship. There must be loving honesty between you as you communicate, confessing any transgression that has destroyed your trust and forgiving with a decision not to bring it up again. Only then will love and the precious fruit of trust begin to return in this relationship.

Do you have this kind of trusting love for your spouse? Do you verbalize your trust to your partner on a regular basis? More importantly, are you living in such a manner that your spouse has no cause to doubt you or your love?

10. <u>Love causes you to commit yourself until there is no remedy</u>. This is the enduring and long-suffering quality of love that works and fights for a relationship. It's the characteristic of love that searches for a remedy even when it must hope against hope that a solution can be found. Love is committed to all the above principles for as long as it takes. Love doesn't back off until it is obvious that no solution can be achieved due to the complete unwillingness of the other party. Love only retreats to wait it out. Paul described this quality when he said, *"Love suffers long…bears all things, believes all things, hopes all things, endures all things. Love never fails"* (1 Cor. 13:4, 7, 8). This again is how God has demonstrated His love toward us.

One of the great examples of this quality of love is found in the history of the nation of Israel. God said that He had *"set His love upon them."* He called them His *"special treasure above all peoples on the earth."* He chose them not for any particular goodness in themselves, but because of His own purposes (Deut. 7:6-8). The history of Israel is one long demonstration of His care, provision, protection, redemption, and long-suffering. At times the people returned the love of God by keeping His commandments. Then they would go back to serving themselves and their vain idols. Their unfaithfulness would result in God's correction and their repentance. Over and over again they would fall away. Yet God kept sending His prophets to correct and instruct them. Some were mocked and others were killed, yet God continued to reach out until *"there was no remedy"* (2 Chron. 36:15, 16). Finally, the people became *"joined to idols,"* as Hosea the prophet said, which demonstrated that they would no longer respond to His reproof (Hosea 4:17). As judgment, God allowed the Assyrians and Babylonians to take them captive for their rebellion. His purpose behind allowing their captivity was to wait it out, all the while hoping for repentance so that He might return them to their land.

As God demonstrated His love to the people of Israel, so He has declared the commitment of His love to you. He says, *"I will never leave you nor forsake you"* (Heb. 13:5). What a gracious commitment is promised here. God is very sparing with the word *never* because few things qualify. It is only used a hundred and ten times in the entire Bible and only thirty-seven times by God in promises to His people. He uses this word to emphasize His full and total commitment of love. Take special note of this principle. God, the One who loves, is never the one to back off in our relationship. If someone departs, it will not be Him. Be assured, He is committed to stay the course. You can count on it!

Do you possess this kind of commitment as you work at your marriage? This kind of patience and commitment is essential if you are to find the solutions you are looking for in your relationship. Both parties must have the willingness to stay the course and not give up. Ironically, I will see one spouse give up, while the other sincerely wants to reconcile and build the relationship. Then eventually the uncommitted person changes their mind and recommits to seeking reconciliation, only to find that the other partner has given up. And the whole situation starts all over again from the opposite side. Don't give up too quickly. It takes time to see a person's heart change, so be realistic in your expectations. Your spouse will be slow at heart to change, so you must not be too quick to take drastic action. Love gives plenty of time for God to work.

Do you see now why love is so essential for building the relationship and companionship you long for in your marriage? The love of God in you will enable you to do all He requires, and it will cause you to stay the course with your spouse when the going gets tough. Knowing and applying these principles of love to your marriage will enable you to become a great companion to your spouse. If you want to begin, here are some steps to take.

Actions To Take
1. Ask God to reveal to you how you define love.
2. Ask God to change your heart wherever your views are contrary to His.
3. Ask God to enable you to begin to walk in love His way.

Review
Let's review before we go on from this section. Each of these chapters presents a foundation stone in building a marriage that will last.

1. You must be willing to do anything and everything that God requires in order to reconcile the conflicts that exist and be willing to work at building your relationship. This heart attitude is essential to begin any change.
2. You must be convinced of the ultimate biblical goal of oneness and companionship. You must be aiming at this goal if you are ever to hit the target.
3. You must have a personal relationship with Christ. This is where you receive the power needed to put into action what God requires.
4. You must yield to the authority of God's Word as your only standard of truth. This reveals to you the plan of action necessary to establish companionship.
5. You need a new definition of love. It will enable you to understand and take exactly the right actions at the right time.

Where do we go from here? Once you are willing to implement God's solutions to build your relationship and have established your relationship with Him, you now need to learn how to resolve conflicts. Without learning how to do this, and initiating reconciliation with each new conflict that arises, you cannot build a new relationship. It is absolutely essential that you first resolve anything that is behind you or you will not be able to go forward. How do you do this? What steps do you need to take? This is the subject of the next section.

Group Discussion Questions

1. List the ten definitions of what love causes you to do.
2. Take each definition of love and apply them to specific actions that you should take in your relationship. How will you think, speak, and act?

WHAT HINDERS YOU FROM BUILDING COMPANIONSHIP & ONENESS WITH YOUR SPOUSE?

Once a contractor has laid the foundation for a house, the building process can get underway. There are always problems with the different materials and joining them together to make one building. Similarly, there are also many problems in joining two very different people into a one-flesh relationship.

In this second section, I want to cover the fundamental issues that battle against growth in your relationship with each other. What are the issues that keep you from becoming a companion and friend to your spouse? Why are there so many conflicts between you, and how can you resolve the recurring arguments once and for all? Let's begin with the root of the problem that hinders the building process from ever starting.

6

DON'T MISS THE ROOT OF THE PROBLEM

"Where envy and self-seeking exist, confusion and every evil thing will be there" James 3:16

If one day you went to the doctor with a very high fever and the doctor determined that you had a serious infection raging inside you, what do you think he would do? Would he treat just the symptoms of your illness by sending you home with an ice pack, or give you two aspirin and tell you to call him in the morning? Absolutely not! A good doctor would do so much more than that. He would examine you fully and run tests to determine the cause of your ailment. He would then take a specific course of action, such as prescribing medication or scheduling surgery to attack the source of the problem. A doctor would never just treat the visible symptoms.

Similarly, I want to begin this new section by striking not at the symptoms, but at the very root of what hinders you from building real companionship and oneness with your spouse. If we can destroy the root of a bad tree, the rotten fruit will naturally wither and die by itself. Don't you desire to plant a new tree that will bear the sweet fruit of love and intimacy with each other? The only way to do this is by laying your ax to the root of the tree of your old ways. John the Baptist told the religious leaders of his day, who had plenty of bad fruit in their lives, that they needed to change their ways and *"bear fruits worthy of repentance"* (Matt. 3:8). He then told them how repentance and change occurs. He said, *"And even now the ax is laid to the root of the trees. Therefore every tree which does not bear good fruit is cut down and thrown into the fire"* (Matt. 3:10). It is imperative that you see what hinders your relationship and then lay the ax to the root of that specific attitude or action. God wants to plant in your heart by the power of His Spirit a fresh, loving attitude toward your companion that will bear the fruit you long for.

What hinders true companionship and creates all the conflicts between you, leaving you distant and unsatisfied in your marriage? Is there a root cause to the disagreements and strife you are experiencing? Think for a moment about the one thing that Scripture requires of us in order to reconcile our conflict with God and follow Him. Jesus put His finger squarely on our greatest need: *"If anyone desires to come after Me, let him deny himself, and take up his cross, and follow Me. For whoever desires to save his life will lose it, and whoever loses his life for My sake will find it"* (Matt. 16:24, 25). Jesus made it clear that the disciples could not continue to live for themselves and follow Him at the same time. Self had to be denied to the point of death. These men were called to go to the cross in their personal lives for the sake of the One who called them. Jesus knows that self has to be dethroned if He is ever to be enthroned as Lord of our lives.

The self-life is what keeps any person at war with God and living an independent life. If you want to follow Christ, living for self will be impossible. In addition, Paul explained this same truth to the Corinthian church as one of the root causes of their many conflicts with one another. He encouraged that since Christ had *"died for all…those who live should live no longer for themselves, but for Him who died for them and rose again"* (2 Cor. 5:15). He explained that living for self is directly opposed to living for Christ. Selfishness is the primary issue that God desires to deal with in every life. Only as you renounce selfish living can you begin to live for Him and be able to truly serve others.

The apostle James also wrote to the church explaining why the Christians in his day were having so much strife. He declared, *"Where envy and self-seeking exist, confusion and every evil thing will be there"* (James 3:16). The word *confusion* means "a state of instability and disorder." Self-seeking is what causes this instability and disorder in all relationships. Envy is equally self-oriented because it is only concerned with getting for oneself what somebody else has. Remember every conflict you have and every hurtful behavior begins with a concentration on self. If you want to deal with the root cause of the conflicts in your relationship, here it is: *selfishness.*

Don't put a Band-Aid on the wounds or just treat the symptoms. If you want to determine what the root of all the problems is in your relationship, start here. Strike at the root of what is bearing all the bad fruit.

WHY IS SELFISHNESS THE ROOT PROBLELM?

The answer to this question is very simple. Self-seeking is completely contrary to love. Paul made this vital truth absolutely clear to the Corinthian church when he explained that *"love does not seek its own"* (1 Cor. 13:5). When you love someone you will always be more concerned about their well-being and not your own. Paul had already taught this truth to the Corinthians when he commanded them: *"Let no one seek his own, but each one the other's well-being"* (1 Cor. 10:24). There-fore, love and selfishness cannot coexist. They are like oil and water. Al-ways remember this fundamental truth: the degree to which you love others equals that of the denial of self.

All the conflicts you are having with your spouse right now result from one thing: *selfishness*. It is the battle between your selfishness and your mate's. It's a battle of wills; who will get their own way and who will get it first. Yet no one wins this battle because selfishness always destroys.

The wisdom of this world is teaching us today that self is to be pre-served; to look out for number one. You need to be self-assertive, self-directed, and possess a high self-esteem. There is even a magazine de-voted to propagating this message. It's called *Self* magazine. However, indulging in self is not exercising the wisdom that comes from above.

The emphasis on self today is a sign of our rejection of godly values. In Paul's last epistle he predicted what the last days would be like. *"But know this, that in the last days perilous times will come: For men will be lovers of themselves..."* (2 Tim. 3:1, 2, underline added). Is this not in-dicative of our times? This is not how God wants His children to live because He knows how destructive this attitude can be to all human relationships.

God's Word teaches us something much different. *"But the wisdom that is from above is first pure, then peaceable, gentle, willing to yield, full of mercy and good fruits, without partiality and without hypocrisy. Now the fruit of righteousness is sown in peace by those who make peace"* (James 3:17, 18). To have peace in your relationships, you must live righteously. He describes this righteousness as being gentle, willing to yield, and merciful toward others. God's wisdom is the opposite of selfishness and yields different fruit. It is God's giving nature being expressed through you.

Our basic nature is not like this. Your nature and mine is selfish to the core. Paul said, *"For all seek their own, and not the things of Jesus Christ"* (Phil. 2:21). This is the way you and your spouse are in the very depths of your souls. However, your nature can be transformed so that you reflect God's love and become a selfless giver. I will talk more about how this occurs in a later chapter.

The second reason why I believe selfishness is the basic hindrance to companionship has been drawn from my personal experience in coun-seling. With every couple I have ever counseled, selfishness was at the root of their marital problems. Not only have I come to this conclusion, but the couples I have counseled have usually come to realize this too.

I have an exercise that I have most couples do at some point. I ask them to go home and make a list of all the areas in which they are living selfishly and come back the next week. They nod and agree. Without fail, they come back with quite a list. Then I simply examine their lists and try to show them how their selfish actions are the central reason for their problems.

WHERE ARE YOU LIVING SELFISHLY?

Stop right now and make your own list. Where are you living selfishly? Where is self still on the throne of your life? How is your selfishness affecting your relationship with your spouse? If you will take the time to be honest with yourself and take my challenge, it will yield abundant fruit. As a word of warning, be careful not to list your spouse's failures. Concentrate only on where *you* are acting selfishly. Remember to *"first remove the plank from you own eye, and then you will see clearly to remove the speck out of your brother's eye"* (Matt. 7:5). Jesus made it clear in this passage that you must first deal with yourself before you will ever be able to see clearly someone else's failures. This is especially true in marriage.

Once you've made your list, consider how your selfishness contributes to the conflicts between you. This is a heart-searching exercise and requires the utmost honesty. As you look sincerely at yourself, you will see how your selfishness is hindering intimacy and companionship with your mate.

Let me first give you some idea of where to look. What does selfishness look like in a marriage? Selfishness has many faces, all of which are ugly. Sometimes self is seen in a very bold and aggressive way when a person verbally insists on having their own way. It's their way or no way. It's the straightforward demand of *me* first. Sometimes this bold demand is accompanied with a violent outburst of anger to ensure its way is obtained through intimidation.

Other times selfishness is very subtle. It can have the quiet face of cunning manipulation with gentle words. But in reality, it is still just a persistent pressure to work it's own will upon you. It also may be seen as that stubborn resistance to bend or compromise over even the smallest issues. When its will is not acknowledged or yielded to, there is a quiet sulking or an attitude of indifference until the other partner finally surrenders.

Whether selfishness is seen in its bold or subtle forms, it is the root of the problems between you. Beloved, be not deceived. When you allow self-righteousness, self-will, self-justification, or self-indulgence to reign in your heart, it can only bring every evil thing to your relationship. Only by laying the ax to the root of this tree will you ever see the fruit you desire in your life and marriage. I encourage you again to stop now and do this exercise. If you and your spouse are reading this book together, please work on your lists separately. This will help to keep you centered on your own selfishness and not on your partner's.

How Can You Overcome Selfishness?

Recognizing your selfishness is a major step in resolving your marital conflicts. If you can do that, you are halfway home. However, you must do more than just recognize where you have been living selfishly. You must overcome it in your daily relationship. God wants to free you from being a servant to self to become a servant to Him and your loved one.

How can you see this change come to pass in practical terms? Here are some steps I encourage you to take:

1. <u>Look honestly at the thoughts and motives of your heart</u>. An honest "self" inventory is essential because selfishness begins in the thoughts and motives of the heart. Before selfishness ever becomes an action in your life, it will surface in the way you think about yourself and your spouse.

This is why Jesus challenged the scribes, *"Why do you think evil in your hearts?"* (Matt. 9:4). Jesus knew their hearts were wrong, so He encouraged them to examine their own thinking that they might see the error within. A person's mindset results from what is in his heart (Matt. 15:19). That is why you must probe your thought life. Close scrutiny will enable you to see if the motives of your heart are selfish or not.

In addition, you must also question how you perceive yourself. Simply listen to what you think about yourself and it will tell you plenty. Paul said, *"If anyone thinks himself to be something, when he is nothing, he deceives himself"* (Gal. 6:3). Do you think you are better, smarter, or wiser than your spouse? Do you think you deserve to be served, agreed with, or placed above your spouse? These thoughts reveal selfish and arrogant thinking that will result in many conflicts and little companionship.

Let me give you another biblical example of how selfish thinking destroys relationships. The apostle James wrote to the Jewish Christians about the problem they were having of playing favorites to the wealthy people in their church meetings. He pinpointed their thought life as the source of their problem. He told them they had *"become judges with evil thoughts"* (James 2:4). They were probably thinking, *these rich believers can give us so many things. We sure better be nice to them and give them the best seats in the house.* James exposed their thinking and motives to be selfish, the complete antithesis to what Christ stands for.

Allow the Holy Spirit to begin to minister to you right now. He can reveal your selfish heart quickly and easily. If you will yield to Him, you will be laying the ax to the root of the tree.

2. <u>Ask for the conviction of the Holy Spirit</u>. This is where all change begins and how the process of salvation began in your heart. Jesus said when the Holy Spirit is come that *"He will convict the world of sin, and of righteousness, and of judgment"* (John 16:8). His conviction caused you to see that sin separated you from God in the first place and brought you to change your thinking and direction in life. When you suddenly see the incorrect thinking and motives that you now possess toward your spouse, that is the Holy Spirit convicting you in order to effect a beautiful change in your relationship.

Paul also taught that conviction is the result of planting the Word of God in your heart. The Scriptures are beneficial for *"doctrine, for reproof, for correction, for instruction in righteousness..."* (2 Tim. 3:16). The word *reproof* in this passage means "to convict." Therefore, when you study the Word, you receive doctrine or teaching. As the Word teaches you, conviction begins and initiates the correction and the ultimate change toward righteousness in your life. This is why I stressed in chapter 4 your need to accept God's Word as your standard of truth; unless you do, the work of conviction will not occur.

When I speak of conviction I don't mean condemnation. Conviction is that sweet and gentle prodding of the Lord that draws you into a willing surrender to Him. Condemnation is just the opposite and comes from the accuser of the brethren (Rev. 12:10). It drives you away from God, making you think you have gone too far and are too sinful to receive forgiveness and undergo change. You must know the difference.

Begin today by asking the Lord to show you your selfish thoughts and how your actions are affecting your spouse. Ask Him to reveal how your actions are causing the conflicts and the lack of companionship. Ask Him for the conviction to change inside and out, and a very different fruit will begin to blossom in your relationship.

3. <u>Choose to deny your selfish thoughts and motivations</u>. Once you have determined where you are living selfishly and you are convicted about it, you have a choice to make. Will you deny your selfish desires and choose to live and act differently, or will you choose to deny the

conviction? It's one thing to know you shouldn't do something. It's quite another to respond to the conviction and stop doing it. It's really just a choice.

Throughout Scripture we see that the key to real life is determined by your choice. Remember Joshua encouraged the children of Israel, *"<u>Choose</u> for yourselves this day whom you will serve"* (Joshua 24:15, underline added). God pleaded with His people through the prophet Isaiah, *"<u>Choose</u> what pleases Me, and hold fast My covenant"* (Is. 56:4, underline added). Moses warned the Jews, *"I have set before you life and death, blessing and cursing; therefore <u>choose</u> life, that both you and your descendants may live"* (Deut. 30:19, underline added).

Choosing to deny yourself and your selfish thoughts is your responsibility. No one can do it for you; it's your decision. Every day you must make the choice to deny yourself, take up your cross, and serve Christ. This includes serving your mate.

Over every issue in which you are selfishly drawing away from your mate, you must make a choice. You may even be making that decision as you are reading right now. At this moment you are in the midst of a spiritual battle between God's conviction, your will, and Satan's lies. Recognize his lies and resist them. Satan has no desire to see you living a selfless life. Until this battle subsides you must choose continually to submit your will to the Lord. Ask God to conform your thoughts to be in harmony with His and to fill you with the victory He promises. Remember, *"Submit to God. Resist the devil and he will flee from you"* (James 4:7).

4. <u>Give yourself to the Lord</u>. Where do you get the power to follow through on your decisions to deny yourself? It's by giving yourself to the Lord. A whole-hearted surrender to Him will enable you to change from selfish living to selfless living. Here is where the power of the Holy Spirit will be manifested in your life. Giving yourself to the Lord brings about this transformation from selfishness to giving.

When you completely yield yourself to Christ, He comes to take full control of your life. This is just what He has been waiting for you to do. As you surrender yourself to Him, He will send His Holy Spirit to fill and empower you to change. The Holy Spirit is the only One who can change a selfish heart to a giving one because He is stronger than your sinful nature that now controls you. The Spirit longs to transform you. As Paul said, this is His work. We *"are being transformed into the same image from glory to glory, just as by the Spirit of the Lord"* (2 Cor. 3:18). If this is how the transformation occurs, are you then daily asking the Lord to fill you with His Holy Spirit? God is more than willing to fulfill this desire. Jesus said, *"If you, being evil, know how to give good gifts to your children, how much more will your heavenly Father give the Holy Spirit to those who ask Him"* (Luke 11:13). Are you asking?

The Holy Spirit is the One who will transform you into the image and likeness of Christ. Is Christ giving? Of course He is! And with His Spirit working in you, He will make you giving too! He will make you like Jesus.

There is another promise from God's Word. If you *"walk in the Spirit...you shall not fulfill the lust of the flesh"* (Gal. 5:16). The flesh is what continually draws us all back to selfish living and fights against us every step of the way. Why? Because the root of our human nature is selfishness and rebellion. That is why you experience that constant pull every day of your life. If you are being filled with His Spirit daily, and walk under His control, He will rule over this powerful draw to selfishness.

To walk in the Spirit you must decide to put the deeds of your selfish nature to death. Paul explained how: *"If you live according to the flesh you will die; but if by the Spirit you put to death the deeds of the body, you will live"* (Rom. 8:13). Paul acknowledges here that you must decide in the matter. Notice the word *if* with each choice. By the power of the Spirit you must deny the deeds of the flesh and trust His enabling grace to help you live. One thing is clear: His life in you will always empower you to serve others before yourself.

The Holy Spirit can and will do this work in you if you will only fully give yourself to Him. Don't miss this work of transformation in your life; it is exciting and very fulfilling to watch and witness the progress! Let Him change and empower you. He is waiting for your invitation.

5. <u>Confess your selfishness</u>. Once you have recognized your selfish behavior and have begun to deal with it before God, it is time to reconcile the issue with your spouse. My suggestion is to obey the command of the apostle James. *"Confess your trespasses to one another, and pray for one another, that you may be healed"* (James 5:16).

If you want your marriage to be healed this is what you must do. Why is this action important? Because admitting our wrong is what Christians do when there has been an offense. What would actually happen if you were to confess what God has shown you concerning your own selfish behavior and ask your spouse for forgiveness and prayer for change in your life? What would be the response from your spouse to this kind of humility and honesty? Don't you think your mate would respond in a loving and gracious way? Wouldn't this action bring healing to your relationship and a new depth of intimacy and love?

God requires this kind of humility and honesty in our relationships. Without it He will not bless our attempt to change these areas of our life. Solomon declared, *"He who covers his sins will not prosper, but whoever confesses and forsakes them will have mercy"* (Prov. 28:13). Don't let the sin of pride keep you from making a complete break with your selfish behavior.

When you confess your needs to your spouse, you will not only attain a deeper intimacy with each other, you will also receive the added benefit of their prayer support. Notice the rest of James 5:16: *"The effective, fervent prayer of a righteous man avails much."* Prayer together will achieve great things that you have not yet seen. You will attain new depth of intimacy if you pray together about these issues! Don't miss this means to oneness.

6. <u>Choose to love in each circumstance</u>. This one action will do more to change your struggling relationship than anything I know. When you begin to love in circumstances where you formerly were living selfishly, your spouse will notice the difference immediately. At first your mate will think it's only a coincidence, but after a while they will begin to believe there has been a genuine change in you because your actions will demand this conclusion.

Real love for your husband or wife will be revealed in your patience or by the softening of that harsh tone of voice and will take over the thoughtless reactions that used to dominate you. When your partner sees you not seeking your own way, but seeking their benefit, it will change their heart. Your example will encourage your partner to respond in a similar manner. God's love is designed to beget more love. Paul said we are to *"consider one another in order to stir up love and good works"* (Heb. 10:24). The word *stir up* means to provoke. In other words, your actions of love will provoke others to love you in return, just as anger and selfishness will provoke the works of the flesh.

Now you may be thinking, *Yes. That may work with some people, but you don't know my husband (or wife). He (she) is so hardened and unresponsive nothing would change him (her)!* Now I have to admit, I have seen some people fight long and hard to resist a spouse's continued attempts to love them. But love is the hardest thing in the world to fight against because there is no rational reason to do so. On the other hand, if someone is resentful and aggressive, you seemingly have a perfectly logical excuse for not being nice in return. (I speak from a human perspective not a spiritual one.) Yet, if you are loved by your spouse, you have no excuse for staying hard-hearted. So then, don't give your spouse an excuse for remaining in an unresponsive position; choose to love your mate in every circumstance. This is the best chance you have for seeing change in your marriage.

Until you love unconditionally, you haven't really given the total commitment God requires. He asks you to love even your enemies. If your spouse is your enemy right now, you are still commanded to love. Choose to do it, and your obedience will please the Lord. I have seen many seemingly lost marriages turned around because one person was willing to obey God and love in every circumstance, and the spouse was slowly softened over time. Full reconciliation can occur, but it takes work and lots of it! That's what love is all about.

As a reminder of what practical love will do, go back and review chapter 5. This will help you to determine how God wants you to love unconditionally.

Group Discussion Questions
1. Discuss with the group how your selfishness has hindered a prior relationship other than your marriage.
2. Without giving names or details, give an example of a marriage you have seen destroyed by selfish behavior.
3. Discuss how your own selfish thoughts and motives have hindered the relationship with your spouse.

7

DO YOU HAVE REALISTIC EXPECTATIONS?

"I know the thoughts I have toward you...
to give you an expected end" Jer. 29:11 KJV

Steve and Donna had been married for about three years when I first counseled them. Donna was a very social person and verbally expressive. She could talk a mile a minute about any subject you could suggest. Steve was just the opposite. He was a very quiet and reserved man who would not speak unless you asked him a direct question. He hardly said a word during each of our counseling sessions.

They had been struggling in their marriage from the very beginning. Donna wanted her husband to become more involved in her social activities. She wanted him to be more friendly and talk with people after church on Sundays. Donna had badgered him until he became more and more resentful and ultimately refused to have anything to do with her on any level of their marriage. She was now at the point of total frustration and asked, "Why can't he relate to people the way I relate to them? He must not really care about me or our marriage. If he did he would act differently! I'm through waiting for this guy to change. I want out of this relationship."

When I heard Donna's statement, I knew where I had to begin. Donna had a totally unrealistic expectation for Steve. This was the underlying key to their conflicts. I could see that Steve really did care about their marriage. He did really love his wife, but he had become very resentful over her constant harassment and belittling of him. He said to me, "She won't be happy until I become just like her. I have tried to reach out and be more friendly, but she is never satisfied. So I have just given up trying."

Throughout each of our counseling sessions I made it a point to explain what realistic expectations for change were in their marriage. Donna listened intently but never fully yielded to the truth and the consequences of clinging to unrealistic expectations. Shortly after this they separated and finally got a divorce.

What was the problem here? It was Donna's unwillingness to see that this was primarily *her* problem. She had unrealistic expectations and refused to take action to change. Ultimately, Donna became hardened in her heart toward Steve simply because he was different than her. Steve was also at fault when he responded poorly, became resentful, and refused to try anymore at reconciling the relationship. Their wrong responses to each other ultimately destroyed their oneness and companionship, and slowly drove them apart.

How about you, do you have unrealistic expectations of your mate? If so, what are they? Most importantly, how can you determine what your expectations should be?

One's expectations are often the central cause for marital conflict; however, it is not one that is generally perceived. An expectation is an insidious enemy because it is in your head as a thought and is unseen, making it very difficult to recognize. Most people think, *This is what I want. I'm right and my spouse needs to change.* This expectation creates a slow, smoldering anger inside when change doesn't occur. Eventually, these unrealistic expectations create an attitude of resentment and frustration that grows with every passing day, creating conflict after conflict, until you finally give up in hopelessness. Many times your spouse doesn't change because your expectations are not in accordance with reality or a biblical definition of change.

Here is an equation I have found to be true: Unrealistic expectations always result in unfulfilled expectations, which result in anger, frustration, and ultimate hopelessness. These negative results in turn hinder the building of your marital companionship and prevent the stability you long for.

Let me give you an Old Testament illustration of this principle. This is not a marital example, but one in which clear expectations were declared and remained unfulfilled. Naaman was the commander of the Syrian army. He was a great and honorable man and had many military victories to his credit. But Naaman had the disease of leprosy. One day a young Jewish captive girl, who was Naaman's servant, saw his leprous condition and told her master of a prophet of God in Israel who could heal him. He immediately left in search of the prophet and found Elisha. As Naaman stood before the door of Elisha's house, the prophet sent a messenger out who told him to go wash in the Jordan River seven times and he would be healed. Naaman became furious that Elisha didn't even grant him the courtesy of coming out to greet him, but merely sent out a servant. Naaman then declared his expectation when he said, *"Indeed, I said to myself, 'He will surely come out to me, and stand and call on the name of the Lord his God, and wave his hand over the place, and heal the leprosy'"* (2 Kings 5:11). Naaman was also upset that the prophet had not told him to wash in one of the cleaner rivers of Damascus. In the end, Naaman did go and wash in the Jordan after one of his servants calmed him down. His servant entreated him, *"My father, if the prophet had told you to do something great, would you not have done it? How much more then, when he says to you, 'Wash and be clean'? "* (2 Kings 5:13). The commander then humbled himself, obeyed the prophet's instructions, and was healed.

Here is a perfect example of a man with unrealistic expectations that resulted in unfulfilled expectations and the anger that accompanies them. Yet, Naaman didn't come to hopelessness because when he realized that his expectations were unrealistic, he dealt with them correctly. He humbled himself and obeyed the Word of the Lord, finding the healing he sought. The story could have ended very differently if he had not identified his unrealistic expectations and corrected them.

Donna and Steve's marriage could have continued if they had only dealt with their unrealistic expectations correctly, but they failed to do what Naaman did. They should have humbled themselves and conformed their expectations to the Word of God.

What will be the story of your marriage? If one day your relationship were to be written down, what would it say? Would it document that you identified your unrealistic expectations, humbled yourself, and obeyed the Word of the Lord? Only by first identifying these unattainable expectations can you correctly deal with them.

WHAT ARE SOME UNREALISTIC EXPECTATIONS?

To identify any questionable expectations you must first listen to the things you say to your spouse in the midst of a conflict. "If you would only _____, then I would be happy." Sometimes our expectations have never been put into words; they may only be in our thoughts. Stop and listen to your own words or thoughts the next time you are angry, and your expectations will become crystal clear. This step is critical to identifying expectations and determining if they are realistic or not.

Let's now look at some expectations I hear quite often. I want to relate them to you as people verbalize them to me. This will help you to identify them better in your own heart. There are obviously more unrealistic expectations than the seven I will give here, but these are the most common ones. Any expectation can become unrealistic if it is taken out of the balance of biblical truth or to a selfish extreme.

1. *"Why does my spouse have these problems?"* Many times people ask this question with great frustration and despair, as if their marriage

partner should have no problems at all. Husbands and wives are unrealistically hoping for someone who doesn't have problems. It's a rude awakening when two people get married. After being on their best behavior throughout the courtship, they suddenly realize their partner is someone with real flaws. The reality of being married to a person who is not perfect shakes one or both parties to the very core. You say, "Do people really expect perfection?" Absolutely, or they would never ask this question. This is the secret hope of many married people. They have a subliminal expectation that their spouses will be free of problems and everything will be smooth sailing just like the courtship. People come to me very angry when they find out after marrying that their spouse is not the person they expected. They discover that their spouse has sexual problems, communication problems, spiritual problems, or a multitude of other things that weren't apparent before marriage.

What is realistic? You have married a person who has problems because you married a sinner. Paul said, *"For all have sinned and fall short of the glory of God"* (Rom. 3:23). This is realistic! Sinners have problems, failures, and weaknesses; this is who we are. We are sinners who will constantly fall short of the glory of God and His expectations for us. Surely, then, we will fall short of the expectations we have for one another.

I have had people confess to me that this is the main reason why they have divorced and remarried again and again. They were looking for someone who didn't have any problems. One woman who was on her fourth marriage confessed to me, "I now realize I was looking for a man that just does not exist." Another man on his third marriage said to me, "All I've done in each new marriage is trade one set of problems for another. My first wife wasn't very sexually passionate, so I divorced her and married one who was. But then she had a problem of not telling me how and where she spent our money. My present wife uses money very wisely, but we have a very weak spiritual relationship."

The fact is, there are no perfect people for you to marry anywhere on this planet! If more people truly believed this, more would be working at their present marital conflicts instead of moving on to the supposed "greener pastures."

2. *"With all these problems, maybe I married the wrong person."* This is a faulty belief that is very similar to the previous one because it again assumes that divinely ordained marriages don't have problems. If you look at Scripture and the divinely arranged marriages you find there, this is not the case.

Consider the example of Adam and Eve. Theirs was surely a divinely ordained marriage. Eve was specifically created from Adam's own flesh to be his helpmate. Adam was directed to take her unto himself as his wife by God himself. You can't have a more divinely directed marriage.

However, did Adam and Eve have a perfect marriage? No, and that's why we don't have perfect marriages today! Eve disobeyed God's command and then tempted her own husband to sin too. They both shifted the blame for their failure to escape taking responsibility for their own sin. Their marriage had problems and fell short of the glory of God even though it had been divinely ordained.

Consider the marriage of Isaac and Rebekah. Abraham's servant was divinely directed to go find a wife for his son, Isaac. Through a multitude of God-directed actions, the servant found a wife for his master's son. When he found her, he worshiped the Lord *"who led me in the way of truth to take the daughter of my master's brother for his son"* (Gen. 24:48). As you continue to read the rest of their story, you will find that the marriage had many examples of lying, deception, and unbelief. Though God had ordained this marriage, Isaac and Rebekeh had times in which they fell dramatically below perfection.

Look at the marriage of Abraham and Sarah. They are described in Scripture as a man and woman of faith (Heb. 11:8-12). Yet Abraham had a weakness concerning the fear of man that caused him to lie regarding his wife twice. He said that Sarah was his sister in order to protect himself from a presumed threat on his life (Gen. 12:11-13; Gen. 20:1,2). Sarah also had her problems. She laughed at the improbability of God's promise concerning a son in her old age, and then she lied to cover it up (Gen. 18:12-15). These were two people God chose to parent the nation Israel and bless the world through their seed. But they were clearly imperfect people.

These examples are to teach you that there are no perfect marriages because there are no perfect people. Don't waste your energy looking back trying to figure out if this was the perfect person you were to marry. By His grace and power, become the person God wants you to be. Put off your selfishness and love the person you are married to now. This could encourage your mate to do the same, and then you will have the marriage you are looking for.

3. *"Why do we seem so different from each other?"* The answer to this question is simply because people are different and always will be. If this were not true we would all be robots, exactly alike. Again, most people

will agree intellectually that we are not supposed to be alike, but then in the next breath, they get angry if their partner isn't thinking and acting just like they do.

No two people are exactly alike. We have all grown up in different families under various parenting styles with different friends, genes, and geographical or cultural backgrounds. We've each lived our own lives differently and achieved distinct goals as a result. Then there are also the dramatic differences between men and women, physically, emotionally, and hormonally. All these differences should naturally teach you that your spouse will never be just like you. This was the central error in Donna's thinking. Remember she asked, "Why doesn't he relate to people the way I do?"

Paul the apostle assumed there would be differences in people's thinking and decision making. The early Christians of his day had conflicts regarding what day they should be worshiping and what foods they should eat. His counsel to them was this: "*One person esteems one day above another; another esteems every day alike. Let each be fully convinced in his own mind*" (Rom. 14:5). Note that Paul naturally assumed that people would have their own personal convictions regarding the gray areas of certain behavior. In non-moral issues, God allows people to form their own opinions. He was basically declaring that it is alright to have personal beliefs that differ over peripheral issues. He merely encouraged these believers to refrain from judging one another because of these differences (Rom. 14:3, 4).

Therefore, you can also assume that you will see many things differently than your spouse. This is a realistic expectation because it is the biblical declaration of what one should expect. It's okay to see things differently than your spouse, but the question is, are you judging or despising them for this opinion? If you are, it is because you have unrealistic expectations. Instead, take this difference as an opportunity to learn how to love.

4. "*Why can't my spouse make me happy?*" I have found that when people are personally unhappy and unsatisfied in life, their marriage can never satisfy them. Seeking happiness from your mate is an unrealistic expectation that can be very subtle because it is very natural for you to want someone to love and to love you. But if you are unhappy or struggling in your own personal walk with Christ, your spouse will never make you happy. Happiness cannot be attained by direct pursuit; it is a by-product. Your unhappiness is caused by searching in all the wrong places, in things that can never satisfy (Is. 55:1-2). No person or thing can ever

make you happy. If you unrealistically believe your spouse is able to make you happy, then you will begin asking for more than your mate is capable of ever giving. You subtly begin to depend upon your spouse for your joy in life. However, this inner void can never be met because there is no physical or emotional experience that can satisfy the deep spiritual need you have. Only one person can satisfy the emptiness inside you, and this person is the Lord.

The Bible is clear as to where true happiness can be found. King David found that only his relationship with the Lord could accomplish this end. He testified concerning God that, *"He satisfies the longing soul, and fills the hungry soul with goodness"* (Ps. 107:9). He also declared, *"Happy is the people whose God is the Lord"* (Ps. 144:15). Solomon said, *"Whoever trusts in the Lord, happy is he"* (Prov. 16:20). If you will totally bow before the Lord and make Him your God by trusting and receiving Him, seeking Him, and following Him, you will find yourself happier than you've ever been. This is the happiness Jesus promised when He said, *"If you know these things, happy are you if you do them"* (John 13:17). Scripture equates your happiness with the depth of relationship you have with God, not who you know or what you possess. Examine yourself to be sure you are not relying on your spouse to make you happy. If you are, you will never find the happiness you long for in life or in your marriage.

Search your heart honestly to see if you are holding this unrealistic expectation. If you allow the Lord to satisfy you, you will then have something to give to the relationship, instead of just looking to receive. This leads us to the next unrealistic expectation.

5. *"Why isn't my spouse more giving toward me?"* I talk to people weekly who are waiting to receive from their spouse and wondering why nothing is happening. It is totally unrealistic to think that your spouse should give to you first, especially when Scripture teaches us just the opposite. When I hear this expectation verbalized I usually ask, "Since you are expecting your mate to give in this area, how are you giving?" The individual usually responds with, "Well, I'm waiting for my husband (or wife) to prove to me that he (or she) really cares, then I will change." If this is your attitude, you will probably be waiting a long time because you are violating every biblical principle I know. It is completely unrealistic to expect your spouse to be this great giver while you are sitting and doing nothing.

This attitude, in reality, is selfishness, and the Bible clearly teaches against this sort of lifestyle. For example, Jesus taught, *"Whatever you want men to do to you, do also to them"* (Matt. 7:12). In other words, what you want to receive, you must first be willing to give. This is what love will do. The writer of Hebrews also declared that we should *"provoke one another to love and good works"* (Heb. 10:24, KJV). It's easy to provoke someone to wrath, but it takes love and good works to provoke another to the same. If you would take these actions, your demonstration of love would be the best encouragement to your spouse to give more to you. This is the only realistic way you will ever see change in your spouse.

Get rid of this unrealistic expectation and begin to take the action of love. Your mate will wonder what happened to you. Remember, don't sit and wait for your spouse to change. You take the initiative!

6. *"Why isn't my spouse changing faster?"* If you have the expectation in your mind that any change will be quick, you will be deeply disappointed. It's not realistic to think that just because you snap your fingers that change will automatically appear in your mate's life. It's not going to happen! Jesus recognized this fact about men when He said to His disciples, *"O foolish ones, and slow of heart to believe all that the prophets have spoken"* (Luke 24:25). Jesus realistically understood that mankind and even His chosen disciples were *slow at heart* to make the changes needed to fulfill their calling as ambassadors to the world. Look at yourself; can't you see this same tendency of slowness to believe? Aren't you slow to change what you think or how you act? How many times has the Lord had to teach you the same truth over and over again? Then one day you see His truth over that same issue, as though it were a totally new concept. Many times in counseling I will share a certain concept, and a husband or wife will tell me, "I've never seen it that way before." The other partner will get upset and declare, "I've told you the same thing many times. Why didn't you hear it when *I* said it?"

This is the nature of man. Did you know that the Scriptures use the metaphor of a wild donkey in describing the natural man and his tendency to be stubborn and rebellious? Job said that men were like *"wild donkeys in the desert"* (Job 24:5). Jeremiah referred to the rebellious nation of Israel as *"a wild donkey used to the wilderness, that sniffs at the wind in her desire; In her time of mating, who can turn her away"* (Jer. 2:24)? He describes the children of Israel as being controlled only by their desire to satisfy themselves. This is primarily why we are so slow at heart to change, because we have the flesh working against us. However, David declared in the Psalms, *"Do not be like the horse or the mule, which have no understanding, which must be harnessed with bit and bridle..."* (Ps. 32:9). This passage means we are given a choice. We don't have to be stubborn and resistant to change according to our natural inclination. We can, instead, yield to the Spirit of God, trust Him, and let Him teach us. Read the entire context of Psalm 32 to see this admonition.

Spiritual growth and change are described by two important phrases in Scripture that reveal this concept of slow growth. First, Paul referred to your inward man as *"being renewed day by day"* (2 Cor. 4:16). This is a daily work that God does, not an instant or once-and-for-all renewal. Second, Paul also uses the phrase *more and more* to describe this same work of transformation in your life. When he prayed for the Philippian church he said, *"I pray that your love may abound still more and more in knowledge and all discernment"* (Phil. 1:9). To the Thessalonian church he urged them to *"abound more and more, just as you received from us how you ought to walk and to please God"* (1 Thess. 4:1). It is clear from these verses that Paul did not expect an instant change, but a gradual one to take place in the lives of those to whom he wrote. This should be your expectation for change as well. It is realistic.

If you understand this truth about yourself and your spouse, it will take great pressure off your marriage and will bring patience to your heart as you give the Lord time to work. It is reasonable to understand that by your mate's very nature, they will change slowly. I explain this to people in premarital counseling to prepare them for the reality of living with another sinner. I usually demonstrate this by holding my two fingers up completely aligned one in front of the other, explaining that there are a few things in life such as certain spiritual goals, childrearing, or recreation that is enjoyed in which they will think exactly alike. These things are what has attracted them to each other. Then I move my fingers about two inches apart to illustrate that there are many other things they agree upon, but not exactly the same. Finally, I put my fingers about two feet apart to represent that there will also be a few things in which they disagree to the point of conflict. Every marriage has issues of intense opposition. Most couples discover these issues after the wedding ceremony. After I finish this illustration I explain, with my fingers two feet apart, that these issues will change very little. I illustrate this by moving my fingers back to about a foot and a half. This visual aid gives people a realistic expectation of just how much to expect these differences to change over a lifetime in their marriage.

How about you? Do you have a realistic view of change for yourself and your spouse? If you do, this will cause you to be much more patient with each other. Yet, if you are expecting your spouse to change in one of those areas in which they are extremely opposite from you, you will be greatly disappointed and frustrated because it's not going to happen. This brings me to my last unrealistic expectation.

7. *"Why do these things never seem to change?"* Consider my example of Steve and Donna. This is a perfect example of why some things never change in a relationship. Should Donna have ever expected that Steve would become as outgoing as she was? No; not any more than Steve should expect Donna to become a quiet and reserved woman that never says anything. Steve was reaching out more to others, but Donna's expectation was so high and unattainable that this was never good enough for her. Small changes can occur, but the basic person and personality will remain the same. A quiet homebody will never become a social butterfly. God takes the person we are and rules over our personality by His Holy Spirit. He changes our moral character by giving us a new nature to enable us to love Him and others, but our basic personalities will stay the same.

The best example of this truth can be seen in the apostle Paul because we see him before and after coming to Christ. Before Paul met Christ on the road to Damascus, he was a driven, motivated, aggressive, and zealous individual for the Law of God. He was so zealous he persecuted the church unmercifully (Phil. 3:3-6). Did Paul remain the same man in his basic personality after he was born again? Yes, he did. After Paul came to Christ, he was the same motivated and driven man. Once driven by hatred and anger for Christians, he was now driven by a new passion, his love for Christ and the Gospel. Paul said of His drive and motivation, *"the love of Christ constrains us"* (2 Cor. 5:14). He became just as zealous in following the Lord as he had been following the Law. He said at another time, *"I press toward the goal"* (Phil. 3:14). The Greek word Paul used for *press* means "to pursue or to persecute." Before Christ, he persecuted the church, but now he pursued Christ with the same persecuting zeal, yet for a godly end. The basic man remained the same, but his moral character and heart were radically transformed.

So be careful about your expectations. Are they truly realistic? Are you expecting your spouse's basic personality to change or their moral character to change?

How Do You Determine What are Realistic Expectations?

First, you must determine and define what your expectations are. Your expectations are simply your hopes or those things that you anticipate and expect that your spouse should do. The Hebrew word *expect* literally means "something that you hope for." This is exactly what Donna was doing. She was hoping and expecting Steve to be and act a certain way. She hoped that he would ultimately do the same things she did, even though it violated his own personality. Of course Donna's hopes were destroyed!

God desires to spare you of unnecessary pain and to give you realistic expectations that can be fulfilled. He wants godly hopes and desires to govern your entire life, and those will come directly from the Word of God. When the children of Israel went into captivity God told them that He wanted to give them an *"expected end"* (Jer. 29:11, KJV). The New King James version translates this phrase as *"a future and a hope."* At this point in its history, the nation had been overrun by the Babylonians. God gave the people an expectation and a hope by making specific promises to them about their future. These promises gave them the hope they needed in the midst of their present distress. God didn't give them unrealistic expectations by making wild promises He would never fulfill. That would have only caused despair. He told them realistically that they would be disciplined for seventy years in captivity in Babylon. After the seventy years were fulfilled, they would be brought back into their land and restored (Jer. 25:11, 12; 29:10).

God's Word, including the promises and commands He declares, are the source of all realistic expectations for us just as they were for the Jews in captivity. These promises and commands will give you a hope for what is possible in your life and marriage. Scripture is the most realistic expectation that you could ever hope to find.

Take all the expectations you have for your spouse and line them up next to the Word of God. If they are in harmony with Scripture, then they are correct and realistic. If they are not, ask God to teach you what the Word prescribes regarding each of your expectations. Your expectations either come from the Scriptures or they come from yourself and are, therefore, selfish.

It is critical for you to determine the source of your thinking. Sometimes your expectations come from what other people have told you or what you have seen in your own family growing up. Are these expectations biblical? If you are hopeless, despairing, or resentful, unrealistic expectations may be one very important cause. The fruit of God's Word is hope (Rom. 15:4). If you are hopeless, you must be believing a lie. Search the Scriptures to become sure that what you are believing and expecting is in line with the hope God has set before you.

Here are some realistic expectations to get you started in your search of the Word:

1. You should expect your spouse to surrender to Christ (Phil. 2:10, 11).
2. You should expect your spouse to deny him or her self (Matt. 16:24).
3. You should expect your spouse to seek first the kingdom of God (Matt. 6:33).

4. You should expect your spouse to be willing to work for change (2 Cor. 3:18).
5. You should expect your spouse to love as Christ loved (Eph. 5:25).
6. You should expect your spouse to speak with respect and to edify you (Eph. 4:29).
7. You should expect your spouse to be a sacrificially giving individual (1 John 3:16).

After reading this list, remember your spouse will also be expecting you to take the very same actions. Expectations go both ways! If you verbally buffet your spouse with these expectations, you had better be expecting these words to come right back at you.

Group Discussion Questions

1. What are some general unrealistic expectations you have had over your life as a whole that have changed over time?
2. What changed these general expectations in your mind?
3. Without giving names or details, discuss a marriage that you have seen struggle because of the stubborn resistance to change unrealistic expectations.
4. Without revealing any information that might embarrass your spouse, explain some of your unrealistic expectations and how you have overcome them.

8

WHAT DO YOU NEED TO KNOW
ABOUT CONFLICTS?

"God was in Christ reconciling the world to Himself...and has committed to us the word of reconciliation" 2 Cor. 5:19

Conflicts, conflicts, conflicts, this is all we seem to have in this marriage. I am sick and tired of the constant conflict. The same things just happen over and over again and we never seem to solve anything. Every time we agree on a solution, my husband doesn't stick to what he agrees to do. We have to start resolving some of these issues. Surely other couples don't go through this, do they, Steve? Is this normal, or are we some kind of weird exception?"

The frustration was obvious as Cindy began to tell me the story of her marriage. She had no concept of why these conflicts kept occurring, and more importantly, no idea of how to begin resolving them.

Her husband, Frank, was also very confused about their marriage. He couldn't see what all the commotion was about. He thought that the disagreements they had were relatively small and really nothing to make such a big fuss over. He had only come for counseling because Cindy had insisted. Frank's solution to the problems became apparent when he put his hand on her shoulder and said, "Honey, if you wouldn't get so uptight, everything would be fine. We have a great marriage."

When Frank said this, I knew I had lots of work ahead of me. These two obviously did not have a great marriage. They couldn't even agree over whether there was a problem! Even if they had agreed that their marriage had problems, they still did not know how to resolve them. Cindy wasn't even sure if conflicts were normal or if they were the exception.

One of the most common problems in marriages today is the great confusion over how to resolve conflicts. Many couples just like Cindy and Frank don't know how to resolve the disagreements between them. Unresolved conflicts destroy intimacy, oneness, and companionship in any marriage and create intense frustration in the relationship, which only generates more conflict between two people. The unresolved conflicts of the past then become fuel to the fire of the next conflict and are often used to beat the other partner into submission. The new disagreement also goes unresolved and becomes more fuel for further destruction of their relationship. It soon becomes a vicious cycle spiraling downward. If partners can't solve the problems between them, eventually they build a wall between them that is so high and so thick that they ultimately have no relationship at all. With no relationship, couples then realize there is no reason for staying together. This is why learning how to resolve conflicts is so important.

First, let's consider whether conflicts are normal. Then we will look at what causes all the conflicts in your marriage. Last, in the next two chapters, we will explore how to reconcile and solve them once and for all so that you won't keep covering the same old territory over and over again. The issues you are about to learn must be understood and practiced daily if you are to grow together and build the marriage you desire. Incidentally, they will also be helpful and effective in resolving the conflicts in any relationship you have.

ARE CONFLICTS NORMAL?

Are conflicts normal? Yes! One of the most interesting things about reading the Scriptures is that the sins and faults of its characters are never hidden. You get to see their great successes and their bitter defeats. All of the great Bible characters had conflicts, revealing that this is a very normal occurrence with sinners. These men and women had conflicts with God, friends, and family members. Let me give you a few examples for your study. I would encourage you to read these passages in their context.

1. Abraham and Sarah had a conflict when Isaac was mocked by Hagar's son, Ishmael, (Gen. 21:1-12).
2. Michal despised her husband, David, after he danced exuberantly before the Lord when the ark of the covenant was carried into the city of Jerusalem for the first time, (2 Sam. 6:6-23).
3. Miriam and Aaron had a conflict with Moses over his taking an Ethiopian woman as his wife, (Num. 12:1-16).
4. Paul had a conflict with the hypocrisy of Peter and Barnabas when they refused to eat with the Gentiles because they feared certain Jews that arrived from Jerusalem, (Gal. 2:11-14).
5. The early church had a conflict over the neglect of certain widows that were not being taken care of properly by the apostles, (Acts 6:1-7).

These are just a few of the conflicts recorded for us in the Scriptures, and they reveal that conflicts are normal, even between those who were greatly used by God. Yet in each of these conflicts, with one exception, a solution was found. It is important to note that these men and women did not allow these conflicts to go on and on. They resolved them.

Conflicts are normal occurrences between sinners. Frank and Cindy were not some weird exception, and neither are you if your marriage has conflicts. Their conflicts were very normal and most likely so are yours. What is not normal is for these conflicts to go unresolved because this is in direct disobedience to God's Word. You must resolve your conflicts. Harmony will always be God's plan for your relationships, and especially your marriage. It is interesting to note that in the above examples of marital conflicts, Abraham and Sara resolved their differences but David and Michal did not. Why? Simply because of the way they both handled the conflict.

God wants you to learn how to properly handle the issues that divide you. God is in the business of reconciliation and has given each of us the tools we need to reconcile with one another. Paul declared that *"God was in Christ reconciling the world to Himself...and has committed to us the word of reconciliation"* (2 Cor. 5:19). As Christians, we are called to be peacemakers because we have the ministry of reconciliation. Each of us has the ability to resolve the conflicts in our own relationships and to help others resolve theirs. Best of all, we have the Word of God, *"the word of reconciliation,"* that shows us how.

Jesus instructed people regarding the subject of conflicts and offenses. He was very realistic when He said, *"It is impossible that no offenses should come..."* (Luke 17:1). He realized that it was unreasonable to expect that no conflicts or offenses would occur while living in this world. He considered it very possible that you and I could reconcile these offenses, and He went on to explain just how to do it. He taught the importance of taking the offense directly to the offender to seek reconciliation and forgiveness. His intention is for us to also be realistic and practical about the possibility of true reconciliation.

You must begin by first understanding that conflicts and disagreements will be normal in any relationship. You are not some strange exception to the rule just because you have disagreements. Your marriage has these conflicts for very specific reasons, and you must understand why if you are to ever deal with these issues properly.

WHAT CAUSES THE CONFLICTS?

What causes conflicts to occur between people who really love each other? Understanding the causes of conflict is the first step toward resolving them. Frank and Cindy had no idea what was causing all the problems between them and thus could not even begin to solve the issues. Anything can cause a conflict between you and your spouse, yet there are key attitudes and actions that the Scripture specifically points out to us as suspect. We are made aware of these problem areas so that we might better know ourselves and be able to deal with them quickly. Let's look at some of these fundamental causes.

1. Conflicts are caused by your selfishness. Selfishness is the most fundamental cause of conflict between a husband and wife. When two people both want their own way, the sparks are naturally going to fly. You either willingly and lovingly compromise, or a conflict occurs. Only by the self-sacrificing acts of giving and compromise will solutions be found. I covered this issue fully in chapter 6, so I will only say a few words here.

Paul believed that dealing with self was absolutely essential to a successful marriage. It is important to note how he begins his classic instruction in the book of Ephesians: *"Submitting yourselves one to another in the fear of God"* (Eph. 5:21, KJV). The word for *submitting* in the Greek means "to subdue." And what must you subdue? Yourself! You must subdue the self that wants to rule and dominate your life and marriage.

Paul goes on to explain to both husbands and wives how they are to subdue themselves in their marriage. He tells the wives to subdue themselves to the leadership of their husbands as the head of the home. In addition, he tells the husbands to subdue themselves by rejecting selfishness and to serve and care for their wives as Christ does His church. I will cover this issue of mutual submission more fully in a later chapter. To understand what is causing the conflicts to occur in your relationship, you must determine where you are being selfish.

2. Pride causes conflicts. Solomon made this abundantly clear when he wrote his Proverbs. He declared, *"By pride comes only contention..."* (Prov. 13:10). Again he said, *"He who is of a proud heart stirs up strife"* (Prov. 28:25). This is the attitude that is stirring up the strife in your home. You must recognize it in your own heart and put this off or the conflicts and strife will continue.

Think for a moment. Do you have an arrogant or superior attitude when you talk to your mate? Do you communicate by your attitude that you are always right and your spouse knows nothing? Do you become indignant and refuse to listen when your partner questions your actions or motives? Have you ever thought, *Who does he think he is to ask me that?* If you have thought or done any of these things, it means that pride and arrogance is in your heart. This attitude is causing the strife.

Scripture rather encourages us to *"show all humility to all men"* (Titus 3:2). Humility enables you to be submissive and makes you willing to reconcile with one another. Peter coupled these two attitudes together when he exhorted, "*All of you be submissive to one another, and be clothed with humility, for 'God resists the proud, but gives grace to the humble'* " (1 Peter 5:5). If pride causes the conflicts, humility will always enable you to solve them.

3. <u>Conflicts are caused by the clash of two opposing and independent wills</u>. The best example of this point is the conflict that took place between Paul and Barnabas as recorded in the book of Acts. As these two men were about to go on their second missionary journey, a discussion came up as to whether or not they would take John Mark with them. John Mark had abruptly left them and returned home in the middle of their first journey. Scripture says that Barnabas "*was <u>determined</u> to take with them John called Mark*" and Paul "*<u>insisted</u> that they should not.*" It says that "*the contention became so sharp that they parted from one another. And so Barnabas took Mark and sailed to Cyprus; but Paul chose Silas and departed...*" (Acts 15:37-40, underline added).

Here are two men who independently *insisted* and were *determined* to have their own way and it ended their relationship. It is important to note that they all reconciled this conflict later since they were ministers of reconciliation. Paul declared in his last epistle that he wanted Mark to come to him because "*he is useful to me for the ministry*" (2 Tim. 4:11).

Again, humility and a heart willing to reconcile will always seek a compromise and a way to restore relationship. Paul and Barnabas each could have sought a compromise to resolve the issue instead of stubbornly seeking his own way. Which do you do? Are you the one who arrogantly insists on your way, or do you humbly seek compromise and reconciliation? Your heart attitude will dramatically determine how often you have a conflict and how quickly you resolve it.

4. <u>Conflicts are caused by a multitude of sinful attitudes and actions</u>. When you hold attitudes such as the three I have just covered or take actions that are sinful, it will always bring you into conflict with your spouse. Sinful attitudes give birth to actions that are offensive to others. Here are some examples:

    A. If you hold resentment in your heart toward your spouse, you can be sure that it will erupt in one way or another. Anger just doesn't sit neutral in your heart. It has to come out somewhere and toward someone. "*Hatred stirs up strife...*" (Prov. 10:12).

    B. Strife can also occur simply because of the *way* you speak to each other. "*A fool's lips enter into contention...*" (Prov. 18:6). Do you speak harshly, arrogantly, or boastfully? If so, it will cause contention.

C. Likewise, judgmentalism and criticism cause strife. *"Cast out the scoffer, and contention will leave; yes, strife and reproach will cease"* (Prov. 22:10). The word *scoffer* in Hebrew means "to judge or to mock another." The word *reproach* means "to show contempt." If you judge or show contempt toward each other, the sparks are going to fly.

D. Any substance abuse of drugs or alcohol will also create an immediate contention in a marriage. Solomon asks some rhetorical questions and then gives the obvious answer. *"Who has woe? Who has sorrow? Who has contentions?... Those who linger long at the wine..."* (Prov. 23:29, 30).

E. When there is lying, deceit, or gossip, contention and strife will naturally occur. There is a whole section of Scripture given to this topic. Solomon declares that when you gossip your words *"go down into the inmost"* part of a person (Prov. 26:22). This offense *"separates the best of friends"* (Prov. 17:9). If you are deceitful and lie to your mate, it is really a cover for hatred. It reveals the lack of love you have for your spouse (Prov. 26:24-28).

F. Contentions result from being controlled by your fleshly nature. Paul said that contentions are a work of the flesh (Gal. 5:19, 20). Here, again, is the best reason why you should surrender the control of your life to the lordship of Christ. This is the simplest way to bring harmony to your marriage relationship. If you walk in the Spirit, you will not fulfill the works of the flesh.

Obviously, some of the areas of conflict I have listed here are moral issues. These concerns cannot be compromised over, but must be addressed in a straightforward and firm manner. Conflicts in these areas will be unavoidable for a committed Christian.

All these attitudes and actions separate you from the intimate and rewarding companionship that marriage is supposed to encourage. Are any of these problems a part of your marriage? If so, then you've found the source of the conflicts. Each of these problems must be dealt with to fully resolve the conflicts between you.

WHAT MOTIVATION DO YOU NEED TO RESOLVE CONFLICTS?

Motivation is absolutely essential to reach the desired goal of resolving conflicts because it drives you to take the correct actions necessary (and lots of action is required in most cases). You need proper motivation to enable you to persevere when the going gets tough.

Over the years of working with couples, I have found that motivation is much more important than even knowing the practical steps to take to resolve a problem. A person may know what to do, but at the same time not want to do it. When the motivation is lacking, the action required to resolve the problem will never be taken.

A good example of the importance of motivation is illustrated in the story of a man I counseled years ago. Sam had been a Christian for many years and possessed a thorough knowledge of the Scriptures. However, he had numerous conflicts with his wife that had continued for many years. Sam knew exactly what was needed to resolve these conflicts, yet he simply refused. It wasn't until he went through great turmoil with his business partner that he became motivated enough to resolve the conflicts with his wife. What happened? His business partner had been making some shady deals on the side, and one day Sam found out about them. He tried to resolve the issues with his partner, but to no avail. Sam told me that his partner was unwilling and very bitter at the questioning of his business dealings. It took having his business relationship destroyed before he could see what he was personally doing to his own wife by refusing to reconcile. Sam ultimately reconciled all the issues with his wife. All it took was a little motivation! It is unfortunate, however, that it took losing his business before he could see what was needed in his marriage. You don't have to wait for calamity. If you will ask God in prayer, He will give you the motivation you need.

What are the most important motives or priorities you need to resolve conflicts?

1. You must first be willing. I will not restate this point all over again, but let me say here, if you want to resolve conflicts, you must be willing. Ask God to soften your heart; He will do it.

2. You must be motivated by a sincere desire to please God above all others. Many times people are motivated to find compromises and resolve conflicts, but for the wrong reasons. Some people are only motivated by the desire for a hassle-free existence and will give in to any demand. These individuals hate any and all conflict and will do almost anything to avoid it, without any concern for what is right or wrong. They just want their mates to stop bugging them so they can have uninterrupted time to pursue their own agenda, a hobby, a television program, or a sport. This is a very selfish and dishonest motivation for trying to resolve a conflict, and any commitment that is made over the issue is usually not kept.

Then there are those who will do anything it takes to please their mate, even if it entails violating their own conscience or the Word of

God. They allow their spouse to be abusive or unresponsive without say-ing much just to keep peace in the house. Ultimately, these people get tired of always trying to please their spouses and seeing no response.

Both attempts at pleasing self or your spouse are not godly because you are violating the principles of honesty, selflessness, and accountabil-ity revealed in God's Word. It is not right for you to behave selfishly or to allow your spouse to do so, because you are failing to please God, the most basic of motivations.

We have all been called to please God. This is the highest purpose any person can live by, driving us to take actions that are selfless and, at times, very difficult. We do so because we love the Lord and look forward to hearing Him say, *"Well done!"* one day. This is what motivated Jesus to take the very difficult and selfless actions He did: *"I always do those things that please the Father"* (John 8:29). Again, *"I have come... not to do my own will, but the will of Him who sent me"* (John 6:38). With this as your motivation, you too will be able to take the difficult and selfless actions that are necessary to reconcile your conflicts.

Pleasing God must be what directs all your actions in life, especially with your spouse. Paul told the Thessalonian church that this was the ultimate motivation needed to live the Christian life, teaching them how they *"ought to walk and to please God"* (1 Thess. 4:1). Notice how he associated their correct walk with the desire to please God. Again, Paul commanded Timothy to *"please Him"* who has enlisted him as a soldier in His army (2 Tim. 2:4). When you choose to please God first in all you do, you will not only be striking at the root of all the conflicts, but you will also begin to experience His peace and joy deep in your soul.

Where do you get this motivation when you don't believe you have it? It's a natural by-product of a love relationship with the Living God. When you are in love with Him, you *want* to obey Him and put Him first in your life. Again, here is why it is so important that you renew your relationship with the Lord. If you have continued to read this book and still haven't done this, you need to stop now and do it! Nothing will even start to change in your life or marriage until you first surrender to Him!

Before you go on to the next chapter, won't you ask the Father for the motivation to willingly and whole-heartedly please Him? When you do, the actions necessary to resolve all of the conflicts in your marriage will naturally follow. All you have to pray is, "Make me willing, Lord, to please you in all things."

Review

Let's review before we go on. What is necessary to begin to resolve conflicts?

1. Be assured that the conflicts occurring between you are very normal. What is not normal is to allow them to go unresolved.
2. Before you can resolve them, you need to understand and deal with what causes these conflicts.
3. Last, you need the correct inner motivations to resolve these conflicts.

Now let's go on to the practical steps needed to resolve the conflicts between you and your spouse.

Group Discussion Questions

1. Discuss how your selfishness has caused a conflict with someone other than your spouse.
2. Discuss how your pride has caused a conflict with someone other than your spouse.
3. Discuss how your stubborn and independent will has caused a conflict with someone other than your spouse.
4. Without giving any details that might embarrass your spouse, discuss how these three sinful attitudes have created conflicts in your marriage.

9

PRACTICAL STEPS TO RESOLVING CONFLICTS

"If your brother sins against you, go and tell him
his fault between you and him alone.
If he hears you, you have gained your brother." Matt. 18:15

Now that you understand why conflicts occur in your relationship and the correct motives to resolve them, the big question is: what practical steps should you take to resolve them? You can agree with all of the truths I have just gone over in the previous chapter and still not understand exactly how to put them into practice. Knowing *how* to do something is always the difference between success or failure. This is where much of our present-day preaching has failed. You are taught *what* you should do, *why* you should do it, but few explain *how* to actually put their teachings into practice. However, the Bible is a book filled with practical explanations of how to implement its teachings. If you are truly sincere about removing the hindrances impeding oneness and companionship in your marriage, then this is the chapter for you.

What you need to do, at this point, is to make a list of all unresolved conflicts in your marriage and keep it in front of you as you read through this chapter. Ask yourself each of the questions below. Your answers will determine whether or not you will actually be able to fully resolve your particular problems.

1. <u>Are you willing to take action to resolve these issues</u>? We covered this question in chapter 1 in great detail, so I won't spend a lot of time here. However, it's easy to talk about wanting real companionship with your spouse and to still be stubborn or unwilling to actually work at it. Therefore, look back at your list of unresolved conflicts and ask yourself if you are willing to take action regarding each one.

Remember what Isaiah said, *"If you are <u>willing and obedient</u>, you shall eat the good of the land; But if you refuse and rebel, you shall be devoured by the sword"* (Is. 1:19, 20, underline added). Isaiah coupled these two qualities for a reason; willingness must be followed by obedience or action. It can't be a half-hearted willingness. This is completely insufficient for lasting change to occur. God knows the difference and so will your spouse. How can you tell if you've got a half-hearted willingness? Simply by looking at what actions you are willing to take. If you are whole-heartedly willing, then you will be fully obedient to all God requires of you.

If Scripture asks you to take a specific action that you don't feel like performing, would you do it? You may think, *What about my spouse? Shouldn't they do something too?* We will get to that question later. First, you must take care of your own attitude and actions.

The first thing you need to do is ask God for a willingness to actually go to your spouse and seek reconciliation. There is never a justification for you to avoid the attempt to reconcile with your partner. Jesus gave His disciples no excuse for holding back when they knew there was an unresolved issue in their personal relationships. *"Therefore if you bring your gift to the altar, and there remember that your brother has something against you, leave your gift there before the altar, and go your way. First be reconciled to your brother, and then come and offer your gift"* (Matt. 5:23-24). *"Moreover if your brother sins against you, go and tell him his fault between you and him alone. If he hears you, you have gained your brother"* (Matt. 18:15). These passages instruct that if you have been offended by someone or if you know that someone is angry with you, in both cases, you are commanded to go and seek reconciliation. The emphasis should be on the word *go*. Jesus doesn't want you to come and worship Him when you know there is an unresolved conflict with your brother. Sometimes the reason why reconciliation doesn't occur is the simple unwillingness of one or both partners to go to the other. You obviously can't begin to reconcile anything until you meet face-to-face. That is why you need to begin by asking God for a willing heart to go to your spouse. Prayer can change your heart today if you will just ask. Remember James cautioned us: *"You do not have because you do not ask"* (James 4:2). Before you even continue reading any further, ask God for the willingness to actually go and approach your spouse over the issues that separate you.

2. Are you willing to take action *quickly*? The time factor in resolving conflicts is critical. From my experience in counseling, I have found that most Christians can have an argument with their spouses and let it go unresolved for days. I have even talked to couples who have not dealt with certain resentments for years. One couple I counseled, who had been married for twenty-two years, was still arguing over issues that had surfaced on their honeymoon. This should not be! Let's consider some of the reasons for dealing with your conflicts quickly.

First, you should resolve your conflicts quickly because this is the clear commandment of Christ. Notice the next verse in the passage I just cited in Matthew 5: "*Agree with your adversary quickly, while you are on the way with him*" (5:25, underline added). Jesus wants you to go get things right with your adversary immediately. He then gives a general principle in dealing with any adversary: "*Agree... quickly.*" This passage would, of course, refer to your spouse also, especially if they are your adversary at this moment. Jesus wants you to seek reconciliation and forgiveness as quickly as possible so the conflict won't get any worse.

The second reason why you should take action quickly is because the longer you wait to resolve a conflict with your spouse, the harder your heart will get. But it's not just your heart. Your mate's heart will grow hard too. This is why the author of the book of Hebrews warned with great urgency, "*Today, if you will hear His voice, do not harden your hearts as in the rebellion*" (Heb. 3:15). Hardness of heart comes from resisting God's voice of conviction day in and day out. *Today* God is pleading with you to reconcile your conflicts with Him and your spouse. There is no doubt that this is the call of God to you!

Likewise, you should move quickly to reconcile with your spouse because time distorts the facts of a conflict in your mind. Even after a short time passes, you can't remember who did or said what, and you will begin to argue over the distorted facts. This solves nothing and only adds further frustration. The best time to solve a conflict is *today*.

When you fail to resolve a conflict, you then begin to have spin-off conflicts from the original one. Secondary conflicts occur because you are already angry with each other. Holding resentment in your heart makes it easy to send a little jab here and a little dagger there. One unresolved conflict begets another and then another. Every conflict you fail to reconcile only builds the wall between you, which is hardly conducive to the companionship you are seeking.

So don't wait. Start reconciling those past issues today and keep a short account of the present issues that come up. Resolve them daily!

3. <u>You must be willing to be completely truthful</u>. Why is truthfulness so important for resolving conflicts? First, if you are not completely truthful, God will not bless your effort at reconciling these unresolved issues. King David realized this when he tried to continue his relationship with the Lord after committing adultery with Bathsheba. He tried to live like nothing had happened, rationalizing his actions and justifying himself, yet he knew things weren't right before God. As long as he hid his sin dishonestly and kept silent, his "*vitality was turned into the drought of summer*" (Ps. 32:1-5). In other words, his spiritual life just dried up.

Once he honestly confessed his sin, David's spirit was renewed and the joy of his salvation returned. He realized what God wanted and declared in his psalm of repentance, *"You desire truth in the inward parts..."* (Ps. 51:6). This is always what God is after in our hearts.

David's example reveals that there is no reconciliation with God without first acknowledging the truth in your heart. Jesus knows your every thought; there is nothing you can hide from Him. He is the one who declares, *"I am He who searches the minds and hearts"* (Rev. 2:23). Therefore, He knows your every intent and motivation. If you are not being completely honest with God or your spouse, He will not bless your attempt to reconcile your marriage. He cannot bless it. If He did, it would make Him a party to deception.

Hiding from your faults also hinders the work of the Holy Spirit in reconciling your marriage because He is called *the Spirit of Truth*. The Spirit wants to first help you to be truthful; His primary mission is to *"guide you into all truth"* (John 16:13). When this is accomplished, He can then be a helper in your marital relationship.

Jesus revealed a fundamental key to the disciples' growth and maturity. He told them that the Word of God needed to be sown in the good ground of *"an honest and good heart..."* (Luke 8:15, KJV). Honesty is essential in order to grow in your relationship with God as well as with your marriage partner.

Your spouse knows whether you are being honest, having lived with you, and knows you better than you think. When your mate sees you being brutally honest with yourself and with God, this will soften their heart to do the same. But if you refuse to be honest, the opposite effect occurs. Your spouse will become hardhearted and lose all hope that anything can be reconciled.

Let me give you an example. I had been counseling a couple for about a month, when one day the wife called me on the phone. She told me that she was not coming back for counseling anymore. When I asked her why, she replied, "It will not make any difference. He has been lying to you the whole time we've been coming to see you. He lied to you when you asked him if he was using drugs. He smokes marijuana almost every day." She said, "This is his pattern, and I can see this is not going to work." She hung up the phone and left him the next day.

What happened here? This woman had lost hope that anything would ever change in her marriage because she knew her husband was not being truthful. He was just playing the game of counseling to appease her. She knew his motivation was totally wrong and realized he had no intentions of changing. After I confronted him about his dishonesty, he still continued to lie to me. Sadly, this marriage ultimately ended in divorce. I have found over and over again that when marriage counseling fails or a marriage fails, dishonesty is one of the root causes.

How honest are you with yourself and your spouse about your faults and failures in the marriage? How honest are you with God? If you truly want a change, ask God right now to cause you to be brutally honest over the unresolved conflicts you've listed. Confess your sins of dishonesty to God and then confess them to your spouse.

4. Are you willing to restrain your anger? Here is where the real work begins, because if you can't control your anger, you won't be able to even start to resolve the issues that divide you. Uncontrolled anger is what keeps every other step in the reconciliation process from ever happening. It destroys and drives you apart, never together. Think of the awful things that you have said to your spouse when you have been controlled by anger. Think of the terrible things you have done when rage and resentment ruled you. After you calmed down, you wished you could take all the words back again, but it was too late. The words were spoken, and you drove the knife deep, going for the quick kill. Your tongue was like a razor that carved up your spouse, but now you realize you didn't mean half the things you said. You didn't really mean to put your fist through the wall, or throw that lamp. But you did it all because you got so frustrated and your anger got the best of you. The worst part about it is that it didn't solve anything. You still had to talk it out all over again anyway.

Does this sound familiar? Is this how your marital conflicts go? If you struggle with controlling your anger, you have probably asked yourself many times, "Why did God even create me with this anger? What's its purpose? Is it possible to restrain and control it?" These are very important questions, so let's look at them.

Is it really possible to restrain your anger? Yes it is! You may be thinking, *That's easy for you to say, but it's another thing to do it.* Yet think for a moment. You have controlled your anger many times in the past. Everyone has done it. Even as a non-Christian you probably did it many times. Have you ever been at work and your boss treated you unfairly? Perhaps he spoke harshly to you or demanded some work to be redone because he didn't like it. Didn't you get very angry inside? But at the same time, you didn't explode or respond in a hateful way. You held it all inside, controlling and restraining your anger until he walked away. Then you let it all out to a co-worker, telling him exactly what you thought of your boss.

Has this or something similar ever happened to you? Sure it has. Even the most verbally aggressive person has buttoned their lip at some time in the past. And what motivated you to restrain your anger? What stopped you from exploding at the boss? Wasn't it because you didn't want to lose your job? That's right, you didn't want to lose that paycheck at the end of the week, so you controlled your anger. It was a simple choice you made because you wanted to keep your job.

The question is, why don't you do this at home? Why do you come home to the person you love the most and blast them with both barrels when there is a disagreement? Why, all of a sudden, is there no restraint when it comes to your spouse? Restraining your anger to keep your *marriage* together should be just as high a priority as keeping your job. It is critical for you to understand that this lack of restraint is slowly destroying your relationship and hindering you from ever resolving your conflicts. Controlling your anger is a must! How do you do it?

First, you must recognize and admit that you have a problem. Here is the honesty I spoke to you about previously. Can you honestly admit your problem with anger to the Lord in prayer? Will you admit it to your spouse? You can't even start to solve these problems until this occurs.

Second, if you believe that you have a problem here, ask the Lord to motivate you toward restraint. How? Remember in chapter 5 I discussed with you how love will motivate you to restrain certain actions? Love is a higher motivation than just keeping your job or financial security. The love of Christ needs to control you instead of your anger.

Also, you have the power of the Holy Spirit to help restrain you. If you will *"walk in the Spirit,"* you will find the strength to resist all of the dictates of your flesh (Gal. 5:16). The Spirit is your *helper*; He will help you to control your emotions if you will just ask (John 14:16).

Likewise, wisdom and discretion enable you to restrain your anger. Solomon says, *"The discretion of a man makes him slow to anger..."* (Prov. 19:11). Why is this true? Because the older and wiser you get, the more you realize that when you explode, nothing is accomplished. You may feel better for the moment, but that feeling is soon followed by conviction or condemnation. Wisdom tells you to slow down and get all the information first, then try and resolve the problem.

Ask God to teach you restraint by His love, by His power, and by His wisdom. You will be amazed by how He can change you if you are only willing.

Third, restraining your anger is a choice. It's a choice to stop a conversation or disagreement before it gets ugly. It's a choice to stop and pray because you can sense the anger beginning to boil inside. It's a choice to hold your hand up and say, "Wait, we are both getting angry here. Let's take a minute to calm down and try this conversation all over again." Sometimes taking a time-out like this is all you need to control and restrain your anger. This is what Proverbs tells you to do. Solomon said,

"The beginning of strife is like releasing water; Therefore stop contention before a quarrel starts" (Prov. 17:14). His analogy of anger compared to the releasing of water is quite fitting because it draws a picture we have all seen. It starts small with just a little anger, but like water coming out of an earthen dam, it eventually erodes the restraints and becomes a gushing torrent. So is anger. When you start letting it out, it erodes all its restraints and does incredible damage. Haven't you sensed the anger build as you began to express it? That's why God's Word says stop the contention before it starts.

Notice another Proverb that teaches the same truth: *"It is honorable for a man to stop striving, since any fool can start a quarrel"* (Prov. 20:3). It's so easy to start a quarrel, isn't it? Any fool can do that, but it takes a wise and honorable man to prevent a disagreement from descending into an angry exchange.

Fourth, don't make the opposite mistake of internalizing all your anger. People often misunderstand the exhortations to stop contentions before they start by trying to hold all their anger inside. However, this will only backfire and ensure a greater explosion later. Anger won't sit neutral inside your heart; it has to come out somewhere. Holding in your anger and angrily expressing it to your mate are both wrong and unbiblical actions. Paul the apostle advised, *"Do not let the sun go down on your wrath"* (Eph. 4:26). This means that you should not let one day pass while still holding anger in your heart. See also Ps. 37:8.

Now you might ask, "If I can't hold anger in my heart and I can't allow it to explode on anyone, what do I do with it?" Allow your anger to motivate you to biblical and righteous action. What do I mean by this? God created you with the ability to get angry. Anger is not an evil or sinful emotion. It has been divinely created for good and to motivate you to godly action. It is the action that you take when you are angry that will determine whether or not you have sinned.

If we never got angry we would lose a very powerful motivator for our lives. Let me give you some examples of what I mean. Scripture records that Jesus got angry at times and didn't sin. Mark reports that when the religious hypocrites of His day sought to trap Him, *"He looked around at them with anger, being grieved by the hardness of their hearts"* (Mark 3:5). This is a great example of how anger was used the way God intended. You have to read the rest of the story to see that Jesus did the right thing, even though He was angry. He first posed a question to instruct the Jews concerning what was right to do on the Sabbath, and then reached out to touch and heal a man with a shriveled hand. He reproved those who were wrong and did what was right.

Even in the Old Testament you can see that when God was motivated by anger He always took righteous actions. Scripture says God was *"moved to anger"* by the Jews turning to idolatry (Deut. 32:21). He responded by sending the prophets to verbally reprove them. Then He sent correction and ultimate judgment upon the nation. Deuteronomy mentions further that He righteously provoked them to jealousy by reaching out to the Gentiles in the attempt to bring them back to himself. However, at the same time Scripture declares that He *restrained* His anger and chose not to cut the Jews off completely (Is. 48:9). To fully understand the balance of what the Bible teaches on the issue of anger, it is important that you see both sides of His example: God himself is motivated by anger to take righteous actions, and these actions are always coupled with restraint.

Since we are to be Christ-like, the Scriptures command us to *"be angry and do not sin..."* (Eph. 4:26). Therefore, it must be possible to be angry without sinning. Why would God command us to be angry? Because we need to be motivated to godly and righteous action. I believe, as Christians, we are entirely too passive at times. We aren't angry enough at what we should be angry at, that is, those things at which God is angry. We need to hate the things He hates and love the things He loves. If we did, all of us would be more committed Christians.

Now let me explain this idea of being angry and not sinning a little more. The only way to be angry and not sin is to be angry at sin. This is what I mean by hating what God hates. We are to target sin in our anger and respond in obedience to God's Word.

When Moses was charged by Korah for supposedly taking too much power unto himself, what did he do? He *"was very angry, and said to the Lord..."* (Num. 16:15). Moses, motivated by anger, went immediately to God in *prayer*. He *"fell on his face"* before the Lord (Num. 16:4). Then Moses *spoke directly with his accusers*; he didn't go off and gossip to others about the problem. He challenged them to stand with him before the Lord to allow Him to decide between them (Num. 16:5-14). Then Moses *trusted God* that He would vindicate him (Num. 16:15-19). All of these responses are godly actions to take when angered, and they entailed godly restraint.

In the same manner, Nehemiah controlled his anger and acted righteously. While he was ruler, news came to him that his fellow countrymen were charging interest of one another for food. Many could not pay the high prices and were forced to sell their land and children into slavery in order to eat. When Nehemiah heard of this he *"became very angry"* (Neh. 5:1-13). What actions did his anger motivate him to take?

First, he went into *serious thought* over the problem (v. 7). He then called a great assembly and *reproved the rulers and nobles*. He could not have done this in an arrogant or harsh way because they were immediately receptive to his directions and counsel. He *reasoned with them* about what was good and righteous (v. 8-13). Anger should motivate you to the same restrained responses. Don't jump up from the couch to immediately go to battle verbally with your spouse. First seriously think through what you should do, what is righteous. Restraint allows you to do this. If your spouse needs to be reproved, do it with the motive to reason with them instead of yelling and screaming.

Likewise, King Saul was motivated to righteous action by anger divinely planted in his heart. The Scripture tells us that when the Ammonites came to the city of Jabesh-Gilead, they wanted to oppress God's people and make them their servants. Yet they also wanted to humiliate and bring reproach upon the Israelites by gouging out their right eyes. According to 1 Samuel, *"The Spirit of God came upon Saul when He heard this news, and his anger was greatly aroused"* (11:1-15). The Spirit of God *aroused anger* in his heart. What did his anger cause him to do? He gathered the Israelites together and *resisted the evil* of the Ammonites by mounting an army against them, and God gave the Israelites victory against this oppression. Saul saved the people of Jabesh-Gilead because he was moved by anger to accomplish righteousness.

From these biblical examples, you must agree that anger can influence you to godly action. The problem is that we usually choose to take the wrong action: explosions of yelling or cursing; accusations are thrown (and sometimes even pieces of furniture); a fist is put through the wall, or perhaps in the face. Sometimes the opposite occurs. You give the silent treatment, where resentment seethes quietly and the distance widens between you every day. All of these actions are sinful and must be repented of before God and eradicated.

I have spent a lot of time on this subject because it is such an important key to resolving conflicts. If you can't control your anger, you will never be able to take the next steps. Ask God to teach you to control your anger and deal in your heart about these issues.

5. Are you willing to listen and understand before you try to prove your point? The skill of listening is only possible when your anger is under the control of the Holy Spirit. What do you feel like when you are trying to communicate, and your spouse isn't listening? Don't you become frustrated and angry because they are communicating to you that your ideas are really not important? Failing to listen will only increase the distance between you, and the conflict will definitely go unresolved.

Are you the one who doesn't listen, or are you the one not listened to? Or, are both you and your mate guilty, not hearing what the other has to say? This is an important question to answer because listening is a critical step to resolving conflicts. Listening is essential if you want to reason or communicate with your spouse on the basis of what they have said to you. If you refuse to hear, you cannot understand, which makes it impossible to even agree over what the problem actually is.

When your mate voices something that upsets them, do you interrupt? Do you try to answer your loved one's concerns before they have even finished talking? Are you really listening, or merely thinking about how you want to respond? These are all signs that you aren't listening. If you aren't a good listener, you won't be able to communicate well because you haven't really understood what your spouse has said. If you constantly hear your mate declare, "No, that's not what I mean," or, "You don't understand what I'm saying," you probably don't! This means you aren't listening very well at all.

If the Holy Spirit has convicted you of poor listening practices, begin by acknowledging a problem exists. Again, this demands the honesty and humility we spoke of earlier. You can't go wrong with these two attitudes. In fact, they are essential to hearing and understanding your spouse.

Next, ask God to show you *why* you don't listen. Let me give you some biblical possibilities that you can choose from. Is it possibly because you don't restrain your anger, as we described in the previous section? You surely can't listen to anyone when you are out of control emotionally. Perhaps you are too busy talking. You can't talk and listen at the same time. James says that if you want to be *"swift to hear,"* then you must be *"slow to speak,"* which ultimately makes you *"slow to wrath"* (James 1:19).

You may not be a good listener because of pride, thinking you are always right. Proverbs says a scoffer (which in Hebrew means an arrogant talker) *"does not listen to rebuke"* (Prov. 13:1). Are you too proud to listen? Another reason for not listening is given by David in the Psalms. There, the heart of God cries out to his people when He says, *"Oh that My people would listen to Me..."* (Ps. 81:13). David had already explained why the Jews wouldn't listen to Him. He revealed that it was because of their *"stubborn heart"* (v. 12). Are you just plain stubborn?

Ultimately, listening is a decision you make. It is the consent of your heart to hear and understand what your loved one is saying to you. This principle of consent is revealed by Moses as he instructs the Israelites concerning false prophets. He explained that when a false prophet came into their midst, the people had to make a choice. He commanded them not to *"consent to him or listen to him..."* (Deut. 13:8). In other words, listening ultimately comes down to choice.

If you want to become a good listener, ask the Lord to convict you every time you fall into one of these traps. Surrender to His conviction, and His power to change your behavior will immediately enter your heart. Practice allowing your spouse to talk while you listen. If you struggle here, you may even have to repeat back what he or she has just said. Ask your partner, "Is this what you mean?" This will help in two ways: first, it will help you to fully understand what your mate is trying to tell you, and second, it will assure your spouse that you truly desire to listen.

Listening allows you to understand your spouse, which is a fundamental key to resolving conflicts. May you grow in this ability. We will talk much more about communication in a later chapter.

6. <u>Will you be the first to humble yourself and confess your faults?</u> Humbling yourself is also a very important step that will enable you to quickly resolve the conflicts between you. When both parties take this step, there is no argument. It's over because you have just acknowledged your fault, and no one has to prove that the other is at fault.

Let me illustrate by describing the dynamics of a typical conflict. Your spouse comes to you with a charge that you have done something offensive. You immediately get angry, defensive, and explode. You deny any fault and then begin to charge your mate with some grievances of your own. You refuse to really listen to your partner's viewpoint because you are too busy shifting the blame and excusing your action because of some extenuating circumstance. Your spouse then believes that you don't think you've done anything wrong. So your spouse tries a little harder to convince you that this offense really has occurred. In the meantime, the anger continues to rise in both of you because of frustration, dishonesty, and the unwillingness to listen. Then your spouse reminds you of another past example of your fault, and this really infuriates you because the past is now being thrown in your face. So you throw out an illustration of your spouse's past failings. The charges and countercharges fly back and forth until you can't even remember what you were originally fighting about. The volume rises more and more until one of you gives up and walks out, slamming the door behind you. Does this sound familiar?

If this sounds like your house, you have got to stop this behavior if you want to build your companionship. How could this conflict have been stopped before it went down this path? By simply acknowledging your fault in honesty and humility, and asking forgiveness right at the beginning. This is the fastest and easiest way to stop a contention before it even starts. Let me explain why.

When you confess your fault, you immediately disarm your spouse with humility and honesty. Your partner doesn't have to prove to you anymore that you have a fault. You remove the weapons of accusation and lay them on the table. As a Christian, you are called to humble yourself, not force someone to humble you by proving you are at fault (James 4:10).

Confessing your shortcomings saves a whole lot of time arguing about *if* there is any fault, and you get to the heart of the problem right away. There are no more fights that seem to go on and on. It can be over very quickly instead of continuing for days. Speedy resolution occurs when two people are maturing in their relationship.

Humble honesty enables you to see clearly all aspects of the conflict. In most cases both parties have fault, but when you refuse to acknowledge your own weakness and shift the blame to your spouse, everything gets confused. Jesus recognized that you must first deal with your own faults before you start picking at someone else's: *"How can you say to your brother, 'Let me remove the speck out of your eye,' and look, a plank is in your own eye? Hypocrite! First remove the plank from your own eye, and then you will see clearly to remove the speck out of your brother's eye"* (Matt. 7:4, 5, underline added). The picture Christ draws is so vivid and powerful. It is ridiculous to try to perform eye surgery on a friend when there is a huge plank sticking out of your own eye. Your personal blindness makes it completely impossible for you to see anything with a proper perspective. It's pure hypocrisy for us to refuse to look in the mirror, and then put a magnifying glass up to the faults of our spouse. Brothers and sisters, until you first look at your own faults, you are really incapable of speaking to your mate about theirs.

What do we do instead of confessing our own faults? We blameshift. One of the most basic characteristics of man's sinful nature is the willingness to shift the blame to others. This was the first thing that Adam and Eve did after they sinned in the garden. When God confronted them that fateful day, Adam said, *"The woman You gave me, she gave me of the tree and I ate..."* The woman replied, *"The serpent deceived me, and I ate"* (Gen. 3:12, 13, underline added). Adam shifted the blame to God and to his wife, even though he chose to eat of his own free will. Then Eve blamed the devil for it all. These two were the first blameshifters in history, and they have trained us all very well.

Are you blameshifting in this same way? Blaming God? Blaming your spouse? Blaming the devil? You can't resolve anything until you take responsibility for your own actions and confess your faults. Don't wait for your mate to begin. You start it first, then the healing will begin.

7. <u>Are you willing to truly forgive</u>? Forgiveness is absolutely essential if you desire to see your marriage fully restored and to build oneness and companionship. The unwillingness to fully forgive your spouse is a main reason why these conflicts are never resolved. Haven't you ever wondered why you hold resentment and anger from the past? Or, why you explode over the smallest infraction of your rules? Or, why you refuse to confess your own faults when confronted? Or, why you are generally unwilling to take the right actions? Can't you see that your unforgiveness lies at the root of these wrong actions?

The refusal to forgive is one of the great stumbling blocks to reconciling any relationship. When you are unwilling to forgive, it's as if your feet are set in concrete and you are completely immovable in your position. No forward progress will be made, and no change for the better will occur in your relationship. In fact, unforgiveness slowly and imperceptibly destroys any relationship that remains. Both hearts just grow harder with each passing day.

Many couples say they are sorry after a conflict is over, but true and complete forgiveness does not occur many times. There is a sorrow for what has happened, but neither partner is ready to forgive as the Scripture commands. Usually no sincere request to be *forgiven* is made, nor is there true repentance so the same issue won't come up again. The unforgiveness is quickly revealed when one or both parties bring up the past issues to use as ammunition in a new conflict. This is *not* what you should do if you want to build your relationship to last.

Notice how differently God deals with you. Remember how you came into a relationship with the Lord? It was according to His mercy and forgiveness bestowed freely upon you. It is the very nature of God to forgive and show mercy. Micah the prophet declares that God *"delights in mercy"* (Micah 7:18). King David said, *"For You, O Lord, are good, and ready to forgive, and abundant in mercy to all who call upon You"* (Ps. 86:5). You don't have to twist God's arm to get Him to show mercy and forgiveness. He's ready to forgive and delights to, if you will only ask. No doubt you have asked Him many times. But, in the same manner, are you willing and ready to forgive others and especially your spouse? Are you willing to forgive as you have been forgiven? You must be willing to let His life be lived through you. Paul entreated us to *"be kind to one another, tenderhearted, forgiving one another, <u>just as</u> God in Christ also forgave you"* (Eph. 4:32 underline added).

If there is unforgiveness in your heart, the issues between you will not be fully reconciled. Make the choice today to forgive before you approach your spouse for reconciliation. Then you will be ready to forgive when your mate makes a request. Only then will you be following the example to forgive as you have been forgiven.

8. Are you willing to communicate in love and explain exactly what attitude or action you want your spouse to change? This is one of the most uncomfortable actions required to resolve a conflict. It's not easy to tell your spouse that you are not happy with the way they are treating you because you anticipate an angry or unpleasant response. To protect yourself, you choose to stuff it down inside and deny or excuse your mate's offenses, but you know down deep that someday you will have to deal with it. Sooner or later you are going to have to talk about it with your mate. Let me explain how to go about that.

After you have taken steps 1-7, you should now tell your husband or wife exactly how you believe you have been offended. This, of course, is only done if your spouse has not already confessed their own faults. Yet, if they haven't, then begin the conversation by speaking with gentle words as opposed to harsh words because "a *soft answer turns away wrath, but a harsh word stirs up anger*" (Prov. 15:1). The last thing you want to do at this point is to stir up more anger. Come with soft words of reconciliation as you discuss how your mate has offended you. There are always two sides to a conflict, and both must be dealt with completely.

Be careful about how you take this action. First, don't be vague with your spouse, speaking of some feeling you have, but be very specific, referring to particular words or actions that have offended you. Note the example of Christ as He reproved the church at Ephesus. He was very specific in addressing their fault. He said, "*I have this against you…you have left your first love*" (Rev. 2:4). This is about as direct and to the point as you can get.

Second, you must have the right goal. Jesus explained to His disciples, "*If your brother sins against you, go and tell him his fault, between you and him alone. If he hears you, you have gained your brother*" (Matt. 18:15, Underline added). The goal is to gain your brother, and this means you must come with that attitude and desire. If you come with yelling, finger-pointing, and accusations, merely venting your own frustrations, the results will be far from profitable, and you won't gain a right relationship with your spouse. You will only alienate them more.

If your spouse refuses to hear you, then you would take the next step referred to in Matt. 18:16. Jesus said, "*But if he will not hear you, take with you one or two more, that by the mouth of two or three witnesses every word may be established.*" The best way I have found to implement this verse in a practical way is to call your pastor. Ask him to call your spouse so that you might try and reconcile the issue together. Many ask me if this isn't violating your mate's trust by revealing the problem to the pastor. Absolutely not. You have biblical basis for taking this action as mentioned in the above verse of Scripture. It should be done because your spouse has refused to hear and reconcile with you. I have seen this approach work very well many times. Jesus knew what He was talking about. Trust Him and do it. I have also spoken in much more detail on the subject of an unresponsive spouse in the appendix of this book.

Finally, another common sense reason to communicate specific offenses is because your spouse is not a mind reader, and they are not going to know what you are thinking unless you spell it out. Many times in counseling, a husband or wife will say, "Why didn't you tell me this before?" There is total amazement on the person's face that this issue has never come up in a conversation. Your spouse can't know or understand what you are thinking or feeling unless you tell them.

The bottom line in reconciliation is that at some time both parties must speak honestly about what has offended them. This enables understanding and the possibility for a real change of action.

9. <u>Are you willing to find agreement through compromise</u>? The goal on the vertical plane is to please God; the goal on the horizontal plane is to find an agreement with your spouse. Remember the command of Jesus we looked at earlier to "*agree with your adversary*" (Matt. 5:25)? Agreement is found as you choose to give in and compromise in these areas in which you have been stubborn or selfish. This will please God and demonstrate love toward your mate. Compromise is how you find agreement with your spouse.

The prophet Amos asked the question: "*Can two walk together, unless they are agreed?*" (Amos 3:3) He was rebuking God's people for their disobedience and unwillingness to agree with God about their sin. The apostle John addressed the same issue. He said, "*If we confess our sins, He is faithful and just to forgive us our sins...*" (1 John 1:9) The word *confess* means "to agree with." When you confess your sins, you are agreeing with God, and this enables you to walk with Him. God will never force His will upon you or force you into an agreement with Him. He waits for you to willingly come to Him and choose to turn from your self-life, thus coming into agreement with Him.

The same thing is true with your spouse. When you both confess your faults, you find immediate agreement together. This agreement is what allows you to find a lasting compromise where you have previously demanded your own way. Compromise is the loving agreement to give, not demand. Forcing and imposing your will is nothing but pride and selfishness on your part, which will reconcile nothing between you.

Choosing to give is a key ingredient to finding compromise and the agreement you long for in your marriage. In fact, compromise cannot be found unless at least one partner is willing to take the first step and give in a sacrificial way. When partners concede they are making the concessions that are necessary for compromise to occur. Giving in this manner will always eliminate strife and restore harmony to the relationship.

Abraham and Lot illustrate this principle well. When strife occurred between these two family members over the issue of grazing land for their large herds, notice the choice Abraham made. He said to Lot, *"Please let there be no strife between you and me...Is not the whole land before you? Please separate from me. If you take the left, then I will go to the right; or, if you go to the right, then I will go to the left"* (Gen. 13:8, 9). This is what compromise is all about. It seeks a way to give in order to eliminate strife. Compromise may even entail giving your partner the opportunity to make the choice and being willing to abide by their decision. Love will always seek a way to give to others in this manner. *"For God so loved...that He gave His only begotten Son,"* in order that He might remove the strife and reconcile us to himself (John 3:16). Love always takes sacrificial action to reconcile conflict.

How about you? Are you willing to give to your spouse in this manner? Will you by love seek a plan to compromise with your mate to remove the point of strife between you? If so, take the biggest issue that is dividing you right now and ask God to show you a creative way in which *you* can give. This may entail restraining yourself from a particular action or taking one to demonstrate your love and desire to reconcile this issue. Don't wait for your spouse to take the first step; you take it.

However, always remember the balance in this issue of compromise. You should only compromise over nonmoral and nonbiblical issues. Never compromise with anything contrary to Scripture or where Scripture has clearly commanded you to act.

10. Are you willing to diligently pray together for reconciliation? God pleads with His people, *"Call to me, and I will answer you, and show you great and mighty things, which you do not know"* (Jer. 33:3). James says, *"The effective fervent prayer of a righteous man avails much"* (James 5:16). Do you believe these promises? Do you believe that God will answer you if you call and that He will show you the things that you need to do? Are you fully convinced that prayer together will really help your marriage? If you believe this to be true, then start praying together today.

Why is prayer together so important in helping you to resolve conflicts? Because prayer brings you both to a place of humility before God and before each other. You have to be honest and totally open with God and your mate when you pray. If you will not come in this manner, both God and your spouse will be aware of it and your prayers will be ineffective.

Start and end your discussions with prayer, and you will be surprised at the harmony you will begin to experience. You will naturally find agreement and compromise because this is the fruit of prayer. Jesus taught that true prayer occurred whenever *"two of you agree on earth..."* (Matt. 18:19, underline added). Don't miss the fruit of harmony that prayer will bring to your relationship. Don't miss the power of the Spirit that is so necessary for a changed attitude or behavior. You need what He is offering!

11. <u>You must possess patience and long-suffering</u>. No one changes overnight. It has usually taken years to establish the habits and the behaviors that drive two people apart, and there is no one who can wave the magic wand and resolve these issues instantaneously.

If you are not practiced in patience, you will lose hope very quickly when things don't change within your time frame. You must have those realistic expectations that we spoke of in chapter 7. Patience is the key to living with the realistic expectation that your spouse will change slowly.

The Father is extremely realistic about the human race. He knows what is in us as fallen human beings and understands what it takes to change. His patience and long-suffering is a key element in the salvation of all mankind. Peter said that we should *"account that the long-suffering of the Lord is salvation"* (2 Peter 3:15). In other words, God's patience extends to us the time that we need to come to Him and be saved.

This is also true for any struggling marriage. Unless both parties have an abundance of patience and long-suffering, that marriage will not be saved. When you have two fallen people married to each other, both needing major change in their lives, only patience and long-suffering will allow enough time to complete the necessary work.

Where does one obtain this patience and long-suffering? Again, this will come as a direct result of your personal relationship with Christ. Patience is a fruit of the Holy Spirit (Gal. 5:22). This is why you must establish and maintain your walk with Christ. Paul prayed for the Colossian church that it might be *"strengthened with all might, according to His glorious power, for all patience and long-suffering with joy..."* (Col. 1:11). Notice, it's His glorious power that will give you the willingness to patiently work for change and to do it with joy. Paul prayed again for the Roman church that *"the God of patience and comfort grant you to be like-minded toward one another..."* (Rom. 15:5). Don't you want this patience He promises and the comfort that comes with it? To be likeminded is the precious fruit of patience.

Here is how to get it. Ask God to fill you with the power of His Spirit and enable you to suffer long with your spouse. Don't give up on His promises before you have truly given God an opportunity to work! Most people I've seen give up way too soon. Remember that Scripture encourages you to *"imitate those who through faith and patience inherit the promises."* Imitate Abraham, who *"after he patiently endured, [he] obtained the promise"* (Heb. 6:12, 15). Remember, reconciliation takes this kind of enduring patience to see the promise fulfilled.

Therefore, will you believe God's promise that with Him *"all things are possible"* (Matt. 19:26)? Don't listen to those thoughts or people who encourage you to give up. You need patience so that after you have done the will of God, you may also inherit the promises of God.

12. <u>Are you willing to take action even if your spouse will not</u>? This is what God has done with you. *"He demonstrated His own love toward us, in that while we were still sinners, Christ died for us"* (Rom. 5:8). He revealed His care for us, even though we were in rebellion. If we are to love others as He has loved us, then we must do the same (John 13:34). Your spouse may be somewhat resistant to change or in full rebellion against you and God. Taking responsibility to change what you know *you* should is all God requires. If you do what is right, this will be the best encouragement to your spouse to also make changes.

Scripture encourages us to *"provoke [one another] unto love and to good works"* (Heb. 10:24, KJV). Jesus said, *"Whatever you want men to do to you, do also to them..."* (Matt. 7:12). I challenge you to apply this principle to your marriage and see what happens. How do you want your spouse to act toward you? Begin to act that way toward your mate, and you will be provoking them to love and good works. This is one of the best and most positive things you can do in your marriage.

Are you fully convinced that only action will change things in your marriage? It's not enough to know what you should do, you must act on what you know. It's not enough to tell people you love them, you must show them by all that you do. Reading this book by itself will not solve your marriage problems or help you to build your relationship. Going to the best marriage counselor in town cannot by itself accomplish it either. At some point you must put into action what this book teaches or what your counselor tells you to do. That is the only way to fully resolve the conflicts. Let me illustrate this principle for you.

Before the crucifixion, on that last night Jesus spent with His disciples, John records a very interesting occurrence. He tells us that Jesus knew that his hour had come, that He was about to depart from this world. Jesus knew that all things had been given into His hands and that He would be victorious and overcome the cross and return to His Father. He knew how much He loved His disciples and that He had loved them even to that last day. Yet He also knew that the disciples didn't understand all of this, especially how much He loved them. Jesus realized that it wasn't enough for Him to know all this. He had to demonstrate by action what He knew in His heart. So He laid aside His garments and girded himself with a towel and began to wash the disciples' feet. What an act of love! He didn't just talk about loving them. He showed them by this incredible act! He took the place of the most humble servant and washed the scum off their feet (John 13:1-20).

This is what the Lord of Glory did because He was interested in reconciling with the world. Jesus' servanthood was a picture of God's heart and soul trying to communicate His ultimate intention. He took an action that clearly demonstrated how much He loved His disciples. Jesus was a man of words and actions. He was convinced that only by living among us and showing us the love of the Father would we ever believe it. He did this all while the men of this world were in rebellion against Him. Jesus even washed the feet of His own betrayer, Judas.

After Jesus washed the disciples' feet, He then turned to them and said, *"I have given you an example, that you should do as I have done to you... If you know these things, happy are you if you do them"* (John 13:15, 17 underline added).

Are you motivated by this conviction that you must take the action of love, lay aside your pride and selfishness, and become a servant? Will you take these actions even if your mate is not willing to respond in like manner? If you will take this action, then you will be following Christ's command, and He will reveal himself to you (John 14:21). In other words, He will reward you with more of himself, for He is our life and He is our peace.

When He is your life (Col. 3:4), you will do just as Jesus has done to you. You will forgive as He has forgiven you. You will serve your spouse as Christ has served you. You will accept your partner as Christ has accepted you. You will be patient even as God has suffered long with you. This is how you wash your mate's feet, and this is where happiness will be found. If you know these things, you can only find true happiness if you do them. Obedience to His commands are the stepping stones that will bring reconciliation and the depth of relationship that you have always wanted. Take the example and begin today to wash your mate's feet.

Group Discussion Questions

1. Without giving the names or any information that might identify the couple, discuss a marriage that you have seen fail because of the violation of one or more of the biblical principles in this chapter.

2. Without giving any information that might embarrass your partner, discuss how you have violated one or more of the principles in this chapter. How did this hinder you and your spouse from resolving the conflict?

3. How have you overcome and changed this behavior in order to resolve this conflict?

10

HOW TO FULLY SOLVE A CONFLICT

"The saying pleased the whole multitude" Acts 6:5

M any years ago, I heard an interview on television with Billy Graham. He was being asked a whole range of questions concerning the state of our nation and the world. The interviewer then began to ask him questions about marriage and the high divorce rate here in our country. Dr. Graham began to talk about his own marriage and how a Christian marriage was supposed to function. He then shared some very personal insights about his own marriage. What he said that day made a profound impression upon me and I will never forget it.

He said that at the beginning of his marriage he and his wife, Ruth, had all the normal conflicts any couple has adjusting in those first years. But now, after many years of marriage, Christ had brought such harmony between them that he and his wife rarely fought or argued anymore. He related further how they had learned to solve their differences and lovingly serve each other.

Now when I heard that statement, I didn't hear much of the rest of the interview. I was truly taken by the fact that Billy and Ruth Graham rarely argued or fought. This statement intrigued me as I thought to myself, *Could this really be possible?* How could two people come to a place where they rarely fight at all? How does a couple ever get to this point?

At that time I was a newlywed myself, and I was going through my own adjustment period with my wife. But I remember that this statement gave me hope. It gave me something to look forward to for my own marriage. Today, I can tell you that I have found Billy Graham's statement to be true in my marriage. After twenty-five years of marriage, I can honestly say that I rarely fight with my wife. Therefore, the truths I am about to share with you truly do work. It simply comes down to learning how to fully solve conflicts, not just resolving them. Now you may be thinking, *What's the difference?* Let me explain.

RESOLVING A CONFLICT VS. FULLY SOLVING IT

There is a truly fundamental difference between these two objectives, and there is much more here than just a play on words. When you resolve a conflict, all you have done is reconciled the two partners together. They have acknowledged their own faults and asked forgiveness, then the warfare ceases. The original problem is resolved, but will the same thing happen again tomorrow? Will these two people find themselves asking forgiveness for the exact same thing all over again? If so, then the problem hasn't been fully solved.

To fully solve a problem, you must discover how and why the conflict happened in the first place. This takes identifying some of the underlying issues and determining if any of them are recurring problems. Then you must devise a plan to avoid falling into the same trap again. This entails coming up with mutually agreeable practical actions to employ in order to head off the problem in the future. If you are both looking for how to prevent offending the other, and are searching for ways to love and serve each other, you strike at that root of all problems, *selfishness*. Ultimately, you will have fewer and fewer problems to deal with, and true marital harmony results. These are always the necessary steps for good problem-solving, whether it's in your marriage, with your friends, or with those whom you come into contact at work.

I'm sure that if you will stop and think for a moment, you will be able to remember certain conflicts that you have already solved in your marriage. These would be issues that you have argued about many times in the past, but not anymore. Why is this? Because you've solved them, and they are no longer a point of contention.

Let's look at the steps to fully solving a conflict between you and your spouse. I would like to take you through a typical conflict step by step, illustrating what hinders you from short-term reconciliation, and continue all the way to a biblical plan for a long-term solution. Then I will show you how the apostles used these same principles to solve a serious conflict in their day. My hope is that you will study these principles and apply them to those stubborn areas of conflict in your marriage.

STEPS TO FULLY SOLVING A CONFLICT

1. <u>Discover what hinders the process of reconciling and fully solving problems</u>. There are two basic actions that hinder couples from even beginning the process of reconciliation. People either concentrate on

attacking each other, or they choose to *retreat* from each other. I would like to give you a progressive diagram to illustrate how this occurs that will enable you to see the process more clearly. I have adapted my diagram from a similar one used by Jay Adams in his book, *The Christian Counselor's Manual.* I have built upon his original idea to further explain the difference between resolving and fully solving a conflict.

Figure 1: A husband and wife will either attack each other or retreat from one another, thus hindering them from ever solving the problem.

First, let me explain what I mean by attacking and retreating. If you are an attacker, you are the more aggressive partner, and therefore, you will usually go on the offensive to verbally blame, condemn, criticize, or denounce your spouse. This offensive behavior may be associated with angry yelling, screaming, hurling insults, throwing up past failures, or belittling your spouse for not having changed at all. The purpose of attacking your partner in this manner is to verbally slash to the bone, to cut your opponent off before they can slash at you.

Oh, how deep the tongue can cut! It can hurt someone quickly and destroy the person you love in a moment of uncontrolled anger. David said concerning those who spoke against him, *"Your tongue devises destruction, like a sharp razor, working deceitfully"* (Ps. 52:2). His enemies' harsh words cut and wounded him deeply. Solomon taught the same thing about the tongue. *"There is one who speaks like the piercing of a sword, but the tongue of the wise promotes health"* (Prov. 12:18).

What is the result of attacking like this? You will simply destroy your spouse slowly day by day. Paul described this attacking method when he wrote to the Galatian church. *"But if you bite and devour one another, beware lest you be consumed by one another"* (Gal. 5:15). He draws the picture of dogs biting, ripping, and tearing at each other. One or both in the relationship will ultimately perish. So, too, will be the result in any marriage where one or both deal with each other in this manner.

Are you attacking your spouse like this? You may feel justified because of the problems in your marriage, but you are failing to see what is really taking place between you. You are tearing your spouse apart slowly, limb by limb and piece by piece. Attacking will never solve the problem because most of the time you will never get to the problem because you are too busy slashing each other. In fact, attacking your spouse personally will only intensify the problems because you have missed what the real problem is–your attacking.

Retreating from each other is just as bad because it does just the opposite. The one who retreats is usually the less verbal individual in the marriage, and this action appears to be the best defensive method for battle with the attacking spouse. The person who retreats in conflict will hold all the anger inside and will usually never bring up areas of conflict because they fear the consequences. This husband or wife will just stuff all the resentment and hurt down inside and stay silent or turn around and walk out of the room. The attacker will constantly be chasing the one who retreats, trying to talk the problems out. The argument will move from room to room, but to no avail. Sometimes, the one retreating is very subtle in their tactics, using words to retreat. Those who choose to retreat will sometimes play word games to never allow the conversation to ever get to the real issues. Sometimes the one retreating learns to lie their way out of everything, again to keep from ever being confronted on issues. Other times, a retreater will just refuse to talk at all.

Retreating in relationships is seen in Scripture in many places. Jeremiah the prophet spoke of this tendency in man to retreat from God when he said, *"they have turned to Me the back, and not the face; though I taught them... yet they have not listened to receive instruction"* (Jer. 32:33). Isn't this what we often do with the Lord? We retreat and turn our back and refuse to listen to Him. Yet we also do the same thing in our marital relationships when confronted in a conflict. We turn our back to our spouse and run away, refusing to deal with the issues. We don't want the confrontation, so we retreat as quickly as we can.

From the moment of the very first sin, man has taken this action to avoid being confronted with failure. After Adam and Eve sinned, what did they do? They ran and hid from God in the garden to avoid being confronted for their disobedience. We looked at this verse earlier, but look again at Adam and Eve's action in the light of this concept of attacking and retreating. When confronted by God, Adam then turned and attacked God to justify himself for his own sin. He said, *"It's the woman you gave to me."* He was basically telling God, *It's really your fault that I've sinned.* Note, Adam first retreated and then attacked by attempting to shift the blame to God for his own failure. It is possible to take both of these actions in the midst of a conflict. The men who argued with Stephen in the book of Acts took on this dual role of retreating and attacking. *"Then they cried out with a loud voice, stopped their ears, and ran at him with one accord; and they cast him out of the city and stoned him"* (Acts 7:57-58). This is an extreme example of men who first refused to hear by stopping their ears and then physically attacked him. Hopefully this is not what is occurring in your home.

Remember, every time you put off resolving a conflict to another day, you are retreating. Every night you go to bed angry with unresolved issues between you, you are retreating. Whenever you turn your back and walk out of the room in the midst of a conflict, you are retreating. Each time you refuse to reconcile a conflict and roll over in bed and face the wall, you are retreating. This will solve nothing because in the morning you have to talk about it anyway.

Both of these actions are totally unproductive for resolving or fully solving conflicts. These are sinful actions that will only drive you further apart from each other and hinder a final solution. You must identify which of these activities you are prone to do. Are you the one attacking or the one retreating? You also may switch back and forth between attacking and retreating as Adam. When both partners are attackers, it is usually a very stormy marital relationship. If one spouse is an attacker and the other is constantly retreating, there will be less conflict, but it is frustrating because one spouse will have to chase the other to face the issues. If both choose to retreat, it usually takes a very serious incident or issue to get these two to deal with a problem. Two retreating spouses can usually stay together for years even with very serious problems in their marriage simply because they just don't deal with the problems between them.

If you can identify how you tend to react, then you are much more able to take it to God in prayer and ask Him to change your thinking and behavior. When you realize how unproductive these two actions are, a change of direction can occur. Remember, when you are attacking and retreating from each other, you are violating all of the principles I covered in the previous chapter. What is your alternative to attacking or retreating?

2. <u>Agree to attack the problem</u>. As you consider the next part of the diagram, you will see that attacking the problem is the only productive action to take when dealing with conflicts. It is what allows you to resolve it. See the next part of the diagram.

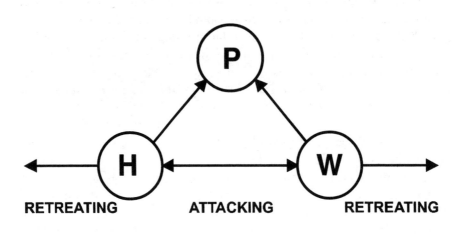

Figure 2: Attack the problem instead of attacking each other.

How do you attack the problem? First, you must refuse to attack or retreat from your spouse. You willingly make this decision because you understand that attacking or retreating accomplishes nothing, and you also encourage your spouse to do the same. In the midst of a conflict you might say something like, "Honey, you are attacking (or retreating) right now. This isn't going to get us anywhere," thus encouraging your mate to turn from this method.

For the best long-term results, you must determine what the real problem is. But you may be thinking, *How do we do that?* It's very simple, but not easy. You must ask yourself what *you* have done wrong to cause your conflicts. This will entail examining yourself with brutal honesty to determine your own fault. Like David, ask the Spirit of truth to search your heart to reveal if there is *"any wicked way"* in you (Ps. 139:23, 24). God's Spirit will surely help you to find the truth, and as you do your fault will become obvious. Where *you* have failed is the problem you want to attack! Every time you attack the problem, you are choosing to apply all of the principles of the previous chapter.

If there is an attitude or action where you have failed many times, it is important to recognize it as a *key issue* that has probably caused other conflicts too. What do I mean by key issue? It is any issue that comes up over and over again as a source of conflict or a place of failure in your relationship. When an individual can't recognize the key issues, he is doomed to repeat the same pattern. One of my primary responsibilities in marriage counseling is to help people to see what the key issues are and what the Bible declares they should do about them. If people fail to change regarding the key issues in which they are stumbling, they will never fully solve anything.

Let me give you an example of some key issues in one couple's marriage to make this more practical. Dan and Paula had been married for eight years and had very severe financial problems. In our first counseling session, I immediately asked how they had gotten into this predicament. Dan replied that he had been fired because of using drugs while at work. Afterward, he descended into depression and refused to look for work, even though his wife constantly encouraged him to do so. The bills began to mount up, so they put all their debts on a credit card until they reached the card limit. Finally, Dan got some part-time jobs, but the earnings did not take care of the family's needs. Dan, still struggling with his guilt over being fired and his failure to provide for his family, began to drink secretly and to lie about why the money was disappearing. Paula caught him in several lies, which ultimately brought them to see me.

After counseling with them for several months, I found that Dan had several key issues that he needed to solve. First, Dan had a lying problem. Paula told me of many times in the first few years of their marriage that she had caught him in clear-cut lies. I explained to Dan that until he was ready to be totally honest with God, his wife, himself, and with me, nothing was going to change.

Second, Dan had a problem of refusing to face his problems. He would simply choose to deny that a problem existed until things got out of control. When he did choose to deal with a problem, he would not deal with it in a biblical way. I told Dan that this was a key reason why he was in so much trouble right now. He needed to receive God's instruction and follow His solutions if anything was to change.

Third, Dan had no real personal relationship with the Lord. He had grown up in the church for most of his life but would rarely pray or read his Bible. I explained that his personal relationship with the Lord was where he would find the inner satisfaction and fulfillment he was searching for in the drugs and the alcohol.

Paula had some key issues to deal with as well. She was trying to be a good and submissive wife and, therefore, would never confront him, even though she knew he was lying to her. The only time she said anything to him was when it was so obvious that it was awkward for her not to confront him. Generally, though, Paula would rarely confront her husband about anything. He would speak harshly to her, and she would take it and not respond. He would fail to keep his promises, and she would say nothing. I explained to Paula that she is required by God to confront her husband when he sins against her (Luke 17:3; Matt. 18:15). Ultimately, Paula realized that this was a key issue and was the reason she had so much turmoil and anger in her heart toward Dan.

Paula also spent very little personal time in reading Scripture or in prayer. She realized this was a key issue that needed to change as well. All of these issues had to be identified and dealt with if they were to fully solve anything in their marriage.

What are the key issues in your marriage that cause the same conflicts to recur? This is how you attack the problem: identify where you are failing. If you have failed in a certain area many times before, be assured that this is a key issue in your life. These issues must be dealt with if you are going to see your conflicts fully solved.

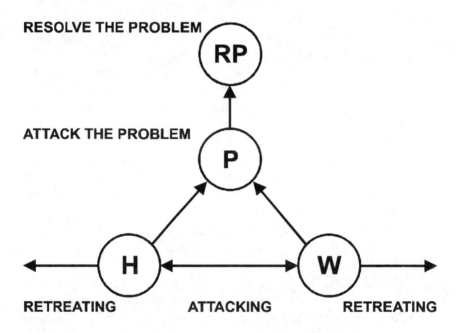

Figure 3: Resolve the conflict.

3. <u>Resolve the immediate conflict</u>. Once you have started to attack the problem by identifying your faults, now you can resolve it by confession, forgiveness, repentance, prayer and all the principles given in the previous chapter. See the diagram.

There are two aspects to resolving a conflict. Reconciling your sin before God and then with your mate. Therefore, first ask God to forgive you for your part in the conflict. *"If we confess our sins, He is faithful and just to forgive us our sins and to cleanse us from all unrighteousness"* (1 John 1:9). Ask for God to completely cleanse you and purify your heart before Him. This reconciles the issue before God.

Next, confess your fault to your spouse and ask their forgiveness. James says, *"Confess your faults one to another, and pray one for another, that you may be healed"* (James 5:16, KJV). If your spouse will also confess and ask forgiveness, then you can resolve the conflict completely. Then pray together for tender hearts and for grace to return to a right relationship with each other. This reconciles the conflict with your spouse.

However, remember that resolving the conflict is only your short-term goal. The long-term goal is to fully solve the problem, to change the way you relate to each other from this point forward. Most couples stop when they reach the short-term goal of reconciling the immediate conflict, believing everything is fine simply because they are not arguing anymore. They think that because they have acknowledged their fault, asked forgiveness, hugged each other, and maybe even shed some tears, all is well. This is not the case, however. If you stop here you are only doomed to repeat the same behavior all over again. The circumstances will be different, but the underlying problem will be the same. Your ultimate goal must not only be to resolve this conflict but to solve the underlying key issues once and for all. How do you do that?

4. <u>Find a lasting solution</u>. Finding lasting solutions to your conflicts must be your ultimate aim and objective. If you ever want to grow in your relationship to the point where you will rarely argue with each other, this final step is essential. One day you should be able to give the same testimony as Billy Graham. Don't you want that in your marriage relationship?

How do you find a lasting solution? It takes spiritual maturity to find lasting solutions because of the path you must take to get there. It takes emotionally controlled communication and a willingness to compromise with your spouse. It takes honesty and humility to acknowledge your own faults and to see that you are no longer single, but one flesh, taking into consideration your spouse's feelings, thoughts, and opinions. All these qualities require you to live in an unselfish manner and require a practical knowledge of Scripture to truly enable biblical solutions to be formulated. You also need the personal discipline to follow through on your plan so that the conflict won't happen again. Learning how to live in a loving way with your spouse is what fully solves a problem and what stops a recurring offense, bringing lasting harmony to your marriage. This kind of spiritual maturity comes only from a committed personal relationship to Christ. Here is where the power comes from! No one can act in the above manner in the strength of the flesh. Now let's look at some of the specifics of finding the solution.

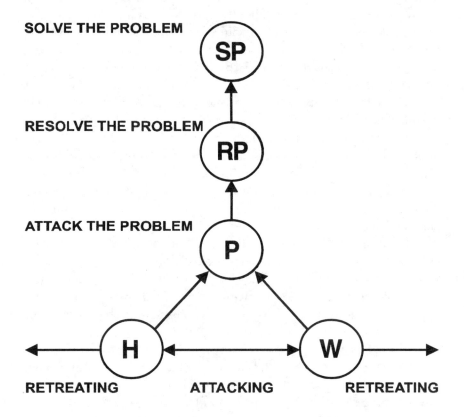

Figure 4: Finding a lasting solution.

To find the solution you need to search the Scriptures to learn exactly what is said concerning the problem that you have identified. For example, if you are struggling with over-commitment and lack of priorities for the family, you need to understand what God views as important priorities and what counsel He gives about the problem. Sometimes you will find direct commands in the Scriptures; other times you will find general principles or examples given.

Once you have this insight, then communicate with your mate and think creatively to determine how to obey God's commands or how to implement biblical principles to change your behavior. This may take some counseling with your pastor to gain further insight. Some conflicts are very complicated and need the objectivity of a biblical counselor who is outside of the situation. But remember, these changes of behavior always require loving compromise from both husband and wife to find the lasting solution. Don't give up before you find it.

Last, you must discipline yourself to work your plan and keep the promises you have made to each other. This is where many lasting solutions break down and a couple goes back to the same old behavior that caused the conflict in the first place. If you find a mutually agreeable solution, it is imperative that you remember what you said you would do and do it.

The important thing is not to give up in your endeavor until you find these lasting solutions. I want to give you hope because it is truly possible to find them. As I said earlier, you have probably already found some lasting solutions over issues you previously fought over when you were first married. You don't fight about these problems anymore. Why? Possibly because one or both of you have retreated from each other and have not resolved the issue. More than likely, you have already chosen to wisely and lovingly compromise and solve your problem. You did this because you wanted to show love to your spouse and, of course, to stop the arguing over the problem. My point is this: if you can do this with any conflict, you can do it with all of your disagreements and differences.

The problem arises when you stop trying to find a way to fully solve these recurring issues. Perhaps you are both stubbornly refusing to fully reconcile and search for the solution. You need to apply what you have learned here and take the action God requires. There is a lasting solution for every conflict between you.

Let me now give you an example from the book of Acts regarding how these steps to find a lasting solution worked in the early church.

"Now in those days, when the number of the disciples was multiplying, there arose a complaint against the Hebrews by the Hellenists, because their widows were neglected in the daily distribution. Then the twelve summoned the multitude of the disciples and said, 'It is not desirable that we should leave the word of God and serve tables. Therefore, brethren, seek out from among you seven men of good reputation, full of the Holy Spirit and wisdom, whom we may appoint over this business; but we will give ourselves continually to prayer and to the ministry of the word.' And the saying pleased the whole multitude. And they chose Stephen, a man full of faith and the Holy Spirit, and Philip, Prochorus, Nicanor, Timon, Parmenas, and Nicolas, a proselyte from Antioch, whom they set before the apostles; and

when they had prayed, they laid hands on them. Then the word
of God spread, and the number of the disciples multiplied greatly
in Jerusalem, and a great many of the priests were obedient to the
faith" (Acts 6:1-7).

There is much to be learned from this story about how the apostles
resolved conflicts in the early church. Notice first of all that there was
plenty of anger and complaining over the neglect of the Greek widows.
The Greeks and the Hebrews had undoubtedly been arguing over this
problem, but to no avail. They were attacking each other, as was evidenced by their murmuring against one another. They brought the conflict to the apostles for objectivity and help in finding a solution. The
apostles identified what the real problem was and why it was occurring.
They agreed that it was the *"neglect"* of the Greek widows. The apostles
didn't waste any time arguing about whether there was a problem, but
honestly and quickly acknowledged what was happening. They could have
attacked and blamed one another for the problem, or retreated and denied
that a problem even existed, but they didn't. Half of the battle is over when
you can at least agree on what the problem is, then you can attack it
together. That's exactly what they did!

The reconciliation and the lasting solution came next. What was
the solution? They appointed seven capable men to specifically take care
of this need of ministering to the widows. The wisdom of the apostles is
revealed in the fact that each of the seven names chosen was Greek. The
apostles didn't just promise to do better or give a long speech and do
nothing. They simply agreed on what the problem was and found a creative solution to fix it. They also took specific and practical steps to keep
this problem from ever happening again.

The apostle's solution made everyone happy. Luke recorded that
"the saying pleased the whole multitude." This should be the result of
every conflict in which a lasting solution is found. The reason for total
satisfaction on all sides was that everyone could see the wisdom in the
solution and all were willing to forgive and work together again. This
satisfaction should also be the result when you solve problems in your
marriage. When you truly solve a conflict, both partners will be pleased
and drawn together again in love and forgiveness just as the early church
was.

Let me give you another more practical example that I'm sure you
can relate to. Years ago, a couple came to me very angry with each other,
asking my counsel over a problem. It began when the husband didn't
come home from work one evening. His wife had dinner ready that night,
and expected him at six o'clock, his usual time of arrival. The kids were

waiting and everyone was hungry for dinner, but Dad didn't show up. The mother and kids finally ate dinner at about seven-thirty without Dad. He came home at about eight o'clock expecting everything to be normal. Needless to say, his wife was a little upset when he walked through the door. The two had a heated exchange of words, then reconciled later that night. The husband explained that he had been out with some of the men from work. He asked her forgiveness, and they kissed and made up. The wife wasn't upset he had gone out, only that he didn't let her know he would be late.

A few weeks later the same thing happened again, only this time his wife was very angry. They reconciled again and all was well until one Saturday afternoon when the husband failed to come home after going to the hardware store. He was gone the whole day. The husband just seemed to always get sidetracked and would fail to call. Each time he asked for forgiveness, but he continued the offensive behavior. Their relationship became very strained, and they decided to come for counseling.

I explained to them that they had reconciled the conflict every time, but they had not solved the problem. What they needed to do was to set up a practical plan to keep the problem from happening again. Failure to devise a plan only guaranteed future conflicts.

I gave them a number of possible solutions; one of which was for the husband *to call* if he was going to be more than a half an hour late. Second, he wasn't in the habit of wearing a watch, which contributed to his losing track of time, so I asked him to purchase one. Finally, I also encouraged him to stick a note to his dashboard as a reminder of his responsibility to call his wife.

This solution worked very well. They came back months later to tell me that there had not been one problem since our appointment. Why? Because they fully solved the problem! They took creative and practical steps to keep it from ever happening again.

How many recurring conflicts do you have right now? How many of those issues have you asked forgiveness for many times? What you need to do is to fully solve the problem by setting up a practical plan to keep it from occurring again. This will eliminate an immense amount of anger and frustration between you. There is a lasting solution to every conflict if you are willing to search it out!

Let's Review
What does it take to fully solve a conflict?
1. Refuse to attack or retreat.
2. Agree to attack the problem.

3. Resolve one problem at a time using the principles found in the previous chapter.
4. Find a lasting solution that you both can agree upon.

Group Discussion Questions

1. Without giving any information that might embarrass your spouse, discuss how your attacking or retreating has hindered resolving or solving conflicts.
2. When you finally attacked the problem, how did this help you resolve the issue?
3. Without giving any information that might embarrass your spouse, give an example to the group of a conflict that you don't have anymore and how you solved this issue.

✺ 11 ✺

DEALING WITH A HARD HEART

*"If you will hear His voice,
do not harden your hearts"* Heb. 3:7-8

I have previously written at great length about the necessity of a will
ing heart and its effect upon resolving conflicts. Now I want to discuss with you another essential attitude that enables this whole process to begin: tenderness of heart. Tenderness is the key to your becoming willing to work at a relationship, while hardness of heart results in
unwillingness to take the actions described in the last few chapters. A
hard heart hinders all those correct attitudes and actions from ever becoming a reality in you. If you are focusing on all the external mechanics
of change without dealing with the hardness of your heart, very little, if
anything, will change. However, you will see a dramatic change in your
life and marriage if you just allow God to soften your heart and make you
tender toward your spouse.

When Jesus spoke of the cause of marital breakups, He described
hardness of heart as the issue of greatest importance. Jesus always got
right to the underlying and most important issues whenever He discussed
a problem. Notice the great prominence Jesus gave to this issue of the
heart when He was asked why Moses allowed divorce in the Old Testament: *"Moses, because of the hardness of your hearts, permitted you to
divorce your wives, but from the beginning it was not so"* (Matt. 19:8).

Here is the simplicity of the problem as Jesus defined it, *because of
the hardness of your hearts.* Why have you fallen out of love with your
spouse? Why is there so much distance between you and your mate?
Why are there so many conflicts in your marriage that never seem to get
resolved? Once you understand that hard-heartedness is the cause of
marital disharmony, you have also found the key to solving these stubborn problems. You must then deal with this attitude and guard against it
from ever forming again. This is essential for finding the oneness and
companionship you desire and for building a marriage that endures.

How did your heart get so hard? What are the steps that led you to
this sad place? And most importantly, how can you change it?

HOW DID YOU GET SO HARD?

To ever change a hard heart you must understand how you first became this way. It is not a mystery. It doesn't just *happen*, as though some unique process has developed in your heart over which you have no control. No, there is a very specific cause-and-effect relationship.

1. <u>First, hardness of heart is the result of a series of choices</u>. Scripture is clear about this fact. If we are warned and commanded not to harden our hearts, it would necessitate a choice on our part to either take that action or resist it. This is a choice we make every day in every aspect of our lives. The writer to the Hebrews was very concerned about the early Christians and their rebellious attitudes toward Christ. He told them, *"Today, if you will hear His voice, do not harden your hearts as in the rebellion"* (Heb. 3:15). In the Old Testament this understanding is revealed again in reference toward other men. Moses declared to the children of Israel, *"You shall not harden your heart nor shut your hand from your poor brother"* (Deut. 15:7). Therefore, whether it is in reference to God or toward man, you are charged by God not to harden your heart. If you had no choice in this matter, how could God require you to keep this commandment or justly chasten you for disobeying it?

The attitude of your heart, then, is definitely determined by the choices you make. Your heart is as hard or as tender today as the choices you've made. As you will see from the following verses, hardness of heart is a *series* of choices you make to turn away from God's correction, to proudly resist the changes your spouse is requesting, to reject the testimony of God and man, and to refuse to deal with your own sin.

2. <u>Pride and the refusal to receive correction causes hardness</u>. Since pride is one of the basic causes of conflicts, so it is the culprit in keeping you from resolving your hardness of heart. Pride and arrogance make you think that your way is always right, and that you don't need anyone telling you how to run your life. It makes you believe that everything is all right on your side of the marriage, and it must be your spouse who has the problem. Solomon said, *"Every way of a man is right in his own eyes, but the Lord weighs the hearts"* (Prov. 21:2). When you think that you are always right, it is pride. This was also why Pharaoh hardened his heart and refused God's instruction. Moses told him, *"Thus says the Lord God of the Hebrews: 'How long will you refuse to humble yourself before Me?'"* (Ex. 10:3) Pharaoh had great rationalizations for why his way was right. In his pride he rejected God's correction and so hardened his heart.

Pride and the refusal to receive God's correction are what caused the Jewish people to harden themselves, and they were taken into captivity. When Nehemiah was describing the history of Israel, he explicitly declared why they rebelled against the commandments of God: *"Our fathers acted proudly, hardened their necks, and did not heed Your commandments. They refused to obey"* (Neh. 9:16,17). Notice that an arrogant heart is directly associated in this passage with hardness and disobedience. These choices of the heart led God's people into captivity. Likewise, if you allow pride to harden you, you will naturally disobey. If you refuse His command to reconcile, consequently, nothing will get resolved in your relationship.

Another excellent example of how pride hardens you is seen in the life of Nebuchadnezzar, the king of Babylon. The prophet Daniel explains the central reason why this great king was removed from his throne: *"When his heart was lifted up, and his spirit was hardened in pride, he was deposed from his kingly throne, and they took his glory from him"* (Dan. 5:20). Pride hardened this man's heart and ultimately robbed him of all he cared about. Don't allow yourself to be robbed of the family relationships that you care so much about.

3. <u>Unbelief in the promises of God results in hardness</u>. I have seen hardness occur this way many times. Two people will come to me for counseling, and I will explain the wonderful purpose and design God has for their marriage. I share God's promises and how His power can change them and their relationship. Many times I have seen the look on one partner's face declaring their total unbelief that anything could ever change. Guess what happens? Nothing. Unbelief is why nothing changes. It hardens your heart and cuts you off from God, who is your only solution. Unbelief robs you of the transforming power of God and keeps you from even trying to solve your problems. Unbelief causes you to basically just give up. The action required for change will not be taken because of unbelief, and therefore, you harden yourself in your position. When people come to encourage you to work at your marriage, you resist or reject their words.

The best biblical example of how this occurs is illustrated by the disciples upon hearing of the resurrection of Christ. After His death they were very discouraged and depressed. The two disciples on the road to Emmaus said, *"We were hoping that it was He who was going to redeem Israel"* (Luke 24:21). They had lost all hope and were in total unbelief. Little did they know that they were talking to the Redeemer himself at that very moment. Earlier, the women came and testified to the disciples that the tomb was empty and the angels had declared His resurrection. However, they chose not believe this testimony. *"Their words seemed to them like idle tales, and they did not believe them"* (Luke 24:11). Unbelief made the women's assertion sound like a fairy tale.

What did Jesus do when He showed up on the scene? He got right to the heart of the problem. *"He rebuked their unbelief and hardness of heart"* (Mark 16:14). He then showed them His hands and His feet to prove to them that He was really the same man who had been crucified a few days prior. Then He did the most important thing. He gave them a Bible study. He *"opened their understanding, that they mighty compre- hend the Scriptures"* (Luke 24:45). He went through Moses, the Psalms, and the Prophets so they could see the overall predicted plan of God. He did this to give them a basis for their faith that He was truly the Messiah.

What is your response when your friends tell you that there is a solution to your marriage problems? Does this sound like a fairy tale? Do you resist or reject their words? If you do, then your heart is hardened in unbelief. You are forgetting that there is a risen Christ who is *"able to do exceedingly abundantly above all that we ask or think, according to the power that works in us"* (Eph. 3:20). Don't let unbelief harden your heart. Go to God's Word and dwell on His promises. Hear His voice today. You will find Him able, if you will believe!

4. <u>The refusal to repent results in hardness</u>. Here is the bottom line. If you choose not to repent of whatever God is dealing with you about, your heart will only grow harder. This refusal to repent is a resistance to the Holy Spirit, which naturally hardens anyone. Why is this the result? Because when you see the solutions in God's Word, reading that there is a way out of the dilemma you are in, and you choose *not* to repent and accept His solution, you have to harden your heart against the convic- tion of the Spirit. This conviction is the inner battle you experience when you must decide what is right and wrong in any given circumstance. God won't force you to do what is right. He expects you to use the wisdom He has given you, to ask Him for help, and to make the right decisions that are in accordance with His Word. But thank God He does seek to per- suade us by His Spirit.

Paul equated unrepentance with hardness of heart. He told the Christians at Rome that their problem was their *"hardness and impeni- tent heart"* and that they were despising *"the riches of His goodness"* by refusing to turn and repent (Rom. 2:5). God in His goodness is very patient with every one of us. He patiently works and seeks to change our minds and to turn us back to Him, but many times to no avail. Paul also explained in this text that the Romans had no concept of God's goodness and His ultimate purpose. He explained that it is the goodness and pa- tience of God that *"leads you to repentance"* (Rom. 2:4).

Don't harden your heart by refusing to repent of anything that God is showing you in your heart. If there is pride in your heart, rebellion to His commands, or unforgiveness toward your spouse, choose to repent of these right now. If you do not, you will be stiffening your neck and worsening your marital relationship. Nothing good will result. Let His goodness and the patience you have already experienced lead you back to total repentance. It's your choice! If you have taken actions that are sinful or inappropriate, or spoken words unpleasing to God, or retain resentful attitudes toward your spouse, repent of these. If you refuse to deal with these sins, hardness of heart will result because you are fighting against the Spirit of truth and your own conscience. The longer you wait, the harder you'll get, and the harder it will be to turn it around. Remember, *"Today if you will hear His voice, do not harden your hearts"* (Heb. 3:15). Can you hear the urgency in the heart of God? Take the steps to turn this marriage around *today.*

WHAT ARE THE SYMPTOMS OF A HARD HEART?

Take a moment and ask yourself these questions. They will help you to determine whether your heart is becoming hardened.

1. Are you refusing to humble yourself before God?
2. Are you refusing to obey God's commands to love and forgive?
3. Are you rejecting correction from your spouse?
4. Have you given up believing that your marriage could change?
5. Have you been rejecting the testimony of others that God is able to change it?

If you answered yes to any of these questions, then your heart is hard and probably getting harder by the day. This is not a hopeless situation. There is something you can do about it.

HOW CAN YOU BECOME TENDERHEARTED?

To become tenderhearted is very possible no matter how hard you have become. I have seen people who have been divorced for years humble themselves before God and their mate, and reconciliation and remarriage occur. How could this ever happen? It is the result of two people just doing the opposite of all that made them hard. If certain choices and decisions cause your heart to harden, then it stands to reason that the opposite actions and decisions will soften you. This is exactly what Scripture teaches. Let's look at how it occurs.

1. <u>Make the choice to come back to God and ask Him for a new heart</u>. He is the only one who can change your heart because He is the only one who can work on the inside of you. He is the best heart surgeon in the universe and is capable of performing a complete work in your life today. Remember, it's *His* work to make you tenderhearted. It is not dependent on your ability, but upon His! All you must do is *yield* to allow Him to do the work.

Here is the promise God made to the children of Israel before their return from captivity. He promised them a miraculous spiritual heart surgery. *"I will give you a new heart and put a new spirit within you; I will take the heart of stone out of your flesh and give you a heart of flesh. I will put My Spirit within you and cause you to walk in My statutes, and you will keep My judgments and do them"* (Ezek. 36:26, 27).

What a glorious promise! Could this same thing be done in you? Do you want the heart of stone taken out of you? If you will only come to Him, this is exactly what He will do. This work is done by the Spirit of God working within you. Jesus said, *"If you...know how to give good gifts to your children, how much more will your heavenly Father give the Holy Spirit to those who ask Him"* (Luke 11:13). All you have to do is come to Him and ask! If you will do this now, your heart will begin to change, and you will become more and more tenderhearted every day. As often as you ask for His Spirit to do this work, you will see the power of God at work in your heart, making you tender.

Furthermore, notice in the Ezekiel passage that once their hearts were changed, they would be empowered to obey His Word and to walk in accordance with His statutes. The same transformation will happen in your life and marriage too. When God goes to work in your life and fills you with His Spirit, you will *want* to obey His Word, and you will find the power to do exactly that. I challenge you to come to Him wholeheartedly and see what happens. It's up to you. He won't force you to come.

2. <u>Make the choice to humble yourself, hear, and respond to His Word</u>. As you come to the Lord, you must come with an attitude of humility and an openness to hear from Him. You must humbly want to hear what God has to say about the problems in your life and marriage. If you have a humble heart to take His advice, His grace will cause the softening work to continue in your heart and bring the complete change you desire.

How does this humbling process take place? Scripture declares that you are to *"humble yourselves under the mighty hand of God, that He may exalt you in due time"* (1 Peter 5:6). This, again, is your choice. Don't make God humble you. That's the difficult way to get rid of the hardness. I have heard people pray many times, "God just humble me so I will be a more faithful servant." God will do this, but it is not His first desire. He wants you to *humble yourself.*

In the Old Testament there is a perfect illustration of how humility and tenderness of heart work together. Josiah became king in Jerusalem after many years of idolatry and national corruption. He began to seek the Lord and sought to purge the temple and restore the true worship of God. When the workers were cleaning out the temple one day, they found an old copy of the Law of God. One of the scribes brought it to King Josiah and read it to him. When the King heard the words of God, he wept and tore his clothes in humility and repentance.

Through Huldah the prophetess, this is what God said to him: *"Because your heart was tender, and you humbled yourself before God when you heard His words against this place and against its inhabitants, and you humbled yourself before Me, and you tore your clothes and wept before Me, I also have heard you," says the LORD"* (2 Chron. 34:27).

Josiah chose to humble himself, and God equated this decision with a tender heart. God also associated his tenderness with Josiah's willingness to listen to God's Word. God's response to a heart like Josiah's, that is, humble, tender and willing to hear, was a promise that He would hear the prayer of Josiah. If you want God to pay attention and respond to your prayers, you need this attitude of heart.

Why does a tender and humble heart get this kind of response from God? Because humility is the honest acknowledgment of your need before God. Humility is revealed in the confession that you don't know how to solve the problems in your marriage. To do this, you have to yield the hard positions of self-sufficiency and pride. Humbleness of mind is the best position you could be in for God to work great miracles in your life and marriage.

Turn to Him now and come with humility before Him. Offer your heart to Him. Ask Him to make you tender inside to His Word and to your spouse. If you want God to hear and to respond to your prayer, humble yourself like Josiah and see what happens.

Likewise, as you come to Christ with this humble and tender heart, allow Him to correct and reprove you with His Word every day as you wait on Him. This is important because *"the Word of God is living and powerful, and sharper than any two-edged sword, piercing even to the division of soul and spirit, and of joints and marrow, and is a discerner of the thoughts and intents of the heart"* (Heb. 4:12). The Word of God is His fine cutting tool, and it can penetrate down to the very thoughts and motives of your heart. This is how God gets to your hard heart and how

He softens it. As He begins to work on the inside of you, then the change begins. How does He do it?

The Word of God brings reproof and conviction to your heart. Like a sword, it has the ability to stab you in the heart right where you are failing in your thought life, attitudes, or actions. Jeremiah said that God's Word was *"like a hammer that breaks the rock in pieces"* (Jer. 23:29). The opposite of hardness is brokenness. God's Word has the ability to pierce and break the most rock-hard heart. If you will receive His reproof and conviction, a tender heart will be the result.

Moreover, God's Word has the ability to instruct you regarding how to correct the problem He has just convicted you of. His initial reproof along with instruction are all you need to change the problem and walk in true righteousness. Paul said, *"All Scripture is given by inspiration of God, and is profitable for doctrine, for reproof, for correction, for instruction in righteousness, that the man of God may be complete, thoroughly equipped for every good work"* (2 Tim. 3:16, 17). It is important to recognize that the Word of God, to the extent that you avail yourself of it, naturally brings the conviction and correction in your life. Then you are equipped for whatever work is necessary in your relationship.

In other words, hearing God's Word will bring you to repentance and correction, and that keeps you from hardness on a daily basis. This is why your *daily* personal time in the study of the Scriptures is so important. It keeps your heart from getting hard and equips you for every need that arises.

Hearing the Word, however, does more than just bring repentance and correction. It also produces faith and hope for all the needs ahead in your relationship. Remember how I discussed with you earlier that unbelief is a fundamental cause of the hardness of your heart? Your daily experience of humbly hearing the Word keeps unbelief at bay. The Word produces the hope and the faith you need to deal with the problems in your marriage constructively. Paul said, *"So then faith comes by hearing... the Word of God"* (Rom. 10:17).

Faith and hope are keys to resolving all the conflicts of any relationship. You must believe there is a solution to your conflicts and that God has the answers you need. Do you have this faith and hope today? Will you allow God to soften your heart so it can be filled with faith? Will you allow Him to use His cutting tool upon you? Get into His Word today and begin by asking Him to show you the condition of your heart as you read. As you hear His voice through His Word, your heart will begin to soften. Don't miss the miracle!

3. <u>Choose to show compassion, mercy, and forgiveness</u>. These atti-

tudes are actually a by-product of the first two points. When you humbly come to the Lord and ask Him for a new heart, He will give you new desires and soften your heart. He will fill you with the fruit of His Spirit, which is love (Gal. 5:22). His love in you will be demonstrated by compassion, mercy, and forgiveness. As you *choose* to forgive and show mercy to your spouse, regardless of your emotions, the hardness will melt from your heart. You can't be merciful and forgive and stay hardhearted at the same time. It's impossible to do both!

Paul said, *"Be kind to one another, tenderhearted, forgiving one another, just as God in Christ also forgave you"* (Eph. 4:32). When you forgive, you are choosing to turn from hardness to tenderness. This is the action of love I explained in chapter 5.

The apostle Peter describes this same action of love when He said, *"Finally, all of you be of one mind, having compassion for one another; love as brothers, be tenderhearted, be courteous; not returning evil for evil or reviling for reviling, but on the contrary blessing, knowing that you were called to this, that you may inherit a blessing"* (1 Peter 3:8, 9).

This is God's counsel regarding how to stay tenderhearted. You need to take the action of love toward each other. This choice keeps a disagreement with your spouse from escalating into a major conflict in which you end up not talking to each other for days. Ever had one of those arguments? You don't speak courteously or softly, but you revile your spouse the same way you have been reviled, and the whole conversation gets quickly out of control. If you choose, instead, to show compassion and demonstrate love, the whole conversation will move in a totally different direction.

No matter where your heart is today, God can soften you and make you tender inside once again. Just hear His voice as you study His Word and choose not to harden your heart. Don't let your pride or unbelief keep you from letting God turn you around completely. Remember, there is nothing too hard for the Lord!

Group Discussion Questions

1. Describe to the group a time in your life when you have become hardened in your heart. What were the primary choices that you made that caused this to occur?

2. What were the choices that brought your heart back to tenderness toward God?

3. If your heart is hardened toward your spouse right now, will you ask the group for prayer to obtain a tender one?

12

FORGIVENESS THAT LASTS

"Be kind... tenderhearted, forgiving one another" Eph. 4:32

In her book, *The Hiding Place*, Corrie Ten Boom relates this true story that occurred years after the end of World War II:

It was a church service in Munich that I saw him, the former S.S. man who had stood guard at the shower room door in the processing center at Ravensbruck. He was the first of our actual jailers that I had seen since that time. And suddenly it was all there — the roomful of mocking men, the heaps of clothing, Betsie's pain-blanched face.

He came up to me as the church was emptying, beaming and bowing. "How grateful I am for your message, Fraulein," he said. "To think that, as you say, He has washed my sins away!" His hand was thrust out to shake mine. And I, who had preached so often to the people in Bloemendaal the need to forgive, kept my hand at my side.

Even as the angry, vengeful thoughts boiled through me, I saw the sin of them. Jesus Christ had died for this man; was I going to ask for more? *Lord Jesus*, I prayed, *forgive me and help me to forgive him.*

I tried to smile. I struggled to raise my hand. I could not. I felt nothing, not the slightest spark of warmth or charity. And so again I breathed a silent prayer. *Jesus, I cannot forgive him. Give me your forgiveness.*

As I took his hand the most incredible thing happened. From my shoulder along my arm and through my hand a current seemed to pass from me to him, while into my heart sprang a love for this stranger that almost overwhelmed me.

And so I discovered that it is not on our forgiveness any more than on our goodness that the world's healing hinges, but on His. When He tells us to love our enemies, He gives, along with the command, the love itself.

You may not have an enemy or an offense to deal with as grievous as Corrie Ten Boom, but the steps to forgiveness will always be the same. You will probably be just as unwilling and also realize the same lack of power to forgive as she did. You will sense the same struggle within, knowing you should forgive, but not wanting to actually do it. As she made the *choice* to reach out her hand, she also sensed the Spirit of God reaching out to touch and enable her to do what she knew was right. Just as God was ready to help her, He is also ready to help you. When the Father commands you to forgive, He will also give you the strength to actually do it. The love of God will flood your soul just as it did Corrie's. You may be wondering, can this really happen in my life?

Your spouse has probably offended and hurt you many times. But has there been true forgiveness? Are you sure? Corrie probably thought she had forgiven the officer, until she saw him standing there before her, face-to-face. All of a sudden, she realized she didn't have what was needed to actually take the step to forgive.

Forgiveness within your marriage is fundamental if you want to have a marriage that is built to last. Your willingness to forgive is what motivates you to take the essential actions that result in reconciliation with your spouse. Forgiveness is also the key to finding the lasting solutions to every problem you face. Let's look at some of the critical issues relating to forgiveness in your marriage. We will first look at some of the basics about forgiveness, such as why you should forgive and then how to actually do it. Failure to fully and completely forgive is one of the greatest reasons why couples drift apart and position themselves against each other. Yet if you will apply the principles you are about to learn, your relationship can be restored to experience the oneness and companionship you once knew.

Why Should You Forgive?

This is a question you must answer first because you need a powerful motivation within your heart to take the sometimes difficult steps of forgiveness. The reasons why you should forgive are just the urging some need to actually take the steps they know are right. Remember Corrie Ten Boom? She knew and had preached of the need to forgive, and this is what moved her to finally reach out her hand to the one who had abused her. You will too if you allow these reasons to sink down in your heart.

1. <u>You should forgive because it is the command of God</u>. This is where you must begin in your thinking. Many couples think that some-

how forgiveness is merely an option they have available to them; something they can take or leave. However, this is not the case. The Word of God declares that you *must* forgive any and all who offend you. This command would, of course, include your spouse. Jesus said, *"And whenever you stand praying, if you have anything against anyone, forgive him..."* (Mark 11:25). This command is all-inclusive, *anything* and *anyone*. Jesus includes all issues and all people in our life so that no one can find an escape clause or loophole for not forgiving. We must all come to the conclusion that Jesus meant exactly what He said. You must forgive everything and everyone who has offended you.

Paul also declared this imperative when he commanded the believers at Colosse to forgive. He encouraged them to bear with one another and forgive one another. *"If anyone has a complaint against another; even as Christ forgave you, so you also must do"* (Col. 3:13). Again, we are commanded that we *must* forgive anyone for the offenses committed against us.

It is clear from Scripture that forgiveness is not an option, but a definite command and responsibility for every believer who has been offended. You must forgive *even as Christ forgave you*. This is your calling as a Christian. There are no exceptions and no excuses you could ever give the Lord for why you would choose to disobey this command.

Will you heed God's command to forgive any and all who have offended you? Will you choose to forgive your spouse for all they have done against you? Have you been obeying this command daily? If not, this is one of the reasons companionship is being hindered in your relationship.

2. <u>You should forgive because this is an expression of your love for the Lord</u>. Jesus said, *"If you love Me, keep My commandments"* (John 14:15). Ultimately, forgiveness is an expression of your love for the Lord, an act of obedience to God because you desire to please Him above all others, even yourself. Forgiveness is the demonstration before God that you care about what He thinks and are willing to bow to His authority and commands for your life. If you love the Lord, then you will forgive your spouse.

When you reduce the act of forgiveness to its essential motivation of love, then you understand why forgiveness is so important to your relationship. Demonstrating love is what reconciles all conflicts. It is important to note that love is also what motivates God to forgive you. Asaph declared this truth when he described God's forgiveness of the Jews. *"But He, being full of compassion forgave their iniquity"* (Ps. 78:38). God's compassion motivated Him to forgive over and over again. When Christ cried out from the cross, *"Father, forgive them!"* He was revealing just how much love He really had for all mankind, and especially those who had just crucified Him (Luke 23:34). How great was God's love that He could forgive even while they were rejecting Him. Likewise, Scripture teaches that you are to forgive even as Christ has forgiven you (Eph. 4:32). Therefore, when you forgive, you are showing the same love you have been shown by God.

Jesus said *"Love one another; as I have loved you"* (John 13:34). This is your calling as a Christian, and this is your calling as a husband or wife. To forgive your spouse is to demonstrate your obedience to His command because you love the Lord, which will ultimately translate as love for your spouse. This is the action of love.

3. Unless you forgive, you have no right to ask God to forgive you. In the Lord's prayer, Jesus made it clear that you must forgive just as you expect God to forgive you. Jesus taught His disciples to pray *"forgive us our debts as we forgive our debtors"* (Matt. 6:12). The Lord assumed that we would make the connection that if we were going to ask for His forgiveness, we would naturally forgive others in the same manner. But sadly this is not the case in most marriages. Most want abundant forgiveness on the receiving end, yet are very stingy when it comes to giving it. How about you? Have you understood the connection that Jesus intended in the Lord's Prayer regarding forgiveness?

This issue is an absolute with Christ. In fact, Jesus made it clear that *"if you do not forgive, neither will your Father in heaven forgive your trespasses"* (Mark 11:26). You may think this is a harsh statement, but it reveals just how much importance He places upon your obedience to forgive. If you are not forgiving, be assured that He is not forgiving you at this very moment.

You have no right to ask for His forgiveness or to expect to be forgiven if you are refusing to forgive your spouse. You must understand the very real consequences of your refusal to forgive and see how God views this sinful attitude if you are ever to change. Don't wait one more day. Obey His command and forgive your spouse.

4. Unless you forgive, you will be the real loser. What do you lose when you refuse to forgive? First, you lose the fellowship or closeness in your own relationship with the Lord. As we saw from the previous point, when you choose to not forgive, God refuses to forgive you. This creates an immediate distance between you and the Father. Within a very short time you will begin to sense a dryness within your spirit. This is God's chastening hand seeking to bring you back to himself. Unforgiveness simply robs you of the peace and joy God intends for your life. Many times the only person you are hurting by your unforgiveness is *yourself.* It

is a simple equation: you can't be happy and be unforgiving at the same time. It doesn't work that way. Solomon observed this truth when he declared, *"The merciful man does good for his own soul, but he who is cruel troubles his own flesh"* (Prov. 11:17). Mercy is good for the soul. On the other hand, if you refuse to forgive, you trouble your own life. If you want to be happy, you must be merciful and forgive your spouse just as you want to be forgiven.

Happiness is always the by-product of obeying God. Jesus said, *"If you know these things, happy are you if you do them"* (John 13:17). If you know that you should forgive, do it, and you will experience the joy that will naturally result.

Second, unforgiveness makes you a loser by robbing you of oneness with your spouse. You can't experience the real intimacy you desire while holding resentment toward your mate. As we saw in the previous chapter, the refusal to obey God's commands will always result in hardness of heart, destroying any chance of intimacy.

Peter explained the only way two people could ever find oneness. He said, *"Be of one mind, having compassion one for another"* (1 Peter 3:8). You must have this compassion for each other if you are to ever experience being of one mind. Only compassion and forgiveness toward each other will result in this marital blessing.

How Do You Actually Forgive Each Other?

The *how to* of forgiveness is of the utmost importance. How does one actually do it? If you take the following steps you can and will forgive your spouse every time they fail.

1. <u>Ask God to open your eyes to your own sin</u>. This is a truth that I have personally found to help me forgive quickly. When my own heart has been hard and unwilling to forgive, this is what I do. I simply ask God to open my eyes to His forgiveness toward me. This is very helpful because many times the real problem with unforgiveness is that of *self-righteousness*. We think, *How could he or she have ever done this to me?* forgetting that we also have sinned against our spouse many times. We can't see the plank in our own eye that definitely distorts the view of others' sin. Jesus said, *"First, remove the plank from your own eye, and then you will see clearly to remove the speck out of your brother's eye"* (Matt. 7:5).

The quickest way to become a person who forgives easily is to ask God to reveal to you your own sin as well as His abundant forgiveness toward you. Once you have seen the plank in your own eye, your attitude toward your mate will change dramatically. This is how Jesus taught Peter to forgive "seventy times seven." He told Peter the story of a man who was required to repay an impossible debt. He asked his creditor for some more time so that he could repay everything. But his lord, instead, was moved with compassion and chose to release him by forgiving the entire debt. This servant, who had been forgiven, then went out and refused to forgive another man a very small debt. His lord returned and asked him, *"Should you not also have had compassion on your fellow servant, just as I had pity on you?"* (Matt. 18:33).

This is a good question to ask yourself. If you truly see how much God has forgiven you, should you not show the same compassion toward your spouse? Ask God to open your eyes to your own sin and the magnitude of His forgiveness in your own life. This will give you a more tender heart toward your mate.

The apostle Paul also associates compassion of heart with the comprehension of being forgiven. He said, *"Be kind to one another, tenderhearted, forgiving one another, just as God in Christ also forgave you"* (Eph. 4:32). Tenderness of heart will generally develop as you *consider* God's forgiveness in your life because it causes you to humble yourself in light of your own failures. Stop right now and think about how much God has forgiven you. However, don't let it merely be a one-time reflection. Make it a daily meditation, and you will walk in lasting forgiveness toward your spouse!

2. <u>Ask God for a willing heart</u>. Many times this is one of the simplest reasons why you refuse to forgive. It's that you just don't want to forgive. You would rather nurse the resentment and punish your spouse for their offense. This is especially true with long-term conflicts that surface over and over again. Your heart grows harder, and your willingness to forgive decreases with each occurrence of the same offense. Ultimately, it's not that you can't forgive, but that you won't forgive.

Once you see your own sin, you now need to ask God for a willing heart to forgive. He will give it to you if you will just ask. Remember, *"It is God who works in you both to will and to do for His good pleasure"* (Phil. 2:13). It is God's good pleasure that you forgive your spouse, so ask Him to begin His work to make you willing. Don't wait any longer. It will never be any easier than it is right now.

3. <u>Choose to obey His command</u>. Now that you are tenderhearted and willing to forgive, it only remains that you make the *choice* to do it. Jesus commanded that every one of us must forgive *"from his heart"* (Matt. 18:35). This is where the choice is made. Before you ever come to seek reconciliation with your mate, you must first deal with it at the heart level. Once you have chosen to forgive in your heart, then you are ready to talk about the offense with your husband or wife.

This choice within your heart does not depend upon whether you feel like forgiving your mate. In fact, your choice to forgive will probably be contrary to your feelings. Personally, I have never *felt* like forgiving anybody, but I do so because I know I am commanded to. Knowing that forgiveness is God's command encourages me to ask for the willingness, and enables me to make the choice to actually do it.

Be sure of this one thing: if you are waiting for some overwhelming feeling of forgiveness before you actually make the choice to forgive, you will never do it. The feelings of forgiveness come *after* you make the choice to forgive, not before. Feelings of love and forgiveness are the result of reconciling with your spouse. Think of the times you have reconciled with your mate in the past. After you forgave each other, didn't the anger and resentment melt in your heart? The tears began to flow and the joy and love returned to your relationship. This was the result of taking the correct action before you felt like it. People struggle with this concept of action-before-feeling because our culture is so feeling-oriented. People today only want to do what feels good or what's easy. However, Jesus taught that we should do just the opposite when it comes to forgiveness.

To prove this, you need to read the entire passage of Luke 17:1-10 in context. Jesus taught His disciples to forgive even if someone should sin against them seven times in one day. The disciples, seeing great difficulty in forgiving this many times, asked the Lord to increase their faith. He told them that more faith wasn't necessary; all they needed was to use the faith they already possessed. Then Jesus told them a story to illustrate how they could exercise their mustard-seed faith and choose to forgive without the feelings. The story was of a servant who came home one day tired from plowing the fields and tending his master's sheep. This servant obviously didn't feel like serving any more that day. But the master requested his servant to go and prepare his dinner and serve him before sitting down himself. In the story Jesus declared that the servant did what his master wanted because he was commanded to do so. In other words, this servant took actions that were against his feelings simply because he was commanded to by his master. Jesus told His disciples, "So *likewise you, when you have done all those things which you are commanded, say, 'We are unprofitable servants. We have done what was our duty to do'* " (Luke 17:10).

The point of this story is that you have been commanded to forgive by your Master, and it's not an option to refuse it. You must make the choice to forgive no matter how you feel simply because you know it pleases God. Once you have done what you have been commanded to do, then you can sit down and enjoy the feast of a heart satisfied that you have done what was your duty to do. What a joy it is to know that you have pleased the Lord!

Forgiveness that is dependent upon your feelings will not last because it is based on emotions that can change quickly. Forgiving based on the choice to obey God's command, even when feelings are absent, will always last because it is motivated by God's Word that doesn't change. Forgive because you are commanded to forgive, not because you feel like forgiving, and the reconciliation will last.

4. Determine to make a promise. Another primary aspect of forgiveness entails a second choice on your part. When God forgives He makes a very important promise to you that you must also make when you forgive your spouse. God says, *"I will be merciful to their unrighteousness, and their sins and their lawless deeds I will remember no more"* (Heb. 8:12). The Greek word translated *remember* means "to hold in a mental grasp, to recollect, or to dwell upon in order to use at a later time to punish." This promise is also made in the Old Testament where God declares, *"I, even I, am He who blots our your transgressions for My own sake; and I will not remember your sins"* (Is. 43:25). The Hebrew word used in this passage for *remember* means "to mention or recount again." The promise God makes here is vital. He is promising that when He forgives you, He will never recount or mention your sin to you ever again. He doesn't hold your sins in a mental grasp to use at a later time. It's not that He forgets your sin. He can't do that because He is omniscient and knows all things. He simply chooses not to remember it against you or bring it up to you again in order to condemn or punish. What a glorious promise! When God forgives, He promises never to throw your sin up in your face ever again.

When you forgive, you must make the same promise because Scripture commands you to forgive *"just as God in Christ also forgave you"* (Eph. 4:32). But you may be thinking to yourself, *How can I do that?* Here are three very specific and practical ways you should emulate God's promise to forgive: (1) When you forgive, you should see it as a promise to never condemn your spouse again with their past faults. To bring these issues up again would mean you have broken your promise to forgive. (2) When you forgive, you should see it as a promise not to recount or mention their failures to anyone else; this would constitute gossip. (3) When you forgive, you should consider it a promise not to ever recount or brood over these issues even in your own mind. If you dwell on these offenses in your thought life, the anger and resentment will surely return. This is the practical meaning of your promise: not to mention these issues ever again to your spouse, to others, or to yourself. If you fail to do this, you are breaking your promise of forgiveness toward your mate. By keeping your promise in this manner, the past will truly be past, and your relationship will be able to grow, even blossom. You will experience a forgiveness that truly lasts!

What should you do when you realize you have broken your promise to forgive? First, go back to God and ask His forgiveness. Then choose again in your heart to forgive your spouse. Often, this choice must be made several times in a day because you are battling your own will that wants to take revenge. If you continue to make the choice to forgive, while at the same time asking God for His power to work in you the total willingness to forgive, you will overcome the resentment. Just surrender your desire for revenge and ask for the love of God to fill your heart.

WHAT FORGIVENESS DOES NOT MEAN

There are many misconceptions concerning forgiveness. I have often found that people want to keep their promise to forgive, but one or more of these misconceptions held in their heart will rob them of the confidence to continue. Consider if one of these misconceptions has not stumbled you at some time in the past.

1. <u>Forgiveness does not mean that reconciliation is automatic.</u> Just because you forgive your spouse in your heart does not mean that everything is reconciled between you. Choosing to forgive in your heart is only where the process begins. You now need to speak to your spouse and tell them that you are hurt and offended. Jesus said, *"If your brother sins against you, go and tell him his fault between you and him alone"* (Matt. 18:15). Your mate may already know there is a breach between you, but if not, you need to verbalize it with the motivation of seeking reconciliation. Jesus went on to say that if your brother *"hears you, you have gained your brother"* (Matt. 18:15). Making the decision to forgive from your heart is what enables you to have the correct motivation to approach your mate and gain the relationship again.

Jesus also said in another place that once you have spoken to the person who has offended you, *"if he repents, forgive him"* (Luke 17:3). But you may be thinking, *I thought I already forgave this person in my heart. What does this mean?*

This is a second aspect of forgiveness, the verbal granting of forgiveness to the offending party. This should only be given when your spouse acknowledges their fault and asks for your forgiveness. Then you can verbally declare to them, "I forgive you." You are only able to verbally grant this forgiveness because you have already forgiven in your heart.

Notice that Scripture doesn't merely require someone to say, "I'm sorry." That's because being sorry is only half of the reconciliation process. A person can be sorry that the problem has occurred, but sorrow must be coupled with a request for forgiveness from a heart of true repentance. When you look at the examples of those who reconciled in Scripture, it is important to notice the specific acknowledgments of sin and the requests of forgiveness. What did the prodigal son say to his father? *"Father, I have sinned against heaven and in your sight"* (Luke 15:21). When Joseph's brothers sought reconciliation they said, *"I beg you, please forgive the trespass of your brothers"* (Gen. 50:17).

Why is the specific request for forgiveness so essential? Why isn't an apology good enough? Because an apology is only a statement of how you feel about the offense. Whereas, when you ask your mate for forgiveness, you are asking them to make a choice to *do something* very specific, to obey God's command to forgive, to erase the offense off the ledger, and to promise to let it go forever. This is much more than a simple acknowledgment that you are sorry.

But what happens when your husband or wife refuses to acknowledge their fault? Should you still verbally tell your mate that you forgive them? Absolutely not; simply because the offense is not reconciled. Even though you have forgiven from the heart, there cannot be complete reconciliation until your spouse acknowledges their fault. Save any verbal granting of forgiveness until this occurs. Let me give you an example of why this is the biblical response.

Consider for a moment the redemption of the world through the death of Jesus Christ. When Jesus was being put to death He prayed, *"Father, forgive them for they do not know what they do"* (Luke 23:34). There upon the cross Jesus purchased the means of forgiveness for the whole world. Through the shedding of His blood Christ *"obtained eternal redemption"* (Heb. 9:12). *"God was in Christ reconciling the world unto Himself"* (2 Cor. 5:19). Does this mean that the whole world is actually forgiven and reconciled with God? Surely not. For complete reconciliation to occur between man and God, a person must acknowledge and repent of his sin and ask God's forgiveness. Only then does God grant the forgiveness He has already determined in His heart. He is ready today to forgive because of the reconciliation that was purchased two thousand years ago. The same principle works in your marriage relationship. Forgiveness cannot be verbally granted until there is an honest acknowledgment of fault and a request for pardon. Yet once you have chosen to forgive from your heart, you are also ready to verbally grant forgiveness to your spouse when they acknowledge fault.

2. <u>Forgiveness does not mean it is deserved</u>. I have seen husbands and wives choose to withhold forgiveness because of this misconception

many times. Refusal to forgive is done for various reasons, none of which are biblical. Some choose not to forgive until it is believed the spouse has paid enough for the particular offense. Others are waiting to see if the offense happens again, trying to determine if they really learned the lesson. Then, when some magic space of time has passed or it just feels right, forgiveness is granted. Things get back to normal until the next conflict, and the whole process begins again.

In reality, no one deserves to be forgiven, nor can *you* ever deserve it. You didn't deserve God's forgiveness when He pardoned you, nor can you ever deserve it by any good work you do in the future. God completely canceled your debt simply because of His mercy, erasing it from your account forever. God didn't wait until He felt like forgiving you. He chose to forgive you because you asked Him to pardon you. He took this action of pardon in complete harmony with His Word that declares, *"If we confess our sins, He is faithful and just to forgive us our sins..."* (1 John 1:9).

Likewise, you must not wait until you believe that your spouse deserves your forgiveness before you grant it. They will never be good enough to ever deserve pardon. Your husband or wife can never promise not to fail in the future any more than you will be flawless. Don't set up an arbitrary standard that they can never attain before you think complete forgiveness is deserved. Forgive based on the command of Christ, not on your feelings or some standard you have set up. God has set up a standard of confession and repentance, and yours shouldn't be any different. Only the most supreme arrogance and hardness of heart would require your mate to live up to a standard you yourself couldn't keep. On the contrary, you are required to *"be merciful, just as your Father also is merciful"* (Luke 6:36). Mercy is a gift freely given.

3. Forgiveness does not mean you condone what your spouse has done. Many think that when they repeatedly forgive an offense that they are communicating to their spouse that the transgressions are excusable or all right. Is this true? Of course not! If this were true, then, when God forgives you over and over again, it would mean that He also condones sin, and this is definitely not the case. When God forgives you repeatedly, He is communicating to you His love and commitment to show mercy. God hates sin. It repulses and offends Him, but He still forgives it. This is why Jesus asked the woman taken in the act of adultery to *"go and sin no more"*(John 8:11). God expects a change of lifestyle when He forgives because this is what true repentance is all about. If He didn't require a change of attitude and action from us, God would be condoning our sin.

Therefore, in your martial conflicts if you hate what has occurred between you, forgive, and then require changes that will keep this problem from happening again. This is what Paul called *"works befitting repentance"* (Acts 26:20). To see these changes will entail some serious conversations in which you should discuss practical solutions. This was the subject and goal of chapter 10 "How to Fully Solve a Conflict." When you are fully solving your conflicts, you will never have to be concerned if you are condoning your spouse's sin. This issue may also require you to get counseling from your pastor. A third party can many times greatly help in determining if you are condoning sin or not.

There are solutions to every conflict that divides you and your spouse if you are willing to search them out. Refusing to forgive and holding resentment in your heart is not part of any solution and will only create more problems. Forgiveness is the first step to seeing these changes become a reality. Don't miss the blessings God has in store for your marriage by being unforgiving. *"Blessed are the merciful, for they shall obtain mercy"* (Matt. 5:7).

Review

If you know there is unforgiveness in your heart right now and you want to begin to reconcile these issues, take these actions.
1. First, make a choice to forgive because this is God's command.
2. Ask God to open your eyes to your own sin.
3. Ask God to forgive you for your hardness and unforgiveness.
4. Ask God to give you His forgiveness and compassion for your spouse.
5. Go in humility and make the attempt to reconcile.

Group Discussion Questions

1. Without giving the person's name or any specific details of the conflict, share with the group about someone you have had a conflict with where you held resentment and unforgiveness. What excuses did you use to justify your action?
2. When you chose to forgive this person, what was the result in your life and how did this heal the relationship?
3. Without giving any information that might embarrass your mate, explain how forgiveness toward your spouse has enabled you to continue in your relationship together?

SECTION THREE

KEYS TO BUILDING YOUR RELATIONSHIP

Once you have removed the hindrances to companionship and oneness in your relationship, you want to proceed to build the intimacy you desire. There are clear and definable biblical principles to enable you to do this, just as a blueprint is laid out before a contractor to provide the means for him to build a house to the right specifications. What are these biblical guidelines for building your marriage to stand the test of time? Read on.

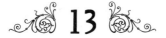 **13**

BUILDING SECURITY THROUGH
TOTAL COMMITMENT

"For the mountains shall depart and the hills be removed,
but My kindness shall not depart from you,
nor shall My covenant of peace be removed,
says the LORD, who has mercy on you" Isaiah 54:10

Have you ever used these words? "If you don't like what I'm doing then, divorce me." Or, "If you don't do what I'm asking, I'm leaving you." These words, I am sad to say, are all too often used in Christian homes today. I know this to be true because I hear them regularly when I counsel couples. These destructive words strike at the very foundation of your companionship and cut deep to the heart. I believe these threats should never come out of your mouth because they are a rejection of your covenant and commitment before God. Even contemplating thoughts of divorce is totally destructive to your relationship. To threaten the total ruin of your relationship is to undermine and damage one of the most fundamental needs in your marriage: security.

I begin this final section with the first building block necessary for a marriage to grow in oneness and companionship. This foundation stone is the security of a total commitment. Your spouse needs to know that you will never forsake your commitment to your marriage covenant. This must be your solemn pledge "so long as we both shall live." This is the vow you made before God on your wedding day, and your mate expects you to fulfill it.

Do you regularly declare your total commitment and faithfulness to your spouse? "I am totally committed to you and our marriage no matter what our differences," or, "I will never stop loving you and working to make our marriage better," are statements that your spouse longs to hear. Words like this coupled with the action to back them up is a fundamental building block of a marriage built to last. There is tremendous security in knowing your mate cares for you to the point of giving, sacrificing, and enduring long enough for love to grow deep.

WHY IS YOUR COMMITMENT SO IMPORTANT?

When you make a commitment to your spouse what happens between you? What is the fruit that is born in your marriage? What does this communicate to your mate?

1. It's a declaration of your love and faithfulness to your spouse. When you declare your total commitment, you are taking a position of love that will be clearly understood by your spouse. Only love will commit itself in this manner. The love that produces this depth of commitment is described by Paul as that which *"bears all things, believes all things, hopes all things, endures all things"* (1 Cor. 13:7). In fact, this kind of love *"never fails"* (v. 8). This is the sense of security your spouse needs, that your relationship will never fail, because you are committed to believe, hope, and endure all the way to the end!

When God declared His commitment through His covenant with the nation of Israel in the Old Testament, He assured them, *"For the mountains shall depart and the hills be removed, but My kindness shall not depart from you, nor shall My covenant of peace be removed,"* (Isa. 54:10). Everything as we know it will one day disappear, but His love will never pass away, nor will He ever break His covenant with His people. The Israelites chose to reject His love and walked in their own way, but He never stopped loving His people. This is why you read in Scripture the often declared promise, *"I will never leave you nor forsake you"* (Heb. 13:5; Deut. 31:8; Josh. 1:5). God has made it clear about His care and love; it will never change! He is committed to loving you and me as long as it takes to fully conform us into the image of His Son.

We need to be assured of this message when we are struggling in our Christian walk. We need to know that God is not going to dump us and run when we have a few problems. We need the assurance that He is totally committed to working with us to the end to fully change what is wrong in our lives. We all count this as a fundamental proof of His love, and it gives us security and confidence knowing that He means it. *"Being confident of this very thing, that He who has begun a good work in you will complete it until the day of Jesus Christ"* (Phil. 1:6).

Likewise, when you make this same commitment to your spouse in word and deed, they will count it as an absolute proof of your love. It gives the assurance and security that you are totally committed to working out all the problems; to *bear, hope, and endure all things*. It gives you both a sure foundation to build your relationship upon. Won't you make this kind of commitment to your loved one today? Tell your mate, "I will never leave you or forsake you. I am committed to you until we are both conformed into the image of Christ." This is a commitment to a marriage that will last!

2. It's a declaration of your faithfulness to God's Word. When you think or verbally threaten your spouse with divorce, in reality, you are proposing to violate God's Word, which declares *"what God joins together, let not man separate"* (Matt. 19:6). You are also asserting that you do not believe the Scriptures, which declare, *"My grace is sufficient for you, for My strength is made perfect in weakness"* (2 Cor. 12:9). Yes, you may find yourself in extremely difficult circumstances today, but violating God's Word and rejecting His promise of strength is not the solution to any of them.

On the contrary, what you need to do is commit yourself to God's solutions, not reject them. God's solutions are found in His Word. Purpose in your heart to obey whatever the Scriptures require to change your relationship for the better. Commit yourself fully to giving and loving your mate with the strength that He gives by His grace. This will please the Lord and give your spouse hope that the best is yet to come in your relationship. This is what it means to commit yourself to God's solution.

When individuals keep the commitment and covenant of marriage, it is actually a declaration that you believe God can solve anything that's wrong in your life. You are asserting that your wedding vows before God really meant something. They weren't just words you repeated for the sake of the minister. You are saying to all, *I will not please myself, but God who commands me not to divorce.*

Let God's command not to separate and His promise to strengthen you take hold of your heart. What God promises, He is able also to perform in your life. Trust Him to do it. Commit yourself to His Word and declare it to your spouse.

3. It's the attitude necessary to fully solve problems. I have found that when one or both partners in a marriage think or threaten divorce, something subtle occurs. Neither one looks for answers or works toward solutions to the problems in the marriage. This is because one or both parties are simply captivated by looking for a way out of the relationship. No one can sincerely be trying to solve marital problems while at the same time they are looking for a loophole in their marriage commitment. You can't do both. It's impossible to build anything when you are thinking or verbally threatening to destroy it all.

Only total commitment to your marriage will enable you to solve every issue that divides you. God's long-term commitment to you is what motivates Him to labor at transforming and conforming every aspect of your life to be in harmony with Him. Paul declared that *"all things work together for good to those who love God, to those who are the called according to His purpose"* (Rom. 8:28). How can we be assured of this? In the following verse, Paul reveals how long God has been committed to fulfilling this work in you, *"For whom He foreknew, He also predestined to be conformed to the image of His Son..."* (Rom. 8:29). God has known you a long time and has been committed to working out His plan in your life from before you were ever born. He is totally committed to a relationship with you and is therefore totally committed to conforming you into His image in every way.

As you are completely committed to your marriage relationship, you will also be committed to solving every issue that divides you. With this attitude of love, commitment to His Word, and enduring pledge to your relationship, you will be conformed and transformed into the man or woman God wants you to be. Your marriage will also have the security and strength needed to stand the test of time.

WHY DO PEOPLE THREATEN DIVORCE?

The answer to this question is difficult to determine because of the diversity of people and the variety of different marital circumstances. Some are finished trying to fix their marriage, while others are truly seeking help. What is absolutely clear is that when anyone threatens divorce, it means there are fundamental problems in that relationship. Talk of divorce should indicate to you that the most fundamental commitment of your relationship is in serious jeopardy. Something must be done as quickly as possible, or this threat will become a reality. To answer this question of why people threaten divorce, let me give you some examples of what I've seen. Examine yourself to see if any of these have been your motivation.

Some people threaten divorce because they are crying out for their mate to recognize that there are real problems in the relationship. It's a declaration that they are extremely unhappy and want real change. This spouse is most likely very tired of talking about problems and not finding any solutions. Threat of divorce is not a game they are playing, it is a statement that the status quo is unacceptable. Such a spouse is declaring that they can't go on living the same way without a dramatic turnaround in the relationship.

You don't have to threaten divorce, violating God's Word to get your mate's attention. Many times we go from one extreme to the other, from not saying anything about the problems (hiding them from everyone, denying that they exist), and refusing to go to counseling, to the other extreme of simply giving up and getting a divorce. We are often creatures of extremes. Practice moderation by simply declaring to your spouse, "It's time to deal with our problems and differences. Let's get some counseling." Please realize that your marriage is important enough to exert some effort to make it grow. If this is your mate's motivation for the threat, hear their cry for change and take action.

Others threaten divorce because it is a game of manipulation. They want to see if they can control or manipulate their spouse into becoming more submissive. I have seen both husbands and wives use this strategy, and it is motivated by a selfish desire to be in control. Such a person doesn't really want a divorce. They simply want you to back down and give up your demand over an immediate issue. If you determine that control and manipulation are the motivation, you must firmly and lovingly confront this issue.

Control and manipulation are very subtle forms of force or pressure. Real love will never grow in this kind of environment because love can only be given from one's free choice, never because of force or manipulation. The Father declared that His free choice was the basis of His love for His backsliding people. He said, *"I will heal their backsliding, I will love them freely"* (Hosea 14:4). The word *freely* means "voluntarily or willingly." God was not forced to love them, nor would He ever try and manipulate His people to love Him in return. He freely loves you and He wants you to freely receive from Him and willingly choose to respond to Him in love.

It is important to note that the Bible ends with this free invitation of His love: *"Whoever desires, let him take the water of life freely"* (Rev. 22:17). A marital relationship is just the same. You must be giving and receiving freely because of love and not from pressure or manipulation. One atmosphere promotes the growth of love and the other destroys it. This issue must be addressed before any other issues can be dealt with. Don't allow yourself to be manipulated or controlled! It's destruction to you and your marriage.

Another reason why people threaten divorce is because they fully intend to go through with the threat. In fact, the threat of divorce is a vague way of letting you know this is the direction they are headed without coming right out and saying they are leaving next week. This is their way of breaking the news to you slowly. I have seen this occur many times. One partner will threaten divorce, and the other will immediately ask for counseling. The one who has made the threat will even agree to come for counseling once or twice, yet in reality, this person will have no intention of ever reconciling. Sometime later I will find out that they had already made plans to leave and may have another person already waiting.

My point in this discussion is this: always take the threat of divorce as serious, and that a serious problem exists between you and your mate. This threat attacks the most fundamental aspect of your relationship. Don't try to hide the problems or deny that they exist. Don't play games with each other, but deal with the issues at hand as quickly as you can. Your marriage relationship depends on it. If you truly want to build your marriage to last, don't allow anything to undermine your commitment to your marriage covenant.

What Should You Do If You've Already Threatened Divorce?

If you have been contemplating or threatening divorce, what should you do now? Have you ruined everything, or can you still turn the marriage around? Is there a way out of this downward cycle of threats and counterthreats? Yes, absolutely! Here is what to do.

1. First, ask God to forgive you. Since your thinking (or threatening) is a violation of God's Word and the commitment you pledged on your wedding day, ask the Lord to forgive you. The prophet Malachi declared to the people who were divorcing, *"The Lord has been witness between you and the wife of your youth...Therefore take heed to your spirit, and let none deal treacherously with the wife of his youth. For the Lord God of Israel says that He hates divorce..."* (Mal. 2:14-16). Take note that the Lord is witness to every thought and every threat, and He sees that your spirit is not right before Him. Therefore, you must take heed to your spirit and get your heart right with Him first. Without your heart right before God over this issue, you will not receive the grace sufficient to keep your commitment to Him or your spouse. First reconcile your failure with the Lord, and His power will be evident for what follows. Remember, *"It is God who works in you both to will and to do for His good pleasure"* (Phil. 2:13). Your marriage is a work of God, so let Him work in you right now.

2. Ask your spouse to forgive you. Next, you must reconcile this issue with your mate. When you come in honesty and humility, acknowledging failure on your part, it will truly touch your spouse's heart. This acknowledgment is sometimes where an entire relationship will turn around. I've seen it happen many times with people sitting in my office, asking forgiveness with heartfelt tears. Don't miss this miracle because of your pride or unwillingness to acknowledge your own sin.

3. Verbally commit yourself to your spouse. Once you have asked for their forgiveness, immediately commit yourself verbally to your spouse.

Resolve to work on solutions instead of loopholes. Tell your mate that you intend to work out every issue no matter what has occurred in the past. Declare to your loved one that you realize divorce is simply not an option for two Christians who personally know the One who has reconciled the world to himself. Continue on a regular basis to verbally declare aloud your commitment to your spouse and to the marriage. Your spouse will definitely appreciate the regular expression of love and reassurance.

4. Take action that proves you mean it. Many times couples who are contemplating or threatening divorce will begin to take actions of separation. For example, some couples begin sleeping in separate bedrooms or they start separate bank accounts. Some start going to different churches and keeping company with a different set of friends. These are circumstances that must change if your actions are to be in harmony with your words. As I have encouraged you before, you should always "*do works befitting repentance*" (Acts 26:20).

Remember that oneness and companionship is the fundamental purpose of your marriage. With this purpose in mind, order your life and relationship in every aspect to come into agreement with this goal. These changes will only build your relationship. Make a list of all of the actions that have promoted separateness and change them to promote companionship. It may also be important to take the action of getting biblical counseling to deal directly with some of the more stubborn issues that divide you.

5. Determine to never use the word *divorce* again in relation to your mate. To honor this decision, you must first deal with the supposed option of divorce in your thought life. If you think and dwell on the idea of divorce, the word will eventually come out of your mouth. When the thoughts of giving up on your relationship begin to flood your mind, stop them there.

Many Christians I have encouraged wonder if it is really possible to control their thoughts. Can you truly control what you think? I want to confirm to you emphatically that you can! You must make a choice over what you will allow yourself to dwell upon in your mind. Paul did this when he was in Rome. He had been imprisoned on false charges and could have had many angry and indignant thoughts going through his mind. (I know I probably would have had a real struggle here.) How about you? What would you have been thinking if you were in his place? Writing from prison, Paul encouraged the members of the Philippian church to make a choice over their thoughts as he had learned to do. He told them, "*Whatever things are true, whatever things are noble, whatever things are just, whatever things are pure, whatever things are lovely, what-*

ever things are of good report, if there is any virtue and if there is anything praiseworthy; meditate on these things...these do and the God of peace will be with you" (Phil. 4:8, 9). He chose to think about the things that were important to God from His perspective, despite his surroundings, and not to allow all the other thoughts in his head. The result was true peace of mind and freedom.

This is exactly what you must do too. If your thoughts are not in harmony with God's Word, reject them. If you don't, they will ultimately turn you from doing the right thing. Thoughts of giving up, of hatred, of taking revenge are plainly not of God. Instead, dwell upon the forgiveness of God, how you ought to demonstrate love, how faithful and true His Spirit is dwelling inside each believer, and how willing God is to change your life. Think of what you can do to improve your relationship instead of giving up. Your thought life is very important for your own personal peace and the peace of your marriage. If you remain Spirit-controlled here, it will build your relationship instead of tearing it down. Be committed to your spouse and to your marriage because this is what God wants you to do for your own sake as well as His.

You may be thinking, *Aren't there any exceptions to my total commitment? What happens if my spouse commits adultery or divorces me? What should I do then?* I will deal with these and other questions in the appendix to this book. For right now, I'm assuming that both partners are willing to build a relationship, not destroy it.

In conclusion, I want to encourage you to fully reconcile all these issues between you. If you do, a tremendous security will be built into your relationship. Your mate needs to know that you are totally committed to the marriage. Your partner must also hear you say it periodically and see actions that prove your intentions. The strength of this commitment will enable you to build your marriage to last. Commit yourself to your loved one today!

Group Discussion Questions
1. Describe for the group what it means to you when your spouse makes a verbal commitment to not divorce.
2. How would this sense of security affect the other areas of your relationship?
3. What other ways could you express your commitment to your spouse and your marriage?

14

BUILDING YOUR RELATIONSHIP GOD'S WAY

"Obey My voice...and walk in all the ways
that I have commanded you,
that it may be well with you." Jer. 7:23

A few weeks before I personally gave my heart to Christ, an old friend of mine was witnessing to me about God's plan for my life. He explained to me that only by following God's will would I ever find true happiness in life. I resisted his assertion that I needed to make a change of direction and follow Christ. Suddenly, my friend stopped our conversation and asked me directly, "Steve, are you happy with the way your life is going?"

I thought for a moment and replied, "No, not really."

He then said to me, "What do you have to lose then by giving your life to Christ? Your way has surely not produced the kind of life you really want, so why not make a change? Why not ask God to forgive you and begin to live your life God's way, obeying Him and His Word, and see what happens?"

The conversation ended that day with me continuing to stubbornly resist the conviction of what I knew was right, but didn't want to admit.

Not long after that conversation I finally surrendered my heart to Christ while driving down the street in my car one night. I have never regretted that decision, not one day. Christ has delivered everything He promised in His Word and more. He has given me the happiness I had longed for and had searched for in so many other places. Living my life His way has truly been the solution I was looking for all along.

A few years later I married my wife, Susan, and we went through the normal adjustment period with our share of newlywed conflicts. But one thing became clear to me: the more I ordered my life and marriage in harmony with God's commands, the better my marriage became. The more my wife and I have sought to live our lives in harmony with God's way, the more harmony and happiness we have experienced. Today, our love for each other is more intense than I ever dreamed possible. I'm a happy man!

I want to challenge you with the same question my friend gave to me. What do you have to lose by reordering your marriage to be in total harmony with God's plan? If you aren't happy with the way your marriage has turned out, try His way and see what happens. If you choose to fully obey God's plan in your personal life, the Scriptures promise that you will be *"rooted and built up in Him"* (Col. 2:7). The same thing will occur in your marriage when you order your relationship according to His precepts. You will become rooted and built up together in Christ because you are building your marriage upon the sure and steadfast rock of His Word.

GOD'S PLAN FOR MARRIAGE

What is God's plan for your marriage? How do you find it? The simplicity of God's plan is revealed in all the Scriptures that deal with the marriage relationship. Let's begin to look at these passages and see what God's way is and how to implement it into your life. In this chapter I want to present the basics that are needed in *every* marriage, without exception. These principles transcend time, cultures, and all creeds. They are God's principles for all couples.

1. You must make your spouse your first priority. On the vertical plane of your life, you must have Christ as the first priority in your spiritual life. I have already discussed at great length how important it is to *"seek first the kingdom of God and His righteousness..."* and to allow Christ to rule in your heart (Matt. 6:33). On the horizontal plane, your spouse must hold the first position over all other things in this life.

To have your husband or wife as your number one priority was God's intention from the very beginning of time. When God presided over the first wedding there in the garden, He stated clearly what His intention was for all marriages thereafter. He said, *"Therefore a man shall leave his father and mother and be joined to his wife, and they shall become one flesh"* (Gen. 2:24). The word *leave* used in this verse means "to leave off or forsake." The word *joined* means "to cleave and stick together like glue," or it can also mean "to follow hard after another person." This command was intended to encourage all married couples to forsake and relinquish their position in one family and start a totally new family structure. This new couple is to be welded together as one. They are to follow hard after one another, seeking to be the primary companion of the other. The ties of authority and decision-making are to shift from their parents' family structure to their own. Clearly then, this command is to encourage you to cleave to your spouse and make them the priority of your life.

Your spouse is to be the one you follow hard after, giving them preference in all things and above all others.

If this command were completely obeyed, many marital problems would never occur. Yet so often I have counseled couples where this principle is being violated with serious repercussions to the marriage. When you allow anyone or anything other than your spouse to take priority in your home, major problems result. Let me give you two very common examples of how this can occur.

The interference of in-laws often violates the priority principle, which results in great marital disharmony. The problem begins like this: well-meaning parents see a need in their child's marriage and interject unsolicited counsel into the midst of the problem. They try to direct their son or daughter in a sincere attempt to help, but they are usually met with stiff opposition by the spouse. Why? Because it is an invasion of the "leave and join" principle. These in-laws are usurping the right and responsibility of the new family unit who need to make decisions without outside pressure. If the adult child appears to be swayed by the opinion of the parent and not by their own spouse, a major conflict will result. But you say, "My mom and dad are my family too." That's right, they are; however, they are your *secondary* family now. It's an issue of priority. Your primary family is your spouse. For example, who do you seek counsel from first, your parents or your mate? Whose opinion has the greater weight, your parents or your spouse? Who do you listen to first when there is a difference of opinion, your parents or your marriage partner?

The solution to this problem is very simple. From this day forward, set your mate as the number one person in your life on the horizontal plane. Lovingly thank your parents for their input and gently explain that you and your spouse will make the decision and let them know what you decide. This is how you gently draw the boundary line between your family and theirs. If you fail to do this consistently, your partner will feel betrayed and believe you value your parents more than you do your own spouse.

Another area in which the priority principle is violated is when children come into the home. This is a very difficult and subtle problem because they are a part of your primary family, and you consider their needs a very high priority. Before you had children, it was just the two of you and your total focus was on each other. Then along came Junior, and you became a dedicated servant to this infant for his every imaginable need. Now your focus became divided between your partner and your child. Time alone with your mate seemed to disappear. This is usually when couples begin to experience a strain on their relationship. As new parents they get distracted from each other's needs just by the sheer weight of the new needs of the infant. It now becomes extremely difficult to carry on a complete conversation without the baby crying for something. Time out together is dramatically reduced, if not eliminated, because new parents usually hesitate to leave their newborn with anyone, or there is simply no money for that romantic date. Distance grows between husband and wife, sometimes completely unnoticed. At this point, it is necessary for one or both partners to realize that something must change for their relationship to continue.

There is a solution to this dilemma. It is important to remember that children are temporary to your homelife. One day they will move out and establish their own families, and you will be alone again. Since your spouse is permanent to your home, they must be your priority, even over your children. Did you know that the highest divorce rates are not only in the first five years of marriage but also again after twenty years of marriage? That is because often after twenty years of marriage when the children are all gone, at this point, a couple finds that there is little relationship left between them. These couples have poured everything into their children and forgotten the priority of their own relationship. Make sure this doesn't happen to you! How can you be sure it doesn't?

In general, the answer to this question is given in each of the chapters in this last section of this book. It is vital that you make every effort to keep your spouse at the top of your list. Make it your habit to ask yourself, *What are my mate's needs today?* If you spend all your energy on your children and everyone else who comes to your house, you may be in danger of having little time or strength left to spend on your spouse, who then feels betrayed. If you make children and family time the sole priority, the spark between you and your mate will slowly fade. One thing my wife and I did to combat this problem was to evenly divide all outings into family time and *our* time. One week we went out to eat as a family, and the next time my wife and I went out alone. One evening we would take a walk with the kids and the dog, the next time we walked by ourselves. One ski trip we went as a family, the next time my wife and I went alone. In following this plan, no one felt neglected.

Never let anyone or anything keep you from following hard after each other. Don't let parents, children, jobs, or friends divert you from seeing your mate as your *first* love among all others on this earth. This is God's way of building your relationship into what He desires it to be.

2. <u>Establish mutual submission to each other</u>. Submission is another very important key to a successful marriage. Building your marriage God's way requires both husband and wife to mutually submit them-

selves to each other, as clearly explained in Paul's teaching on marriage in the epistle to the Ephesians. As you read this passage, it is important to note that before Paul gives any individual instruction to husbands or wives, he first explains this mutual responsibility: *"submitting yourselves one to another in the fear of God"* (5:21, KJV). Most of the time when people begin to read this section on marriage, they begin with verse 22, *"Wives, submit to your own husbands, as to the Lord."* But this is taking the passage out of context. All the biblical commands for marriage should be rooted in the principle of mutual submission if you truly want to build your marriage God's way. Paul begins with this point so that none will miss its importance. It is also important to realize that all Christians, married or single, are to have this attitude toward each other. Therefore, mutual submissiveness is a key character quality necessary for all human relationships, and especially needful in marriage, the most intimate of relationships. How do you submit yourself one to another, and what will this do for your relationship?

The word *submit* means to "subdue, subordinate, or yield." The first question you must ask is *what* must I subdue and subordinate? The answer is, subdue yourself! *You* are the one who needs to yield. If you would simply subdue the self that wants its own way all the time, what harmony would reign in your marriage! Isn't selfishness the biggest problem in any marriage relationship? It has been in mine, and I'm sure it has been in your marriage too. All of chapter 6 was spent dealing with this issue. Note that Paul, with great wisdom, deals with this fundamental problem of self and its need to be subdued before getting down to specifics for husbands or wives. When selfishness is subdued, the power struggle disappears between two people. Decision-making becomes much easier because both partners are not insisting on their own way. Your entire relationship is simplified because you are seeking to agree and to give instead of seeking to have control.

I want to stress that I do mean *both* partners must subdue themselves. Submission is not only a female responsibility, as many think. A husband must subdue his selfishness just as much as his wife. The root cause for a man's lack of spiritual leadership in the home is selfishness, which is also responsible for a man loving himself more than loving his wife. It keeps a man from loving and cherishing his wife as Christ loved the church. Selfishness will cause a man to dictate and bark orders instead of reasoning with his wife. It is what fuels that refusal to help with the chores or the children after work. These are just a few ways self must be subdued by a husband. Remember, Jesus humbled himself, made himself of no reputation, and gave himself as a servant for the church that He loved. He denied all self-interest, and so must the husband and wife who truly desire to build their relationship. I will cover this subject further, for both husbands and wives, later in this chapter.

3. <u>Submit mutually to God</u>. It is important to note why both partners should submit themselves to each other. Paul said, *"submitting yourselves one to another in the fear of God"* (Eph. 5:21, KJV). Both husbands and wives should take this action simply because they fear God, that is, out of reverence or respect to God. Remember, the power for any godly action in a marriage is a person's spiritual relationship with Christ. This is what motivates and enables you to perform in ways that are totally contrary to your selfish nature. Because both of you fear God, you will naturally submit yourselves to Him and to each other.

Mutual submission to God will keep a perfect balance to the marriage relationship. If a husband is in submission to God, he will never take his authority as head of the home to an extreme or unbiblical position. He will lead with a servant's heart because he is the servant of Christ. This husband will lovingly lead his family because he is led by the Lord. He will use his authority correctly because he is a man under the authority of Christ. If a wife is in submission to God, she will never allow herself to be controlled or used as a doormat by her husband. She will only submit herself *"as is fitting in the Lord"* (Col. 3:18). Neither will she try to control or manipulate her husband because this would demonstrate her lack of submission to Christ. Mutual submission to God will dramatically change every aspect of your marriage relationship.

Because you reverence the Lord, will you begin to take these actions? Will you surrender yourself to Christ and at the same time subdue the selfishness you demonstrate toward your spouse? Will you let the selfishness die in order to build your relationship to last?

4. <u>Husbands are to lovingly lead</u>. Men, if you want the best marriage you can possibly have, becoming a loving leader in your home is God's way to obtain it. Paul explains this responsibility to the Ephesians: *"Husbands, love your wives, just as Christ also loved the church and gave Himself for it..."* (v. 5:25). Just prior to this statement he told them *"the husband is the head of the wife even as Christ is the head of the church..."* (v. 5:23). Notice that there is a direct relationship in this context between loving and leading. A husband is to lovingly lead and manage his house because he cares for those in it. Love is the obvious balance and key to his leadership. In addition, Paul further defines this position and responsibility in 1 Timothy 3:4. When he is describing the qualifications for church leadership, he requires that a man first be a leader in his home, one *"who rules his own house well."* The word *rule* means to "manage,

care for, or lead." Therefore, a loving leader is an appropriate description of a husband's position in the home.

How a Husband Leads

You may be thinking, *How can I practically love my wife like Christ?*

A. This can be done by following Christ's example. Jesus said, "*I have given you an example, that you should do as I have done to you*" (John 13:15). However, when I explain this truth to men, many have responded: "I'm just a man. How can God expect me to do what He did?" Yes, it is true. You are just a man, but there is more. You must also remember that if you are born again, you are a man enabled by His powerful Holy Spirit. God has chosen to fill you with His Spirit to bring about a supernatural work in your life. He has the ability to completely change you so that you might be "*conformed to the image of His Son*" (Rom. 8:29). Be assured that what God commands you to do, He will also enable you to do.

Yet, God's purpose and plan to conform you into the image of His Son can only be accomplished by your complete surrender to His Spirit. Paul explains how this change occurs: "*We all...beholding...the glory of the Lord, are being transformed into the same image... by the Spirit of the Lord*" (2 Cor. 3:18). As you surrender to Him, the Spirit of God accomplishes this transforming work in you. Peter also taught us that a person's soul is purified "*in obeying the truth through the Spirit*" (1 Peter 1:22). Therefore, the Holy Spirit will help you as a husband to obey all that God requires of you. Be confident that as you behold the glory of Christ's example daily through His Word and as you yield your heart to obey, God will transform you to love as Christ loved. You have a part and He has a part.

This decision to surrender is not a one-time decision but a continual one. Paul instructed that the inward man must be renewed "*day by day*" (2 Cor. 4:16). If you are seeking God daily for His transformation and renewal in your heart, then begin by asking Him to reveal to you specifically where and how He wants to change you so that you might more completely follow the example of Christ.

B. To gently lead your wife as Christ does the church, you must deal with your selfishness as I have already discussed. You can't love and be ruled by selfishness at the same time. Your selfishness must die. If you love your wife as God requires, you must

be willing to lay your life down for her in all the practical things
of daily life.

C. Furthermore, to lovingly lead your wife, you must become a
servant around your home as needs arise. Now you may be thinking, *Wait a minute. I'm the head of the house, so why do I have to
be a servant?* That's right. You are the head of the house, but
that means you are called to become the head servant in your
home. You must remember that even the head of the church,
Jesus Christ, came not *"to be served, but to serve..."* (Matt. 20:28).
Scripture also teaches that we all are to serve one another by
love (Gal. 5:13). Therefore, service to your wife is love demonstrated by such things as sharing in the household chores when
your wife needs a break, caring for the children when she wants
to go out with a girlfriend, running an errand, or cooking a meal.
I use these examples because I have often heard complaints from
wives that their husbands refuse to do such things. How about
you? Are you following Christ's example of service in your home?

D. To lovingly lead as Christ did, you must also minister spiritually
to your wife. This is what Christ did as He loved His disciples.
He gave them spiritual leadership, counsel, prayer, and encouragement. Christ gave himself for the church "that He might
sanctify and cleanse her with the washing of water by the word,
that He might present her to Himself a glorious church, not
having spot or wrinkle or any such thing, but that she should be
holy and without blemish" (Eph. 5:26-27).

How can you follow Christ's example of spiritual leadership and set your wife and family apart? First, you must have a
passion for the things of God, and especially the Word of God.
Remember Jesus sanctified the church with His Word. Before
you can ever minister the Word to your wife and family, you
must become a student of the Word yourself and allow it to sanctify you. As you surrender to the Scriptures, spiritual leadership
naturally follows because you are placing yourself under God's
authority by yielding to His instruction. It then will become
natural for you to initiate conversation regarding spiritual things
with your wife and children. As God speaks to you from His
Word, you can share with your wife what you are learning and
ask her to explain what she is learning from her devotional time.
As you do this the spiritual fellowship between you will blossom
and grow. You can also sanctify your wife by initiating prayer
with her and for her. James said, *"The effective, fervent prayer of*

a righteous man avails much" (James 5:16). Do you believe this? If you do, make her your prayer partner. As you pray for each other and for others, the oneness God intends for your marriage will become a reality.

You should also take spiritual leadership with your children. At night when your children go to bed, as often as you can, lead them in prayer. In the same manner, several times a week you should lead a devotional with your children. If you are ever to impart to your children the importance of God's Word, they must see that you consider it important enough to communicate it to them. On Sunday mornings and at mid-week service, you be the one to suggest attending church. As you take spiritual leadership in this way, you will not only be following the example of Christ, but you can be used of God to instill within your family's hearts a passion for Jesus.

E. To lovingly lead your wife, you will provide for her needs, nourish, and cherish her as you do your own flesh. Paul exhorts, "*So husbands ought to love their own wives as their own bodies; he who loves his wife loves himself. For no one ever hated his own flesh, but nourishes and cherishes it, just as the Lord does the church*" (Eph. 5:28, 29). How do you take care of yourself? How much time and energy do you spend to feed, cleanse, and clothe your own body? You are to care for your wife in the same manner. You provide for her by going out to work every day. The labor of love that you provide for her and your family is the way you serve them and nourish them in a physical way. An emotional nourishment also comes from caring communication and being sensitive to her needs after you come home from a hard day's work. She has been talking with children most of the day, and now she needs adult conversation and encouragement. Spending even a short time talking will go a long way in meeting her emotional needs. Listening to her tell of her day will demonstrate that you cherish her and your relationship. Are you showing your affection for your wife this way?

F. To gently lead her as Christ does, you will seek to understand her real needs. Peter encouraged this when he said, "*Husbands, dwell with them with understanding...*" (1 Peter 3:7). The word *understanding* means to "know by investigation or study." To grow in love takes an incredible amount of understanding. How else can you love your wife unless you know her thoughts and needs well? You can then act accordingly upon this knowledge to love and care for her. If you know her likes and dislikes, you will plan to give or refrain from certain actions. Fulfilling her needs demonstrates your love for her in a real and practical way. I will cover this subject in greater detail in the next chapter.

G.   Finally, to lovingly lead your wife, you will honor her as Peter also commanded, "Giving honor to the wife..." (1 Peter 3:7). The word for honor means "to value or to esteem as precious and valuable." Your wife should feel valued when you love her as God intended. She will sense that she is very precious to you by your words and actions. Does your wife sense this kind of love from you? This is what it means to love your wife as Christ loved the church. If you want to know if you are loving her in this manner, ask her if she believes that she is precious to you. I will also cover this subject more in the next chapter.

This is what it means to love your wife as Christ does, and it will result in your marriage becoming all you want it to be.

WHAT A LEADER DOES NOT DO

Before I leave the husband's responsibility and go on to explain the next step in God's plan for marriage, let me give you some examples of what being the head of your home does *not* mean.

A.   Being the head of your house does not mean you are the supreme dictator. This would be contrary to the example you have seen in Jesus Christ as servant and loving leader. Jesus did not force His will upon His disciples at any time. Neither has Christ ever forced His will upon you because force is the opposite of love. Force is for slaves, not friends. When Jesus saw that the people were going to take Him by force and make Him a king, He departed. He would have nothing to do with this action because it was not His method. He wanted the people to willingly receive Him because His truth had persuaded them to follow, not because others would force Him upon them. The Scripture declares that the wisdom that comes from above is *"peaceable, gentle, and willing to yield..."* (James 3:17).

Jesus was an example of this wisdom from above. Real love and force can never coexist; they are mutually exclusive. Jesus always made relationship with himself an issue of personal invitation and choice. The last invitation in the Bible declares, *"Let him who thirsts come. And whoever desires, let him take the water of life freely"* (Rev. 22:17). The Father calls and then waits for you to come into agreement with Him concerning the truth. The Scriptures teach us that *"if we confess (agree with Him concerning) our sins, He is faithful and just to forgive us our sins..."* (1 John 1:9). He will not force you to come, nor will He force you to repent. With His love He draws you to come into agreement with Him just as He moved the people of Israel. *"I drew them with gentle cords, with bands of love"* (Hosea 11:4).

This is a critical part of Christ's example if you intend to be the husband God wants you to be. You cannot ever compel your leadership upon your wife. She must willingly agree to submit to it in the same way that you willingly submit to Christ. Why do you willingly submit to the leadership of Jesus? Is it not because of His tender heart of love toward you exemplified through His sacrificial life and His death on the cross? Jesus doesn't have to force His will upon you because you already are convinced of His unconditional love and patience toward you. You are also sure of His mercy regarding your failures and His interest in you as His number one priority. You naturally want to surrender to Him and His authority over your life because you are absolutely confident of these facts.

Instead of forcing your will upon your wife, become an example of Christ's leadership and lovingly seek agreement with her over all the issues that divide you. Paul advocated solving problems in this very manner in the context of sexual issues. He told the men and women of the Corinthian church not to defraud one another *"except with consent..."* and then to *"come together again..."* (1 Cor. 7:5). The word consent in this verse means "to come to an agreement." Notice that Paul doesn't encourage the husband to force his will upon his wife to gain her consent. He wanted couples to lovingly agree together to find a solution. If this is the way you are to make decisions in the most intimate facet of your marriage, how much more should this be the rule in lesser aspects? Love seeks to find agreement and never uses force. When you make decisions this way, it solves the "I told you so" statements that come when you find out later that the decision was a bad one. Save yourself the arguments down the road. Don't rule over your wife; invite her into the decision-making process. You will be glad you did.

B. Being the head of your house does not mean that you should try to control your wife's personal decisions. Many times women tell me that their husbands are trying to dictate and control every detail of their lives. If they refuse, they are charged with being unsubmissive. For example, one woman told me her husband wanted to control what her hair length should be. Another wife was being told to put the dishes in a certain cabinet, or she was not being submissive. This is not love. This is arrogant and selfish control. It's important to remember that even God doesn't try to control your every decision. There are a multitude of non-moral issues that God wants you to decide for yourself. The entire fourteenth chapter of Romans is given over to this discussion. There, Paul deals with the decision of what day of the week to worship on, or whether you eat meat or vegetables. In this chapter he reveals the overriding principle: *"One person esteems one day above another; another esteems every day alike. Let each be fully convinced in his own mind"* (Rom. 14:5). If Christ, who is the head of the body, doesn't try to control our every decision, why should any man think that he can control his wife in such a manner? It will only inhibit real love from ever being built between you. Husbands, give your wife the respect and freedom to make her own personal decisions.

If you will love your wife in this manner, you will be following the ultimate model of the perfect servant leader, Jesus Christ. Your wife will naturally be drawn to love you in return because God's way of loving leadership is very attractive to a woman. Your wife will find it easy to follow your leadership when she sees this kind of man leading her.

A Wife's Role in God's Plan for Marriage

Wives are to lovingly help. After God created Adam He said, *"It is not good that man should be alone; I will make him a helper comparable to him"* (Gen. 2:18). This word *helper* means "one who is sent to support and aid another." From the beginning, God knew that man needed the help of a companion. Therefore, woman was created to be his perfect helper to fulfill a special design that only she could accomplish. God created her with unique emotional, intellectual, and physical abilities to enable her to fulfill her husband's need for help and companionship.

Does this role as your husband's helper mean that you are inferior to him? Doesn't it imply a second-class position in the marriage relationship? Not at all! The Scripture reveals that God is *our* Helper, and He is obviously not inferior to us because He wants to help us (Ps. 54:4). You need not consider your position as helper as degrading to you as a person in any way. On the contrary, you should see your role as one who has come alongside of your husband to work with him in whatever capacity God has called you to as a team; family, ministry, etc. To be a part of a winning team, you need the help of every player or the entire team fails, and this is also what makes a winning marriage.

Remember, God didn't create Eve better than Adam, nor did He make her to be inferior to him. He made her comparable and equal to him. The word *comparable* means "one who is a counterpart or one side of a matched pair." The woman was created to be the perfect comple-ment to her husband just like two matched gloves.

To fulfill God's design for you as a wife, it is important to under-stand where and how to complement your husband, that is, to determine where your husband needs your support or team effort. Finding this need and meeting it is fundamental to experiencing the satisfaction God in-tends for you as a wife.

This need will most likely change from day to day, but God wants to give you eyes to see it and a heart to fulfill it. Perhaps your husband needs your spiritual encouragement because of some personal struggle occur-ring at this time in his life. Could he use your counsel over a difficult decision that he is about to make regarding his job or business? Does your husband need help in organizing things at home? You are the best one to help him because you know him better than anyone else. Solomon affirms this truth when he said, *"Two are better than one...woe to him who is alone"* (Ecc. 4:9, 10).

What are some other responsibilities of a godly helper? God has also called you into a role of loving submission. Paul taught that the younger women should *"love their husbands and their children, to be self-con-trolled and pure, to be busy at home, to be kind, and to be subject to their husbands"* (Titus 2:4, 5, NIV). *"Wives, submit to your own husbands, as to the Lord"* (Eph. 5:22). Paul is describing here a woman who is first submitted to the Lord. In order to achieve perfect balance in the marital relationship, both husband and wife must first be submitted to Christ, and then to each other. This is the context of these Scriptures. If this teaching is taken out of this context, it is unworkable in the lives of any couple.

SUBMISSION: GOOD AND BAD

Before I talk about your responsibilities as a wife, let me first focus on the idea of submission. I know that even the word *submit* sends chills up many a woman's back. Some even consider it a dirty word, and I would venture to say that your neck muscles are beginning to tighten right now. If the idea of submission rubs some of you the wrong way, it is probably because your experience has not been a biblical one. Will you take another look at this subject with me?

First, submission is something we all have to learn in every aspect of life. You as an American citizen must learn to submit to the laws of the United States or be thrown into jail. You must submit to the traffic laws or face a ticket and fine. As an employee, you must defer to your boss and do what he requires of you. As a student, you have to submit your assignments to the teacher on time. Even as a friend, you must honor requests to curb offensive behavior. When you go to the doctor and he diagnoses your illness, you must choose whether or not you will submit to his treatment. No one escapes the issue of submission. Because of the many negative ideas about submission, let me begin by defining what submission is *not*.

A.   Submission does not mean you are inferior to your husband. Scripture everywhere affirms the total equality of a woman to a man. Paul was the one who explicitly and dramatically raised women to equal status with men: *"There is neither Jew nor Greek, there is neither slave nor free, there is neither male nor female; for you are all one in Christ Jesus"* (Gal. 3:28). This was a totally revolutionary statement for Paul to make in the first century because women were considered as mere chattel or the personal property of their husbands. In light of this passage, Paul cannot accurately ever be charged with chauvinism.

The apostle Peter also believed that wives are equal to their husbands. After affirming that a wife should submit to her husband, he then goes on to state that wives are *"heirs together of the grace of life..."* (1 Peter 3:1, 7). There is no second-class citizenship in the kingdom of God. This is essential for a husband to believe or he will never be willing to care for his wife as Christ commands. If she is somehow inferior to him why should he care for her as his own flesh?

Consider the definition of submission in regard to Christ's relationship to the Father. He was equal with the Father in every way, yet in complete submission to Him. Paul describes the harmony of this equality and submission when he taught of Jesus that *"being in the form of God, [He] did not consider it robbery to be equal with God, but made Himself of no reputation, taking the form of a servant...and humbled Himself and became obedient to the point of death..."* (Phil. 2:6-8). Jesus didn't consider His equality with the Father something to be demanded or taken by force. He voluntarily handed over this right in order to become a servant. Because of the incredible oneness and glory of their relationship, the Father and the Son worked together as a team to fulfill the plan of salvation for the world. You, too, can adopt this same attitude as helper toward your husband, being conscious of the equality you possess with your mate, while at the same time, submissively working to fulfill God's ultimate plan in your home. This plan and purpose for your family is that of raising godly offspring in the way they should go (Mal. 2:15).

An even more amazing example of the glory of Christ's humility is seen as He submitted to His own mother and father. He was superior by His very nature, but he willingly placed himself in submission to them (Luke 2:51). Submitting when you know you are equal is one thing, but submitting when you are by nature superior is quite another. If Christ could submit in this way, you can surely submit to your equal! Therefore, submission in no way makes you inferior to your husband any more than Christ was inferior to His Father. You submit to other equals every day when you go to work, so why is it such a big deal to do it at home?

B. Submission does not mean you are to be your husband's personal slave. You can't be an heir together with your husband and a slave at the same time. These two positions are completely contrary to each other. Jesus didn't even call His disciples slaves; He called them friends (John 15:15). This is the relationship that should exist between a husband and his wife because this is the picture of Christ and His church. To be someone's slave means that you do whatever you are told. Friends don't command each other to do this or that. They ask.

Nowhere does Scripture teach that submission on a human level requires unquestioned obedience. There are always limits to submission. Paul says that a wife is only to submit *"as is fitting in the Lord"* (Col. 3:18). The word *fitting* means "that which is due in the Lord." This means that any request made by your husband must be in agreement with the Word of the Lord. If your husband asks you to do anything that violates Scripture or your conscience before God, you are required by Scripture to obey God rather than man. This is a completely biblical principle. See Acts 5:28, 29; Rom. 14:21; Acts 24:16.

The ultimate model for your submission as a wife is the church of Jesus Christ. As Paul said, *"Just as the church is subject to Christ, so let the wives be to their own husbands in everything"* (Eph. 5:24). All you have to do is ask yourself this one question, "Would Jesus ever ask me to do this?" If not, then submission to Christ demands that you refuse your husband's request.

C. Submission does not mean that you never open your mouth and give your opinion or counsel. This is not what you see when you view godly women in Scripture. Let me give you some examples. Abraham's wife, Sarah, is a good place to start. She is referred to in Peter's epistle as a good example of a submissive wife. When there was confusion and conflict in their family that Abraham was not taking care of, Sarah did not keep silent. She had observed Abraham's first son, born to Hagar, mocking Sarah's son, Isaac. Sarah spoke up to ask her husband to remove Hagar and Ishmael from their home. Her request greatly upset Abraham. Then God intervened and spoke to Abraham, telling him, "*Whatever Sarah has said to you, listen to her voice*" (Gen. 21:12).

Now, this is not the picture of a subservient slave who never opens her mouth. On the contrary, Sarah saw a very grave problem in her home and knew that immediate action must be taken. She then informed her husband of the problem and gave her counsel. As Abraham responded to God's counsel, agreement on a course of action was determined. Obviously then, submission does not mean you can never speak up and give your opinion or counsel on a subject. What is essential is that you speak up with the right attitude.

There are other examples you should study on this issue. Notice what the virtuous wife of Proverbs 31 does: "*She opens her mouth with wisdom, and on her tongue is the law of kindness*" (Prov. 31:26). A good woman speaks wise words to her husband with the added virtue of kindness. Or, you can study the example of how the wife of Manoah counseled her husband over his problem of fear (Judges 13:21-25). Priscilla, with her husband, ministered the Word to the great preacher Apollos (Acts 18:26). Each of these examples reveals the positional balance of a godly wife.

In examining where you stand as a Christian woman, remember that your ultimate model is the relationship between Christ and His church. Ask yourself: would I say these things to Jesus? Would I talk to the Lord with the same attitude I have just spoken to my husband with? These kinds of questions will keep you in balance!

Now, let's look at what submission *does* mean. What will you do and how will you act if you are in submission to your husband?

A. Submission is first an attitude. As a husband must have an attitude of love, respect, and gentleness, so must his wife. This is what mutual submission means. Paul ends his teaching on marriage in Ephesians with this exhortation to mutual love and respect in the home. He says, *"Let each one of you in particular so love his own wife as himself, and let the wife see that she respects her husband"* (Eph. 5:33). Submission is first an attitude that results from the fruit of your submission to God, and the fruit of the Holy Spirit reigning in your life. As you surrender to the Lord Jesus Christ, His patience and gentleness naturally control you, your tongue, and all your actions. When this attitude reigns in your life, the rest is easy.

B. Submission means that you subdue your desire to rule your husband. Beware of the power struggle that can often rage in a home. It's the battle of who is in control. For those of you who have a man who is not taking his position as the leader, you will have an even greater temptation to rule. You will have to resist your desire to take over and begin to run things because he is not. At the same time, real submission means that you won't fight your husband when he attempts to lead simply because you want to remain in control. You know when this is happening. Submission means that you deal with this attitude quickly, then give your husband the encouragement and counsel he needs to lead as he should.

    You will relinquish control because you willingly accept the position God has given your husband as the head of the family, not because he is superior to you, but because this is the way God ordained it. Remember, Paul said, *"For the husband is head of the wife, as also Christ is head of the church"* (Eph. 5:23). This concept comes from the beginning of time. After the fall of Adam and Eve in the garden, God said to the woman, *"And he shall rule over you"* (Gen. 3:16). This is why God requires men to take the leadership in the home and for wives to submit to this leadership. The Father was simply creating a chain of command that similarly existed in the Godhead. Note the chain of command all the way from God the Father down to the family. *"I want you to know that the head of every man is Christ, the head of the woman is man, and the head of Christ is God"* (1 Cor. 11:3). It is interesting to note in this context that even your physical body was created to support only one head to manage your entire body. Why is that? Because it brings order and harmony to your entire body. Can you imagine what a power struggle there would be if you had two heads both fighting for control? Likewise, God in His wisdom knows what works best in the family He created.

Think of your own relationship with Christ for a moment. I hope that when you submit to Christ you don't fight Him over what He wants to do in your life. You willingly submit to His position as Head of the church. Likewise, you must yield to your husband this position, too, even as he yields to Christ. You cannot deny that Jesus is an easy person to submit to because of how greatly He has demonstrated His love for you. If a couple finds this balance, in spite of the fact that the media, the mouthpiece of this present world, scream otherwise, then the joy and companionship that God intends for your marriage will be realized and the power struggle will end.

C. Submission means being the helper God has called you to be. Wives, God created you to be a helper. Remember, this was God's original intent. He said, *"It is not good that man should be alone; I will make him a helper comparable to him"* (Gen. 2:18). I have already explained that your husband needs help. God would not have made woman to be his helper if he didn't need help. He created a comparable helper so that man wouldn't have to be alone. The word *comparable* shows the equality and partnership intended by God for a man and wife in marriage. Therefore, if you are called by God to help your husband, don't be a hindrance by always fighting for control. Find where your husband needs help, and then give it to him. In doing this you will become the perfect counterpart to your spouse. If he needs support, help him. If he needs reproof, give it. When he needs counsel, give him all the facts and information you can gather on the situation. Let him know what you think about the situation, encourage him, and pray with him. Encourage a solution in which you are both in agreement, then help him to implement the decision.

Personally, I have found my wife to be my best counselor. She has keen insight and practical wisdom that has helped me many times. She also has a real compassion for people that has balanced me when I would have been harsh. Her decision-making abilities are thoroughly grounded in the Word and have often greatly influenced me. I would be a fool not to take full advantage of this incredible resource living right under my roof.

What will be the result of ordering your marriage after this model? The power struggle between you will die and loving companionship will blossom. When there is a mutual response, both of you will then begin to look for places to serve and give to each other instead of seeking only to take. Love will begin to grow more and more each day, which ultimately bonds your marriage. Think about it. What do you have to lose? I assure you that if you apply these principles, you will lose nothing; you will only gain a marriage relationship that is built to last.

Group Discussion Questions
1. Without using specific names or details, discuss with the group how you have seen other priorities destroy intimacy in your marriage or a friend's.
2. Discuss what are some of the greatest hindrances to mutual submission that you have discovered in your marriage.
3. How has your submission to God and your daily walk with Him helped to transform you to become the husband or wife He is calling you to be?
4. Wives, discuss with the group what you consider the most important qualities in a husband and leader and why.
5. Husbands, discuss with the group what you consider the most important qualities in a wife and helper and why.

15

BUILDING UNDERSTANDING, HONOR, AND RESPECT

"Likewise you husbands, dwell with them with understanding, giving honor to the wife" 1 Peter 3:7

Often when counseling couples I hear this statement: "I just don't understand him. What is his problem? Why does he think that way?" Or, "Why is this issue so important to her?" I also frequently hear this: "He doesn't have a clue as to what I'm saying. It's as if we are talking about two totally different things." These type of statements reveal the reality of a great lack of understanding between two people, which greatly hinders the building of the relationship. If you don't understand each other, how can you grow together in real companionship and friendship? How can you be sympathetic, accepting, thoughtful, or tolerant of each other when you have little or no grasp of what is really motivating your spouse? Ultimately, you end up working against each other because you don't fully comprehend what your mate is thinking or feeling. Understanding for each other is a very important key to working together as a team for common goals and to real friendship.

That is why the apostle Peter encouraged husbands concerning their wives, *"Likewise you husbands, dwell with them with understanding, giving honor to the wife, as to the weaker vessel, and as being heirs together of the grace of life, that your prayers may not be hindered"* (1 Peter 3:7). Peter believed that understanding your spouse was critical for dwelling together harmoniously and essential in order to honor your wife as heirs together of all that God promises. Peter also warned that failure in this area of the marriage would result in a frustrated or cut-off prayer life, individually as well as jointly. Understanding for your mate must be seen as a fundamental key to building the kind of godly relationship that will enable you not only to dwell together peaceably, but to grow together as well. In this chapter I want to look at why couples struggle to understand each other. Once you see why you struggle here, it's simple to see how to gain the understanding you need and enjoy the blessing that will result.

It is important to note that this passage is specifically addressed to husbands, indicating that husbands have a greater problem in this area and should be especially receptive to the instruction given in this passage. It has been my experience that men, in general, do struggle more in this area of understanding than do their wives. However, this in no way means that wives don't have a problem here as well. Just because there is not a specific instruction to wives doesn't let you ladies off the hook. Temptations are suffered by both men and women (1 Cor. 10:13), and everyone has the potential for failing to understand their mate.

WHY DO WE HAVE SUCH LITTLE UNDERSTANDING?

To gain insight regarding any perceived lack of depth in understanding your mate, you must ask yourself the all-important *why* question. Many secular counselors caution against the use of this word in examining self or others, explaining that it causes people to become defensive, put on the spot. However, if you compare the instruction of these counselors with the example of Scripture, you will find quite a contradiction. The *why* question is asked over four hundred times in the Bible. It was first used by God when He asked Cain, "*Why are you angry?*" (Gen. 4:6). And it was a favorite used by Jesus to nurture growth in those to whom He ministered. He asked such questions as: "*Why do you worry?*" (Matt. 6:28); "*Why are you fearful?*" (Matt. 8:26); "*Why did you doubt?*" (Matt. 14:31); and specifically on our present subject, "*How is it that you do not understand?*" (Mark 8:21).

Why is the *why* question so important? Because when you ask yourself this question, it forces you to reason through an issue and come to understand it and its solution. Understanding is half of the problem of resolving any issue in your marriage. Once you understand why you are taking an action, the biblical solution becomes obvious. For example, if you realize that the reason you are still seething with anger toward your spouse is because you have not fully forgiven, it is only reasonable to conclude that you must take that action if you are to solve the impasse.

You must ask yourself why there is so little understanding toward your spouse. When you come up with an answer, the solution will become clear. What are the reasons given in Scripture for why men and women struggle with understanding?

1. <u>A selfish refusal to listen</u>. In chapter 6 we looked at this issue in great detail as the source of all interpersonal problems. Solomon taught in Proverbs 18:2: "*A fool has no delight in understanding, but in expressing his own heart.*" When anyone is more interested in expressing his own thoughts than listening to others, coming to any true understanding is impossible, simply because of the self-focus. When you interrupt your spouse before you have fully listened to what they have to say, that is also

motivated by selfishness. What you are declaring to your spouse is simply, *I don't care what you have to say and I have little desire to understand what you think*. You must *listen* to your spouse. No true understanding will ever be gained when a selfish attitude reigns in your heart.

If this is your problem, you must be totally honest with yourself and God. Ask God to bring the conviction necessary to stop you in the midst of your next discussion. When you sense that you are only interested in being heard, recognize it as selfishness and hold your tongue. Begin to truly listen and try to understand first what your spouse is seeking to communicate. The selflessness of listening is the tool that produces understanding. If you have little understanding of your partner, this is a great place to begin your self-examination.

2. <u>Failure to communicate</u>. Many times in counseling I will hear a husband or wife say, "Well, I've never told you this before..." and then reveal some long-held resentment. Or, after one partner shares an explanation for a specific action, the other will say, "Now that you have told me this, I can understand why you took that action." When I hear such statements, it becomes immediately clear that this couple has much work to do before they will grow in their understanding of each other. Good communication always equals good understanding, and failing to communicate always results in misunderstanding. Truthfulness and a complete explanation allow your partner to understand why you do the things you do.

Solomon said, "*My son, pay attention to my wisdom; lend your ear to my understanding...*" (Prov. 5:1). Good understanding comes from taking the time to communicate, to pay attention, and to lend your ear to hear. Failing to speak to your spouse or to lend your ear to each other will always result in a lack of awareness, insight, and comprehension of what your spouse is thinking and feeling.

3. <u>Not remembering important information</u>. Once you lend your ear, and if you have truly paid attention, then you must remember what you have heard. Little by little, your spouse will reveal to you certain things about themselves, such as attitudes or actions that are annoying or appreciated. Your spouse will continually communicate regarding places they would like to go or of certain gestures that would be considered romantic. You will be blessed if you remember these "revelations" and act upon them for love's sake and out of a desire to please. When you fail to do so, your spouse correctly assumes that your love is in word only.

Jesus also made this point to the disciples when He spoke about the leaven (or hypocrisy) of the Pharisees. They had completely missed the point of what He had been telling them, so Jesus asked them, "*Why do you reason among yourselves because you have brought no bread? Do you not yet understand, or remember the five loaves of the five thousand and how many baskets you took up?"* (Matt. 16:8, 9). Note that remembering and understanding are directly related here. They were puzzling over getting bread because they had failed to remember His great power in miraculously feeding the five thousand earlier in their ministry.

Often in marriage, one partner misses the point and grapples with issues that have nothing to do with what is actually bothering their mate. It's as if they are talking about two totally different things. Each seems to miss the other person in the conversation completely. It's like two people trying to hear the same radio broadcast on different frequencies. Of course, you will hear two different messages. This is what it is like to try to communicate without remembering what you have previously learned from your spouse.

Does this sound familiar? Do you feel as though you are on two different radio frequencies as you attempt to communicate? Are you convinced that your spouse many times doesn't have a clue as to what you are trying to say? Or, perhaps you are the one who doesn't understand. If so, it may be because you are failing to simply remember the important things. If you really care about what your mate thinks and feels, you must concentrate and purpose to remember. The payoff will be worth it.

4. <u>Hardness of heart</u>. One of the biggest causes of a lack of understanding is a general hardness of heart. Mark explains this concept in commenting how the disciples marveled at Jesus walking on the water and calming the storm. They did not comprehend how He could control even the physical elements of nature. Why were they so amazed? Had they not just witnessed the miraculous feeding of the five thousand (6:37-44)? Mark attributes their amazement to a lack of understanding due to the condition of their unyielding hearts. *"They had not understood about the loaves, because their hearts were hardened"* (6:52). They had not understood about the calming of the sea for the same reason. Their hearts were not in a tender place before God, as was evidenced by their constant argument of who was the greatest among them.

When you communicate selfishly or regularly fail to remember those things your spouse has already revealed, resentment and hardness of heart occur in both hearts. Only by listening, remembering, and acting on what your partner has expressed can you keep a tender responsiveness between you. If not, the hardness will continue to increase in the relationship because of the resentment that will be held in your spouse's heart from not being heard and understood. The result is a distance that grows between you every day you continue in this same path.

This hardness of heart must be surrendered immediately if you desire to build the understanding you desire. If you recognize that this is the state of your heart, ask God to make you tender toward Him and toward your spouse. Don't wait a moment longer because every day that you procrastinate only promotes greater hardness.

How Do You Gain Understanding of Your Spouse?

If understanding is hindered by pride and a lack of communication, then it stands to reason that it can be gained by taking the opposite actions. Understanding is gained as a result of a continuous exchange between two people who talk, listen, and respond to each other in a loving way. Your relationship as a whole will grow in the same proportion that you gain understanding of each other. As two people grow in understanding, they also fall more in love, building a marriage that lasts. Therefore, how can we reverse the process and gain understanding?

1. Humble yourself and ask God. I believe humility is the most important way to gain understanding for your spouse because this is the most obvious example given in Scripture. When Solomon was anointed king of Israel, God appeared to him and asked him what he wanted. Solomon humbly acknowledged: *"I am a little child; I do not know how to go out or come in...Therefore give to your servant an understanding heart to judge your people... "* (1 Kings 3:7,9). It pleased the Lord that Solomon had acknowledged his lack and asked for help, so God confirmed to him, *"I have done according to your words; see I have given you a wise and understanding heart..."* (10 -12).

Here is God's answer to a prayer for an understanding heart–granted! Solomon ultimately became one of the wisest men ever to live on this earth. We still have much of the wisdom and insight granted to him recorded for us in the book of Proverbs. Solomon's prayer for understanding and the answer he received is an excellent example and encouragement for each of us. It pleases God when we humble ourselves and acknowledge that we don't have what we need, and then request it from Him. It would please the Father even now if you were to make this request for yourself and your marriage relationship, because He longs to grant it. Are you willing to ask? The first step is to acknowledge your need and request His help.

To motivate you to ask for this understanding, you must first see that He is the primary source of all of the insight you need for your spouse. David said, *"Great is the Lord, and mighty in power; His understanding is infinite"* (Ps. 147:5). If His understanding is infinite, then He is able to give whatever you need and to whomever He chooses. He knows your spouse better than anyone, but He wants you to humbly ask for help.

James says, *"You do not have because you do not ask"* (James 4:2). Don't let this be the reason that you lack understanding. Be assured, God is more willing to give than we are to ask and receive. Paul was absolutely confident that it was God's will to impart understanding in every area of our lives: *"Consider what I say, and may the Lord give you understanding in all things"* (2 Tim. 2:7). It is His desire to give you understanding in all things that pertain to living a loving and godly life. Believe that God's promises are for you and your marriage today. If you do, you'll find the encouragement you need to seek the Lord for this understanding. Remember, *"Those who seek the Lord understand all"* (Prov. 28:5).

2. <u>Search the Scriptures</u>. Another way God gives us His understanding for our mates is through His Word. As you seek Him for wisdom, He will direct you to His primary source for understanding all things: the Bible. Solomon declared that by studying the Proverbs you would come *"to know wisdom and instruction, to perceive the words of understanding"* (Prov. 1:2). If you want to understand yourself, and the responsibilities God has given you for life, and especially for your marriage, just study the Word of God. As you begin to understand yourself you will also begin to understand others, including your wife or husband. The Scriptures enable you to understand the common struggles of our human nature and the divine solutions to these struggles. As you obey these heavenly instructions, your life and marriage will naturally come into harmony because you understand the truth and are acting according to God's ways.

Even after reading the above passages, many have questioned the possibility of truly understanding their mate. People say to me, "I've tried, Steve, and it hasn't happened yet." For those of you who are really struggling, let me give you some assurance: it is possible! This is why I have encouraged you to go to God in prayer and to seek Him in His Word. He will help you if you ask! You must be confident that it is possible to gain the insight you need because God has already helped you once by breaking through the complete misunderstanding you had concerning Him to bring you to Christ. John declares, *"We know that the Son of God has come and has given us... understanding, that we may know Him who is true..."* (1 John 5:20). If God can take you from the darkness with all its inherent confusion and bring you into His marvelous light and clarity of truth, He can surely equip you to understand your spouse. Trust Him to do it.

3. <u>Ask your spouse questions</u>. Not only should you ask God for an understanding heart, but you must also ask your spouse. Remember 1 Peter 3:7: *"Dwell with them with understanding."* The word *understanding* means "to know by investigation or inquiry." This means you must be about the business of investigating and continually learning more about

your spouse on a daily basis. Understanding your mate is, of course, a lifelong pursuit. It is the result of lots of time together as companions and frequent communication. A godly spouse will care enough to regularly investigate such things as how their partner is doing spiritually, or inquire about their mate's personal struggles, needs, and fears. Genuine interest entails listening well and remembering what has been said for future reference. This is what all couples do who value real friendship and companionship.

4. <u>Listen to your spouse</u>. If you are a good listener, and you lovingly want to please your spouse, understanding can be very easy. Whenever there is a conflict and your mate tells you that this or that is offensive, listen. At that moment your spouse is giving you understanding. Remember to lend your ear and pay attention. Along these lines, Solomon gave us another powerful encouragement: *"He who disdains instruction despises his own soul, but he who heeds reproof gets understanding"* (Prov. 15:32). All you have to do is humbly listen to your spouse and heed the reproof. This is how love acts. If you refuse your mate's valid request to be more loving or responsive in some way, you are really despising your own soul. Your refusal will only drive your spouse further away and will create more conflict, ultimately ruining the peace in your own soul and your own home.

Listen to the general rationale Paul gives for a husband to love his wife. *"So husbands ought to love their own wives as their own bodies; he who loves his wife loves himself. For no one ever hated his own flesh, but nourishes and cherishes it, just as the Lord does the church"* (Eph. 5:28, 29). The point that Paul is trying to make is this: since you are one flesh with your spouse, love, cherish, and nourish her just as you already do your own body. No one in his right mind would neglect or seek to destroy his own body. On the contrary, we make sure we feed, groom, and pamper it often because it benefits our own soul.

Likewise, if you will listen to your mate's correction, you can gain great understanding of them. What's the last thing your spouse has reproved you for? Did you listen and take action? If so, you are becoming a wise and understanding person. As you continue to take similar actions, the blessings of God will be evident in the love and intimacy between you.

5. <u>Remember your partner's answers</u>. One couple I counseled years ago had a severe problem with understanding each other. The husband rarely remembered anything his wife had revealed to him. She had told her husband many things that she liked and disliked, but he kept right on doing those things that annoyed her. Conflict after conflict occurred. She said to me, "I have told him many times before, but he *chooses* not to

remember! I'm sure of this because I see him remembering things that are important to him. But the next time the same conflict comes up between us, I have to go through the whole explanation all over again. I'm totally frustrated. What can I do?"

The root of the problem was a selfish unwillingness to listen and remember. That man did not care enough to remember what his wife had said or asked, and the problems just kept recurring. The solution I gave them took a little work. I told him the first thing he needed to do was to ask God's and his partner's forgiveness for his selfish insensitivity. Next, I explained, that in order to help his memory out, he needed to write down every one of his wife's likes and dislikes as well as any issues that were important to her. If she made a request, he was to jot it down in his pocket-size notebook. To make it fair I asked the wife to do the same. The next week they brought their lists back so we could go over them. They did pretty good. For their second homework assignment, I asked them to begin to do the things listed on their papers. Before any action was taken that would affect the other person, the list must be consulted. This would aid the memory and ultimately change the behavior. It solved the problem.

Most couples don't need to go to this extreme, but whatever way is effective for you, do it. When you remember and act upon what your spouse requests, you can't help but grow in your understanding of each other.

6. Give explicit information. When you are discussing a problem, be sure that you explain exactly what attitude or action has offended you, and relate specifically what you would have preferred instead. Without this explicit information you are talking in broad generalities and vague abstracts. For example, if you are feeling unloved by your spouse, you might normally say, "I know you don't really care about me." It would be more effective to address your loved one specifically: "When you refuse to look up at me and respond when I talk to you, that makes me think you don't care about me." Or, if you want to advise your mate on their behavior, don't say, "I wish you would be more loving to me," because that is too vague. Instead say, "Honey, if you would talk to me tenderly and want to spend time with me as you did before we were married, I would probably feel that you still cared."

God is very explicit when He speaks to us about what He wants us to do and not do. He has always been very specific to declare, *"You shall not do this thing"* (2 Kings 17:12). The Father is in no way vague or abstract because He wants us to understand His heart on these issues. Neither is He too general when giving us positive instruction. In the New King James version, there are 1,498 references of the words *You shall*. Jesus told the disciples, *"You shall say..."* and gave them the exact words to use when searching for a colt to ride upon (Matt. 21:3). He also told the disciples exactly what they should do when offended, *"You shall forgive him"* (Luke 17:4). Even His last words on the earth were specific: *"You shall receive power...and you shall be my witnesses"* (Acts 1:8).

Likewise, tell your spouse exactly what could be said or done in the future to communicate love and consideration. In doing this, you promote understanding every time.

7. <u>Keep talking</u>. As I have stated before, companionship is the fundamental purpose of your marriage, and real companionship takes lots of communication. There is no substitute for these two priorities. When partners think that they can live independent lives and still grow in their relationship, there will be a rude awakening one day that usually takes place when a major conflict occurs or when the children are all gone. This is when couples ask me, "How did we get so far apart? Where did the love go?" The answer is simple. Each of the points I've made in this section requires a great deal of communication. To ask questions, listen to a response, and give explicit information all demand that you keep talking. When loving communication continues in a relationship throughout the years, no couple will ever grow apart. You can count on this companionship because the more you communicate, the more you will grow in understanding of each other.

WHAT IS THE RESULT OF GROWING IN UNDERSTANDING?

The most important consequence of your growing in understanding will be that your marriage and home will become more established, stable, and secure. In Proverbs 24:3 Solomon declares, *"Through wisdom a house is built, and by understanding it is established."* The Hebrew word here for *established* means "to be firm and stable," which is the result of growing daily in your love and companionship with each other. God wants to bestow this blessing upon you and your spouse. However, this can only be accomplished by following the guidelines given in the Bible. Understanding is a fundamental key to building your marriage to last. Don't miss the blessing.

Now, let's go a little further into why your marriage becomes established. We have been looking at 1 Peter 3:7. He goes on to say, *"Dwell with them with understanding, giving honor to the wife..."* What is the meaning of the term *giving honor*? What is honor and how do you give it to someone? *Honor* is a word that has lost its full meaning in our culture today. We rarely hear people talk about it in regard to relationships. Yet we must define this word because Peter describes it as naturally following the act of living together in understanding.

In this context it means to consider someone valuable or precious, or to show respect for an individual. Peter was actually describing both the cause and the effect of gaining an understanding of your mate. Honoring and respecting your spouse will naturally cause you to seek a better understanding of how to meet their needs. At the same time, as you grow in understanding, it naturally deepens your companionship and the sense by your mate that they are truly counted as precious in your sight. Being esteemed and valued creates a stable and firm relationship that will not be easily moved.

What does it look like, in a practical sense, to honor your spouse? First, you will verbalize your belief that your spouse is the most precious and valuable person in the world. This expression of love allows your spouse to hear one of the most important things that can ever be said between a man and his wife. When was the last time you said this to your mate? When you said it, was it received because your loved one believed you sincerely meant these words? Or, perhaps these feelings are just not voiced because of fear or embarrassment. Jesus was never embarrassed or afraid to tell people that He loved them. He even verbalized His love to other men without fear of being thought weak or effeminate. He said to His disciples, *"As the Father has loved Me, I also have loved you..."* (John 15:9). To verbalize to your mate that you consider them as the most valuable and precious person in your life is the highest honor you can give. When you dwell with understanding, you realize that your spouse needs to hear this regularly.

You can also honor your spouse by believing that their ideas and opinions are valuable and precious. Instead of belittling your mate's suggestions, acknowledge them as having importance and weight. An individual with true understanding acknowledges that he doesn't know everything and welcomes the input of other trusted friends. Paul said, *If anyone thinks that he knows anything, he knows nothing yet as he ought to know"* (1 Cor. 8:2). Don't let pride keep you from acknowledging the importance of your spouse's ideas. And don't merely tolerate your mate's ideas, but seek their counsel whenever you have need. What more trusted friend do you have than your life companion who knows you so well? Who better to have as your confidante and counselor than the one who cares about you more than any other?

If you honor your mate, you count their part and labor in the family as valuable and precious. Husbands, you must understand that your wife is laboring with children, laundry, cooking, and cleaning all day long. She is working just as hard as you are. If your wife works outside the home, her job is even tougher. Wives, you must understand that your man is out laboring every day to bring home the needed support for your family. Many times he labors with a job that he doesn't even like, but he guts it out for you and his children. To honor each other, regularly communicate to your spouse that you count their labor as precious and that you are thankful for a faithful partner.

Finally, one of the greatest ways you can honor your partner is by giving him or her preference. You give preference by serving or giving in an unselfish manner whenever your spouse asks for your help. Paul specifically defined honor as putting others first and preferring others before yourself: *"Be kindly affectionate to one another with brotherly love, in honor giving preference to one another"* (Rom. 12:10). If each of us would take this action in our homes, our spouses would never doubt that we counted them as precious and valuable. Your unselfish lifestyle would declare loud and clear that your spouse is more valuable than even your own wants and desires. The denial of self is the missing ingredient that can heal and restore any marriage.

Of course, both partners must be giving preference in the same manner for this fruit to be realized. Obviously, if one spouse is controlling or is selfishly seeking to be served rather than to serve, the other partner will eventually become offended by this lack of love and conflicts will resume. Only as both partners demonstrate their honor one for the other will there be a relationship established that glorifies the Lord.

If you want to build your marriage to last, dwell with each other in understanding. Seek it with all of your heart. As Solomon said, *"With all your getting, get understanding"* (Prov. 4:7 KJV). Honor each other as equal heirs of the grace of life and look for the fruit that will abound. This is the proof that you have truly received an understanding heart.

Group Discussion Questions

1. Without divulging any confidential details or referring to any issue that you are currently in disagreement over, discuss personally how you have struggled with understanding your mate. Have you been proud? Have you failed to communicate, forgotten important information, or been hardhearted?
2. Without divulging any confidential details or referring to any issue that you are currently in disagreement over, discuss with the group where you have learned understanding for your spouse.
3. What has been the result in your own marriage from this growth in understanding?

16

BUILDING YOUR COMMUNICATION

"Death and life are in the power of the tongue" Prov. 18:21

Communication is one of the basic skills needed to establish and maintain any human relationship, and in marriage it is especially important. Whenever you find a successful marriage, you will always find two people who have become skilled at communication. Likewise, whenever you find a failed marriage, a communication breakdown is always one of the root problems. Therefore, it is essential that you learn how to become a better communicator.

I hear people cry out every week in counseling, "I just want someone who will talk to me. I want to be married to my best friend and companion, someone that I can share my heart with and who will do the same with me." Yet many times the other marriage partner doesn't value communication or has no skill at it. If you are this person, please give special attention to this chapter.

The ability to communicate is necessary, if not indispensable, for building the kind of relationship you want. To grow in love you must also be able to grow in your ability to talk and fellowship with each other. Real companionship takes a depth of communication that comes from lots of hard work, discussing all the important as well as the everyday issues of life. Effective communication enables you to resolve conflicts quickly, which naturally keeps your marriage growing instead of disintegrating.

Someone once said that communication is the lifeblood of your marriage. Just as blood flows through your veins as a carrier, so communication is essential to the life of your marriage. Your blood carries the germs that infect you with disease, and it carries the white blood cells that destroy that same disease. Interestingly, Scripture declares that *"death and life are in the power of the tongue..."* (Prov. 18:21). Your communication will promote either the life or the death of your relationship. It all depends on *how* you communicate. The tongue is a small body part, but it has great power to turn a relationship one way or the other. Again, Proverbs declares, *"There is one who speaks like the piercing of a sword, but the tongue of the wise promotes health"* (12:18). Which are you doing? Are you piercing and slicing each other with your tongue, or are you using it to promote healing and the health of your marriage? To truly build the relationship you want, you must learn a method of communication that heals. This requires real honesty about where the problems exist and a sincere desire to look for ways to improve your verbal skills.

In this chapter I want to discuss the different ways that partners communicate and explore those things that hinder effective communication. Then I want to give you some practical ways to help build your verbal abilities.

WHAT ARE THE DIFFERENT WAYS YOU COMMUNICATE?

There are two basic ways you communicate with your spouse: verbal and nonverbal. These two methods are the only ways to communicate your thoughts and feelings to your mate. Let's look briefly at both of these methods.

Your nonverbal communication is clearly understood by your spouse and is a powerful means of expressing your love or the lack thereof. Here are some specific gestures.

1. A wink, a smile, or a look. What would you be communicating if you lovingly smiled or winked at your mate across the room at a dinner party? What would be communicated back to you if your spouse refused to acknowledge your smile and frowned at you in return? Wouldn't it communicate that your spouse is not interested in your expression of love? You have both powerfully communicated without saying one word.

Every day you communicate in this manner whether you realize it or not. The nonverbal things you do graphically indicate what is in your heart, and your mate can read your attitude before you have ever said a word. To become a more effective communicator you must consider how your positive and negative facial expressions, gestures, or eye contact (or lack thereof) can affect your relationship.

2. A touch of your hand. Have you ever been sitting in church and your spouse reaches over and puts their arm around you and touches your shoulder? Or perhaps your spouse begins to massage your neck while you are driving the car. Doesn't this powerfully communicate your mate's affection? Or maybe the opposite happens. You reach out to hold hands with your spouse while walking in the market, and they pull away. What does that communicate? Surely, that he or she is not interested. Again, you are communicating very effectively without saying a word.

3. A non-sexual hug or kiss. I say non-sexual hug because this is why some people pull away from their spouse when approached for a hug. Many women tell me that their husbands' hugs usually turn to sexual

caressing almost immediately. The wife perceives this as an *I want* gesture and resents it, resisting any contact with her husband for fear that the encounter is merely a formality in order to have his needs met sexually. Men, if you think this may apply to your marriage, try making a change. The next time you come into the room give a small kiss and a gentle hug with no sexual overtones and see how she responds. Wouldn't this be communicating that you care about her as a person and not just your physical needs?

4. A love note, card, or flowers. These spontaneous gestures are demonstrated for no other reason than to just say, "I love you." Why don't people do this more after they've been married for a while? Perhaps because they are taking each other for granted. They assume that love will grow without continuing to work at their relationship, when actually, just the opposite is true. There are a multitude of ways to express your love in simple and inexpensive ways. These actions are a great way to communicate that you still care.

5. Do anything that you know your spouse likes without being asked. You can be creative here. Make a list of all the things you can think of that your spouse likes and then do them one at a time. Determine what they like to do for fun. What can be done around the house to help? These ideas can range from large to small requests in any area of your marriage, such as those having to do with your spiritual relationship all the way to your sexual relationship. When your spouse says to you, "I just wish sometime you would..." then you should remember that statement! Remember, this is the way you grow in understanding. Don't tell your spouse you plan to implement some of your ideas, just do it when they least expect it. This communicates powerfully that you are listening and want to love your mate.

Before we go any further, consider how you are communicating in these nonverbal ways. What are you telling your spouse? *I love you very much and I am growing in love with you*, or, *This relationship is stale and I am taking you for granted?*

Let's move on to verbal communication. These are the words that you actually say to each other. How do you communicate verbally? There are different levels or depths to investigate so that you can determine your patterns as a couple. As we go through these various levels of communication, ask yourself how often you get to the deepest levels and how often you stay at level one or two.

1. The cliché level. This is the most superficial level of communication that exists. Yet much of the talk between a husband and a wife occurs at this level. An example of this cliché level is when you are asked,

"How goes it? And you reply, "Just hanging in there." This exchange indicates more of a greeting or a verbal handshake and does not require an in-depth reply. There is nothing wrong with this kind of communication as long as you can get to a deeper level right away. The sad thing is that many couples spend way too much time talking to each other in this manner. If you are grunting from behind a newspaper every morning or yelling over the noise of the television, "I'll be there in a minute!" realize that there is not a lot of depth in your conversation.

2. The exchange of the acts and facts of the day. The majority of talk occurs on this level in a marriage. "I mowed the lawn today. What did you do?" This kind of communication is the exchange of information. You are merely divulging the facts about the day with little or no personal thoughts or feelings about what has occurred. Again, there is nothing wrong with this level of communication because facts must be exchanged to carry on the business of the family. Just remember that this is still a very shallow level of communication because you can share facts and not share yourself.

3. The sharing of ideas or opinions. This is a much deeper level of communication because you are beginning to share personal thoughts and opinions about those facts concerning your day. To take this step you must have the confidence that your spouse will listen to what you are saying and receive your opinions. When two people honor each other in this manner, communication flourishes and both will grow in their verbal skills. Remember, that this depth of communication requires the listening ear of your spouse and a loving response. You won't share your ideas or opinions unless this openness and assurance is present in your relationship.

4. Giving and receiving encouragement. This level of communication goes just a little deeper. Giving and receiving encouragement is how you should lovingly respond to the ideas and opinions of your spouse. You will either show you can listen and be encouraging, or you will criticize their ideas, thoughts, and opinions. Your unwillingness to listen and receive will greatly hinder your communication at this point. On the other hand, your demonstration of love to receive and listen will deepen your communication further. Even if you do not agree with the ideas and opinions of your spouse, you can still respond in a loving manner by encouraging your mate to consider your view on the subject and to possibly take another action.

5. Decision-making and planning for the future. When you can share your ideas and opinions with each other and there is receptiveness, love, and an encouraging response, then it's possible to move to this next

level of communication. Why? Because decision-making and planning for the future requires the sharing of many ideas and opinions and the willingness to change. Again, some of these ideas and opinions you will not initially agree upon, and so, the attitude in which you respond to your loved one's ideas will be critical in order for them to open up to share them the next time. To be successful at this level takes many communication skills all working together to enable you to talk, listen, agree, compromise, and to accept the differences you may encounter.

6. <u>Giving correction, reproof, and instruction</u>. When a couple tries to work at this level of communication without first being established in the previous levels, an immediate impasse occurs. This happens because you need a depth of relationship to give and receive correction and instruction. If you don't talk about the facts of your day on a regular basis, share your ideas and personal thoughts with your mate, show your receptiveness and willingness to give encouragement, and compromise over your future plans, you are not building a foundation needed to deal with more difficult issues. It takes a trusting and gentleness in both partners on a regular basis to facilitate conversation of instruction and reproof.

7. <u>Sharing your personal hopes, fears, hurts and goals</u>. Oftentimes when I am counseling a couple, one party in desperation will declare some fear or some hurt from the past. The spouse will then say, "I never knew that. Why didn't you ever tell me?" That's a good question. Why didn't this individual tell their marriage partner about it? Generally speaking, it is because you need an atmosphere of love, support, and receptiveness for someone to believe it's safe enough to reveal such truths without being criticized, laughed at, or put down. Without the skill of each level of communication and a loving attitude, no one will venture to share their hopes or fears.

Isn't this the depth of communication you truly desire with your spouse? Don't you want to be able to share your heart and life with your mate and to have them feel the freedom to do the same with you? This kind of fellowship is what God has always intended for married couples. This is what a one-flesh relationship is all about. Have you found this oneness and fellowship with your spouse yet? If not, something is preventing it.

WHAT HINDERS GOOD COMMUNICATION?

To be able to effect lasting change in the way you communicate, you must identify what you are doing wrong. The Bible has all the instructions you will ever need to explain what hinders good communication and how to change it. It is the instruction manual for making relationships work the way God intended. God's Word explains how to overcome the problems you are facing in communication, enabling you to enjoy a successful marriage. So then, where should you begin to look?

1. <u>Check your attitudes</u>. Your attitude is critical to being an effective communicator and is the basis for what you say and do. Without the correct attitude, your words will always come out the wrong way. You may be totally right in all that you say, but it's the way you say it that many times turns your mate off. Let's look at some of the attitudes to which I am referring.

Do you have an arrogant or superior attitude when you talk to your mate? Do you communicate that you are always right and that they know nothing? Do you become indignant and refuse to listen when your spouse questions your actions or motives? Have you ever thought, *Who does he think he is to ask me that?*

The Scriptures teach that this arrogant attitude of heart is very destructive to any of your relationships and is especially troublesome to a marriage. Solomon declared, *"He that is of a proud heart stirs up strife..."* (Prov. 28:25). Is this attitude the cause of strife in your marital communication? If so, consider Paul's counsel *"to speak evil of no one, to be peaceable, gentle, showing all humility to all men"* (Titus 3:2). Humility is the attitude of heart that keeps you from speaking evil of anyone, or to anyone, and produces a gentle spirit to communicate effectively.

The Scriptures also tell us that *"God resists the proud, but gives grace to the humble"* (1 Peter 5:5). If pride is an attitude that causes God to resist you and causes division in your relationship with Him, would it not do the same in your relationship with your spouse? Don't let this attitude control your heart.

Another sinful attitude that destroys communication is deep-seated resentment or bitterness, which is like poison to your life and marriage. The apostle Peter noticed this attitude when he spoke to Simon the sorcerer. Simon had become envious and bitter at the success of the disciples' ministry. When Simon wanted to *purchase* their spiritual anointing, Peter said to him, *"You are poisoned by bitterness and bound by iniquity"* (Acts 8:23). If you have a bitter and resentful attitude, your spouse will pick this up as soon as you begin to speak. Your tone of voice will reveal the poison of unforgiveness inside. Jesus said, *"If you have anything against anyone, forgive him..."* (Mark 11:25). A heart of forgiveness will be your only remedy for this attitude.

Even when the truth is spoken, many times a partner will take offense, considering you as an enemy and becoming resentful. Often Paul experienced this response when He wrote his epistles. He remarked to the Galatian church, *"Have I therefore become your enemy because I tell you the truth?"* (Gal. 4:16). Paul sensed the attitude of resentment in the Corinthian church after he had corrected them for their carnality. Paul could tell there was a problem by the attitude with which they communicated to him; they closed up their heart from him. He responded, *"O Corinthians! We have spoken openly to you, our heart is wide open. You are not restricted by us, but you are restricted by your own affections. Now in return... you also be open. Open your hearts to us"* (2 Cor. 6:11-13; 7:2). When you nurse anger and resentment against your spouse, you are restricting open communication by *your* lack of affection. When your heart is hardened and closed by resentment, your ability to communicate will be greatly hindered. You need an open heart to have open communication. Ask God to forgive you and open your heart today so that the communication you once had with your spouse can begin again?

Indifference or apathy thwarts your ability to communicate as well. Jesus described this attitude in the parable of the marriage feast. He invited many, yet *"they made light of it and went their ways..."* (Matt. 22:5). This is the same attitude that many experience when their mates try to talk or spend time together. Indifference becomes apparent when you say "not now" or you simply change the subject. When you *make light* of your mate's request to talk or spend time together, you are communicating that they are not really that important to you. Every time you indifferently turn your husband or wife away, it will cause discouragement and a greater distance between you. This attitude is, in essence, a nonverbal slap in the face. It hurts and cuts your spouse to the heart that you would consider your relationship and intimacy unimportant.

Of course, not every time is an opportune time to talk. If you have to postpone a conversation or time together, make sure you communicate your sincere interest and willingness to spend the time it takes to build the relationship. Then be sure you are the one to initiate the next conversation over that same subject. Your spouse will remember your initiative and believe you really care and enjoy talking together.

Can you recognize any of these attitudes in your heart? If you do, they will cut off effective communication. Your mate will sense these attitudes and will naturally want to steer clear of any in-depth communication with you. The Bible describes each of these attitudes as sinful and requires you to put them off. If you do, the whole atmosphere of your time together will change.

2. <u>Check your words</u>. Once you have examined your attitudes or *the way* you talk, now consider *what* you say. What kind of words do you use?

Do you use harsh words? Do you possess the skill to cut and slash your spouse verbally in the midst of an argument? If so, you may win the argument but be daily destroying your relationship. Solomon said, "A *soft answer turns away wrath, but a harsh word stirs up anger*" (Prov. 15:1). David also said the tongue can be like "*a sharp razor*" that can cut and wound a person very deeply (Ps. 52:2). Is this what your tongue is like?

Harsh, critical, and condemning words are incredibly destructive. Think how you feel when a person harshly condemns or belittles you. Doesn't it drive you away from that individual and make you want to retreat? If you speak this way to your spouse, you will see the same results. Paul specifically commanded husbands to "*love your wives and do not be harsh with them*" (Col. 3:19 NIV). Likewise, this command could be equally given to wives. Clearly then, the husband-wife relationship cannot thrive with the use of harsh words.

Rather, let your words be words of kindness. When Solomon spoke of the virtuous woman, one of her characteristics was that "*she opens her mouth with wisdom, and on her tongue is the law of kindness*" (Prov. 31:26). To speak kindly and gently does not reveal weakness, but great strength because it reveals an individual who is self-controlled. Kind words can be forceful and powerful, and can cut to the heart. Solomon again said, "A *gentle tongue breaks a bone*" (Prov. 25:15). When truth comes with gentleness there is no defense against it. You can't shift the blame to *how* these words were said. You must deal with *what* was said. Use kind and gentle words from now on and let the Lord use them to cut to the heart and break down the defenses.

Second, avoid lying or deceitfulness, which will slowly undermine your entire relationship. If you are deceitful and tell only half the story or a doctored version that makes you look good, sooner or later your spouse will catch on. Trust is fundamental to your entire relationship, but lies and half-truths will eventually undermine your credibility. Your spouse will begin to wonder if anything you say is the truth. Then when you do tell the truth, they won't believe you. Any amount of lying to your spouse is like taking an ax to the bottom of your own boat.

If you struggle with lying or deceitfulness, pray what David did, "*Deliver my soul, O Lord, from lying lips and from a deceitful tongue*" (Ps. 120:2). Do what Paul commanded: "*Therefore, putting away lying, each one speak truth with his neighbor, for we are members of one another*" (Eph. 4:25). Put off lying completely by first asking God for the conviction of His Spirit to give you no rest until you stop. As you become sensitive to this conviction and realize within your mind that you are about to tell a lie, choose to tell the truth instead. This is a daily discipline that will take constant attention, but you can change if you truly want to. As a married couple, you are members one of another in every sense of the word; you are one flesh. Don't lie to each other.

Similarly, exaggeration works to destroy effective communication. Are you an exaggerator when it comes to your side of the conversation? Do you hear yourself say, "You always do this," or, "You never do what I ask"? The words *always, never,* or *every time* work like gasoline on the fire of an argument. These words will cause an explosion of anger because your spouse can always think of one time they *did* do what you say *never* occurs. The only solution to exaggeration is *"speaking the truth in love..."* (Eph. 4:15). The truth may be that your spouse *many times* or *rarely* does this or that, as opposed to *always* or *never*.

As we strive to speak the truth, let us remember to speak the truth *in love*, for certain words of truth can also greatly *hinder* your communication. I am referring to the true statements about your spouse's past failures that you bring up to use as ammunition during a conflict. These words cut deep, specifically because they are true, but they are words that should never be used to win an argument. If you have forgiven your spouse for a past failure, then it should be off-limits. Why? Because God talks about your sins this way: *"For I will be merciful to their unrighteousness, and their sins and their lawless deeds I will remember no more"* (Heb. 8:12). The word *remember* means "to hold in a mental grasp or to recollect so that it may be used at a later time to punish." God declares here that once He forgives, He chooses not to remember your sins and will never use them to condemn you. We must forgive in the same manner. Therefore, speak the truth about the present issue only and refuse to drag up all those past issues.

Finally, foul language destroys good communication. I have discovered that many Christian couples, in the midst of a heated argument, will swear and call each other foul names. If this occurs in your home, understand that these words will not be easily forgotten because they demean your spouse and signify your lack of love and respect. Once you have said these words, you can't take them back. That is why Paul said, *"you must also put off all these: anger, wrath, malice, blasphemy, filthy language out of your mouth"* (Col. 3:8). He also said, *"Let no corrupt communication proceed out of your mouth, but what is good for necessary edification, that it may impart grace to the hearers"* (Eph. 4:29). Don't tear your loved one down, but build them up when you speak. Ask God to put that check in your mind before you open your mouth. Pray as David did, *"Set a guard, O Lord, over my mouth; Keep watch over the door of my lips"* (Ps. 141:3). If you ask God, He will answer this prayer.

3. Check your actions. Your behavior is just as important as your attitudes and words in regard to effective communication. The Scriptures, again, have much to say about what you should be doing to encourage communication. Let's look at some of these actions.

Are you a good listener, or are you quick to interrupt when your spouse is talking? This disrespectful action will frustrate your mate and tends to stir up anger. James said you must be *"swift to hear, slow to speak, slow to wrath"* (James 1:19). When you interrupt, it means you are thinking of how you want to respond instead of really listening, and this hinders meaningful and enjoyable conversation with your mate. The faster you are to interrupt your spouse and speak what you want, the more this will encourage your mate to do the same. The conversation moves at an ever faster pace with neither person listening, and then the volume begins to increase. As the volume increases, so does the anger, until neither person senses that anything is being accomplished. Remember, the more quickly you speak, the more quickly you will inhibit any meaningful communication.

A related action to interrupting is sentence-finishing. This occurs when your spouse takes a pause to think about what they are about to say, and you help your mate out by finishing the sentence. Such behavior is, again, extremely frustrating and reveals that you are not listening or trying to understand. It indicates that you have already prejudged their thoughts and declares that you think you know what your spouse is about to say. Solomon said, *"He who answers a matter before he hears it, it is folly and shame to him"* (Prov. 18:13). Rather, allow your spouse to fully complete the thought, then respond. This will demonstrate that you care and are truly listening in order to understand, not just to prove your point.

Explosive anger is another pitfall and is often used only to control a conversation. Sometimes a person will use anger to simply manipulate the other party into doing what is desired, knowing that their spouse will cower and retreat in the argument once the rage appears. Yet this ploy is very foolish because you may seemingly win the argument, but in the end, you risk losing relationship and intimacy with your spouse in the process.

However, there are times when anger is not a ploy used to control someone else. Sometimes an individual just has no control over the emotions that rage inside, due to a lack of desire or understanding about how to control them. Such a person is simply out of control. Irrational anger is what drove the religious people of Jesus' day to attempt to throw Him over the cliff at Nazareth. These religious people were simply out of control. Luke says the people were *"filled with wrath, and rose up and thrust Him out of the city...that they might throw Him down over the cliff"* (Luke 4:28, 29). If you have explosive anger that is not dealt with, you will say and do things you would never ordinarily do. In addition, deep and intimate communication with your spouse will be impossible. No one ever wants to communicate the deepest things of the heart to someone who is raging out of control in an angry fit. Remember, *"the wrath of man does not produce the righteousness of God"* (James 1:20). Your wrath and anger can never produce something good or righteous in your marriage relationship. In fact, Proverbs 14:17 declares, *"He who is quick-tempered acts foolishly."* When anger controls you, you will say and do foolish things you will regret. Some of those foolish things will be: the use of profanity, exaggeration, harsh criticism, and many of the problems already discussed in this chapter. If these are things you do, you need specific counseling from your pastor regarding how to control your anger. The sooner you take this action, the sooner you will learn how to communicate effectively. God wants you to be able to control your anger instead of it ruling you. Solomon taught us that it was imperative to control anger. *"He who is slow to anger is better than the mighty, and he who rules his spirit than he who takes a city"* (Prov. 16:32). Have you surrendered to the Spirit in order to gain this kind of control?

Third, beware of blameshifting. I have spoken about this problem earlier, but let me say a few words about this issue as it relates to communication. Blameshifting is usually done when your spouse points out one of your faults, and you quickly cover yourself by shifting the blame back to your mate or someone else. This is what Adam and Eve did when they were first confronted by God for their sin. Neither Adam nor Eve would take responsibility for his or her own actions. Adam in one breath blamed God for giving him this woman and blamed his wife for giving him the fruit. Eve, in essence, replied, *"The devil made me do it."* What solves this problem? Simply take responsibility for your own actions. Blameshifting is the result of pride and dishonesty. You know what you have done, and your spouse does too, so why not admit it? Without personally taking responsibility for what you've done, all you will do is play the blame game, which only delays progress to a solution. This is a game that no one will win.

The last action that hinders good communication is the unwillingness to confess your faults during or after an argument. This is a problem that results from that same attitude of pride, and to resolve it the apostle James suggests, *"Humble yourselves in the sight of the Lord...Speak not evil one of another...Confess your faults one to another..."* (James 4:10, 11;

5:16 KJV). God requires you to humbly and honestly look at your own actions and not shift the blame. When either husband or wife takes this action of first confessing personal faults, it usually softens the other to do the same, and communication is restored.

But you may ask, *How do I change all these sinful attitudes, words, and actions?* Take heart, there is a way!

WHAT HELPS BUILD YOUR ABILITY TO COMMUNICATE?

Do you truly want to become a better communicator? Are you willing to deal honestly with your faults? If your are, all things are possible with God, who is in the daily business of changing His people. Let's look at some of the most important ways to build your ability to communicate and make the changes you want to see.

1. Establish intimacy with God and find His help for change. A vital relationship with the Lord is where you get the power to change in the areas in which you have been failing. When God is at work filling you with His love and teaching you His Word, you can't help but have something to talk about. Establishing this intimacy with God will inspire the most important communication between you and your spouse–the sharing of spiritual things. When the disciples were filled with the Holy Spirit, they went everywhere sharing Christ. When they were commanded not to speak anymore in His name, their response was, *"We cannot but speak the things we have seen and heard"* (Acts 4:20). God was at work in their lives and they had to share it with someone. David experienced the same drive to communicate what God was doing in his life. He said, *"Come and hear, all you who fear God, and I will declare what He has done for my soul"* (Ps. 66:16). What is the Lord doing in your life? Are you sharing that with your mate? The kind of relationship you have with the Lord will naturally affect your relationship with others and especially with your spouse. Your relationship and communion with Christ is where real communication with your mate begins.

If you are not walking with Christ at this time and have never made a personal commitment to Him, this is the primary reason why you are struggling in your marriage and in your ability to communicate. He can dramatically change your entire life, but you will never experience it without a personal relationship with Him. You can start this relationship by simply acknowledging your sin to Him in prayer, asking Him to forgive you and to come into your life. If you really want to change, He can help you do it. Take a moment right now to communicate with Him in prayer, and ask Him to come into your life. You won't be disappointed!

If you are a Christian, beware of having sporadic devotions or no devotions at all, because when you are spiritually dry, you will have no power or joy to communicate with others. Let me illustrate. Think of a time when you were struggling spiritually and you saw another Christian in town somewhere. What did you do? Did you run up to this person with an overwhelming desire to fellowship, or did you turn and walk the other way so you wouldn't have to talk to him? The answer is obvious. You don't want to talk to another person when you are discouraged or depressed. It's the last thing you want to do. When you aren't growing spiritually, the same thing will happen at home. You won't have any desire to communicate with your spouse either. You will naturally retreat from communication with your partner.

Therefore, return to the Lord and ask Him for His help. Renew your relationship with Him, then the desire, power, and love you need to communicate with your spouse will begin to flow again. When your relationship with the Lord is strong, then the changes you desire will begin.

2. Acknowledge your faults. This will take some brutal honesty in your own heart. Stop now and look back over your attitudes, words, and actions. Where have you been failing in your communication with your mate? You must first personally acknowledge your faults if you desire to see anything change. Remember, don't blameshift by thinking, *I wouldn't explode in anger if he wasn't so lazy and indifferent*, or, *I wouldn't lie so much if she would stop checking up on every statement I make*. Take responsibility for your actions and faults.

Next, go and acknowledge these faults to your spouse, asking their forgiveness. Tell your mate that you truly want to change in these areas. Your spouse will probably be amazed that you would honestly confess to them without being forced to do so. When you take this action, your ability to communicate will dramatically leap forward. Acknowledging and reconciling your faults with your spouse is half the battle. Then ask your spouse to pray with and for you that God would help you to change in each area. It will be a daily choice and a labor of love in order to grow in communication with your mate.

3. Give up all of the excuses. There are a multitude of excuses people use for not building communication with their partner. I think I've heard almost all of them. If a person fails to recognize these excuses, it will be impossible to abandon them, and as a result, communication will not be built into the relationship. Some of the excuses sound like this: "I can't communicate because I've never had a good role model growing up." Or, "I had a verbally abusive father (or mother), so I don't feel comfortable talking to anyone." Or, "I can't communicate; I've never learned how."

Are any of these valid excuses or reasons why a person can't become a good communicator? Absolutely not! Now you may be thinking, *Boy, that seems awfully harsh. There must be some extenuating circumstance that would excuse a person from having to communicate.* Well, let me give you an example from Scripture that will explain why I don't think there are any excuses. You will remember that Moses gave God the excuse of having a speech impediment as a reason for not being able to speak to the Pharaoh and the children of Israel: *"O my Lord, I am not eloquent... but I am slow of speech and slow of tongue"* (Ex. 4:10). It sounds like a pretty good one to me, but did God accept that excuse? Not at all! He responded with a command and then with a promise to encourage Moses to obey. *"Go, and I will be with your mouth and teach you what you shall say"* (v. 12). God overruled his "yeah but" and merely replied "Go." The promise resides in the second part of the sentence and is valuable for all who struggle with communication skills. *"I will be with your mouth and teach you what you shall say."* Did God fulfill this promise to Moses? Absolutely! (However, the Lord did allow Aaron to help Moses in the beginning stages of his ministry to God's people.) As you read further in the text, you will see that Moses ends up being the sole communicator to the children of Israel, and you never observe Aaron speaking for Moses again (Ex. 35:4). Deuteronomy begins, *"These are the words which Moses spoke to all Israel..."* (Deut. 1:1). The entire second giving of the Law was spoken by Moses, not Aaron.

It is clear then that God knew that the seemingly good excuse of a physical speech problem was something Moses could and must overcome. Aaron was only a temporary allowance made by God to encourage Moses to attempt to communicate. God knew that if Moses would simply choose to be obedient, he would learn how to communicate effectively. Obviously, when we read the books that record his words to the people, we can see that Moses did become a very effective communicator.

Consequently, God can overcome any problem you have in communicating if you will simply be obedient. That means you must give up all of your excuses and pray for God to be with your mouth. If you are the one who struggles with communication, start today by asking Him to teach you what and how to communicate with your loved one.

4. Spend time together. Once you have dealt with the failures in your attitudes, words, and actions, have given up all excuses, and have sought God for His power and help, you need to take the opportunity to communicate. Do you set specific time aside to communicate with your spouse? You did this before you were married. You talked on the phone

every chance you could. You went out on dates and would talk about anything and everything for hours. Do you remember how romantic and how much fun it was to talk? This is what must happen again. How?

You need to start dating the one you love on a regular basis. Why not approach your spouse and set something up today? Then make a special effort tomorrow to call your spouse again just to say, "I love you." Talk to your husband or wife about your upcoming date and your anticipation of being together. You may also try turning the television off and sitting after dinner just to talk over your day. Take a bike ride or a walk together. You need to regularly set time aside to just be together because failure to do so is one of the fundamental reasons why many couples slowly drift apart. Other things soon take priority over being together, then slowly and imperceptibly the distance begins to grow between you. This drifting can stop, but it takes constant vigilance to keep time together as a high priority.

Solomon and his wife had the right idea. The Shulamite requested of her husband, *"Rise up my love, my fair one, and come away...Let me see your countenance, let me hear your voice; for your voice is sweet, and your countenance is lovely"* (Song of Solomon 2:10, 14). Do you want the kind of romantic relationship Solomon and his wife had? Then take the same action that they did, and you will experience your best opportunity for real communication to occur. Is the voice of your spouse still sweet? It can be, if you will again make the same effort you did before you were married. Your spouse is worth the time and the effort!

5. <u>Encouragement and praise</u>. If you desire to build good communication with your spouse, try this approach. Each time you are together, look for something that your partner has done well and praise them for it. If you encourage the actions that are godly, loving, and responsible, you will build your mate up and build your overall communication.

Scripture teaches us to encourage. It says that we must exhort one another daily (Heb. 3:13) and speak words that build others up (Eph. 4:29, NIV). Solomon declared that, *"A woman who fears the Lord, she shall be praised"* (Prov. 31:30). This, of course, goes for men as well. We all need acknowledgment and appreciation. But the question is, do you do this? One day Jesus Christ will say to you, *"Well done, good and faithful servant..."* (Matt. 25:21). If Jesus considered these words important to say, shouldn't you do the same?

How often do you say an encouraging word or a "well done?" Your mate must do *something* right, responsible, or loving each day. Look for these things and then tell your spouse that you appreciate them. If harsh and critical words destroy your communication, think of what praise and appreciation will do. Take the time to talk and be together. Be gracious with your words and encourage instead of being harsh and critical. It will build your communication more than you could ever imagine. Remember, *"The words of a wise man's mouth are gracious..."* (Ecc. 10:12). Therefore be wise. Go and give a word of praise and encouragement to your loved one today!

6. <u>Make Christ your example</u>. As I have already stated, Jesus is our example in all that we should do and say. He was sent to communicate with man as the very *Word of God* (John 1:1). He was God who came in human flesh, a real man in all ways with all the same temptations and trials that you and I face every day. He revealed to us the perfect example of what a human being was created to be. One important part of this example was that He was a great communicator. If God desires that you be *"conformed to the image of His Son,"* then it stands to reason that He wants to make you an effective communicator too (Rom. 8:29).

Exactly, what kind of communicator does God want to make you? What will you do and how will you act? The answer is found by looking at your role model, Jesus Christ. Consider His example as you ask God for change in your own life.

Jesus was a man who communicated by His attitude that He was approachable. Children felt comfortable being in His arms, and parents were confident to bring Him their infants that He might pray for and bless them (Matt. 19:13-15). Jesus communicated in all that He did and said that He was a humble and approachable man. Jesus said, *"I am gentle and lowly in heart..."* (Matt. 11:29). This attitude is what made Jesus approachable.

Christ also taught that this humility was essential for anyone who desired to be His disciple. In Matthew 18:2-4 it is recorded that *"Jesus called a little child to Him, and set him in the midst of them, and said, 'Assuredly, I say to you, unless you are converted and become as little children, you will by no means enter the kingdom of heaven. Therefore whoever humbles himself as this little child is the greatest in the kingdom of heaven.'"* It is important to note that when Jesus called this child to Him, the child willingly came. Why? Because of His approachability. Then He encouraged His disciples that their attitude must be humble too, even as this child. Is this what you communicate to others? When your spouse approaches you to talk, do they sense this humility and gentleness?

Jesus had no problem verbally expressing His love for others. He said more than once, *"Love one another: as I have loved you..."* (John 13:34). Now, I have covered this point briefly in the previous chapter, but it is important here in our present context to consider this issue again.

If Jesus is your example of how and what to communicate, you must take this point to heart. I find that men, especially, don't believe it is very manly to go around telling people, *"I love you."* Telling other men that you love them, as Jesus did here, is very uncomfortable and thought by many to be a sign of weakness or of effeminate tendencies. This is simply not the case. If you believe that, then you must believe that Jesus was weak or effeminate, and that certainly was not true.

When you look at the romantic relationship recorded in the Song of Solomon, you see this verbal expression of love back and forth between Solomon and his wife. He verbalized to her, *"Behold you are fair, my love! Behold you are fair"* (Song of Solomon 1:15). Likewise, she responded with how attracted she was to him: *"Behold, you are handsome, my beloved! Yes, pleasant!"* (Song of Solomon 1:16). This kind of loving exchange should be expected between two people who love each other. We will cover this issue more fully in our next chapter on building romance.

Jesus was not afraid to show emotion to communicate exactly what He thought in any given situation. Jesus wept openly more than once never considering that someone might think that He was weak. He wept at the tomb of Lazarus (John 11:35). When Christ stood overlooking the city of Jerusalem knowing of the future devastation that would come upon it, He wept again (Luke 19:41). He could also show His anger and reprove those who sought to trap Him with His own words. Another time the Pharisees watched Him closely to see if He would break their tradition and heal a man on the Sabbath day. He *"looked around at them with anger"* (Mark 3:5). Christ was never afraid to stand up to people and tell them the truth as He did to the religious hypocrites in Matthew 23. Whenever Jesus became angry and spoke to people, it was always in a controlled way, never in a rage. He is our example.

Some of you may be wondering why I would bring up this last point about reproving others when you are angry. You may be thinking, *I sure don't need any encouragement to do that!* But it is important to realize that some people do need encouragement here. Some people hold all of their emotions inside and believe that it is unspiritual to reveal them at all. The person who believes this allows all the emotions to eat away and boil inside without ever saying a word. This is not a biblical or a Christian response. Anger will never go away by stuffing it. That only leads to the next step, bitterness. Conflicts and anger must be resolved if a marriage is to become the union that God has in mind for you, a union in companionship.

Are you following the example of Christ? Do you have the humble and gentle attitude of Christ that draws your mate into conversation with you? Can you warmly and genuinely express your love to your spouse? Are you able to openly express your emotions in a controlled way? If you want to grow in your ability to communicate, you must follow the example of Christ.

Group Discussion Questions

1. What attitudes or actions keep you and your spouse at the superficial level of communication? What issues do you need to work on in your personal life?
2. What positive ways have you and your partner found to deal with some of the hindering factors to communication discussed in this chapter?

17

BUILDING ROMANCE

*"You have ravished my heart, my sister,
my spouse; you have ravished my heart
with one look of your eyes..." Song of Solomon 4:9*

Every marriage begins with some amount of romantic attraction. Some couples start slow in their relationship and the romance builds to their wedding day. Others have an explosion of emotion with an instant attraction for each other that drives them to a quick wedding, simply because they can't stand to be apart. This is the power of romance.

Does the romance continue, or does it slowly die as the years pass by? Should romance grow, or is it just an emotion that is only meant to draw you into marriage? Is romance important for a successful marriage, or is it acceptable to live as companions without it? If romance has died, can it be renewed again?

I believe the Scriptures give the answer to each of these questions. Most of them are simply and easily answered by studying the most romantic book in the Bible, the Song of Solomon.

WHAT IS ROMANCE?

One of the most important questions we must first answer is, *what exactly is romance?* It is essential to define our terms before we can proceed in determining our need of romance or how to obtain it. Therefore, let's define the word *romance* from the best reference source available, the Bible. As I have already mentioned, in the Song of Solomon we have an excellent romantic example left for us by Solomon and his wife.

As you read the exchange between this man and his wife, you realize that romance should first be defined as an excitement of love between two people that is intoxicating. Solomon reveals this when he spoke of his wife, *"You have ravished my heart, my sister, my spouse; you have ravished my heart with one look of your eyes..."* (4:9). He also referred to himself as being held captive by her (7:5). The word *ravished* means "to make the heart beat faster." Solomon was captivated by even one look of her eye, relishing the romance of nonverbal communication. Yet his wife was every bit as captivated by him. She declared, *"Let him kiss me with the kisses of his mouth; for your love is better than wine...my heart yearned for him...I sat down in his shade with great delight"* (1:2; 5:4; 2:3). She even went so far as to say that love was *"as strong as death...its flames are the flames of fire, a most vehement flame. Many waters cannot quench love..."* (8:6, 7). This Shulamite woman described her love like the lighthearted effect given by wine, yet better. She depicted her love as a yearning to be with him, and when she was, she was in great delight. But her romantic love was stronger than just a feeling. It was deeper than delight. It was a fire and a passion that was as strong as death. Her exclamations reveal a sense of the power and strength that romantic love produces.

This strength of passion is why romance is so important in marriage. Romance brings strength to your relationship, a bond that holds you together until death. It is a strong attraction and desire to be with the one you love, to delight in simply sitting with your loved one. There is a fascination and an infatuation with your spouse. It is an emotional, intellectual, and sexual attraction toward your mate, and you need this passionate strength in your marriage.

THE NEED FOR ROMANCE

The need for romance in marriage is quite obvious to me as I sit and listen to couples pour out their hearts in counseling. Both men and women have asked me one question over and over again. "How can we recapture that love and intimacy we had when we first got married?" Couples know that something is missing because of the distance they sense between them. If romance were something that is unnecessary for a marital relationship, why then are there so many who yearn again for such an experience with their mate? In spite of such reasoning, I still hear some Christian speakers discount the importance of romance in marriage. This view has to come from simple ignorance of what Scripture reveals in the Song of Solomon.

Another obvious indication of the hunger for romance in our society is the amount of romance novels purchased. One large publisher of romance novels revealed that over two hundred million books were sold in 1991. And that was only one publisher! I use this example not to condone the message in many of these novels because many of them are clearly not promoting biblical values, but simply to show you the hunger within our culture today. There are also many Christian romance novels being published, another sign of the yearning even within the believer's heart for romance.

WHERE DOES ROMANCE BEGIN?

Again, in the Song of Solomon we have the answer to this question. In the fifth chapter, the Shulamite bride declares her attraction to Solomon. She describes in very graphic terms the beauty of his black hair, his strong muscular hands and legs, and many other handsome features. Yet her romantic attraction is not limited to his physical appearance. She ends her description with the most precious and important aspect of their relationship when she says, *"Yes, he is altogether lovely. This is my beloved, and this is my friend"* (5:10-16).

It is important to see that the Bible relates friendship and marital romance. One begets the other. Consider for a moment if this isn't where your marriage began. You met your spouse and enjoyed their company, and a friendship commenced. As you spent time together, the friendship turned into a relationship that flourished. The attraction and the friendship deepened until you sensed that love and romance had ignited. This romance eventually led you to get married.

After most couples get married, however, they fail to continue to do the very things that started their friendship in the first place. They begin to take each other's friendship for granted, and the relationship loses its power and excitement. This is the case in the majority of the couples that I have counseled in the last twenty-five years of ministry.

To ignite the romance again, you must begin with friendship. Friendship is the ground in which romance grows. Focusing your attention upon becoming friends kindles anew that original bond of love that will spark the romance that is missing in your marriage. What creates this friendship? Let's look at some of the key elements.

1. Be a friend. The wisdom of Solomon is evident in his simple counsel on the subject of friendship: *"A friend loves at all times"* (Prov. 17:17). Love is more than a feeling or an emotion. It is an action that you take. It is commitment. Love always acts in a friendly manner toward others. Therefore, true friendship is created and maintained by *practical* love. Are you demonstrating this faithful aspect of friendship to your spouse, or are you critical, independent, and resentful? The way you are behaving toward your mate will have a lot to do with how they will respond. The Bible declares, *"Whatever a man sows, that he will also reap"* (Gal. 6:7). Consequently, you must first consider your own actions to determine if you are being a good friend or not. Jesus taught this reciprocal principle when He said, *"Whatever you want men to do to you, do also to them..."* (Matt. 7:12). Christ was our perfect example when He initiated friendship and reconciliation between God and mankind.

The problem is that many partners demonstrate that they don't really desire friendship. I hear something like this quite often: "My husband would never talk to his friends at work like he talks to me. They wouldn't stand for it. Why does he think I can be treated this way?" This question is a good one. The truth is, if we treated our friends at work the way we treat our spouse, we wouldn't have many friends. In reality, shouldn't you treat your spouse better than you treat your friends? If your mate is the number one priority in your life, that is how they must be treated.

Therefore, don't wait for your spouse to be friendly; you make the first move. Whatever is required by Scripture or common courtesy, do it, and show yourself friendly. This is the first step toward friendship. As you take it, I'm sure you will be pleasantly surprised with the response you get.

2. <u>Friends always attempt to resolve conflicts</u>. The Bible proclaims that at one time you were enemies of God *"yet now He has reconciled"* you unto himself (Col. 1:21). This work was accomplished because Jesus wanted a relationship with you. He declared, *"Greater love has no one than this, than to lay down one's life for his friends"* (John 15:13). His death on the cross was God's supreme demonstration of love and the offer of friendship. He wanted to be reconciled with you! And His life proved this fact as well. People recognized Him to be *"a friend of tax collectors and sinners"* (Matt. 11:19). Jesus showed himself friendly to those the Pharisees despised, all for the express purpose that He might reconcile unto himself those who were estranged from Him. That was His way of life.

In order to be friends with your marriage partner, this must be your lifestyle as well. You must continually seek reconciliation whenever you become estranged from each other. The moment you begin to hold resentment and bitterness in your heart, the friendship and closeness will begin to disappear. This is true with all your friendships. You can't be friends with someone and harbor anger toward him at the same time because resentment breaches a relationship. The friendship will not continue or grow unless the conflict is resolved.

Paul encouraged Christians to keep a very short account with each other when conflicts arise. He said, *"Do not let the sun go down on your wrath..."* (Eph. 4:26). Yet this is what commonly happens in marriage. Couples go to bed angry and wake up just as upset. They sense the distance between themselves, but in a few days they forget about it. However, underneath the surface the issue still exists. Conflict after conflict goes unresolved, the distance increases, and friendship departs.

Yes, it is difficult to resolve some conflicts, but it can be done. Go back and read through the chapters on resolving conflicts and get to work on the ones that are still unresolved. Examine your own heart for areas in which you can make further changes. If you want the friendship and romance to return, you must solve your conflicts once and for all.

3. <u>Friendship honors requests made</u>. To understand this principle let me use an analogy. If a friend kept asking you to help him fix his gate and you continually refused, don't you think your relationship would become a little strained? Or, if you asked a friend to refrain from smoking cigarettes in your car, and he continued to do so, wouldn't it begin to drive you apart? Sure it would. Why? Because you naturally assume that this person who professed to be your friend might not care as much as previously declared. This is what real friendship means. You listen to your friends' requests and you honor them for friendship's sake.

Jesus taught this same principle concerning friendship when He said, *"You are my friends if you do whatever I command you"* (John 15:14). Granted, our friendship with Christ is of a much higher order than any human relationship because we are called to obey Him in all things. However, if we were to disobey Christ He would, of course, question the sincerity of our profession of love and faith. Our active obedience proves the sincerity of our love. Jesus said, *"If you love Me, keep my commandments"* (John 14:15).

The basic concept is the same in regard to our friendship with each other. If you love your friend, then you will do all that is in your power to keep from offending them, or you won't be friends for very long. Unlike our friendship with Christ, you are not called to absolute obedience to your marriage partner. However, you had better be responsive to their requests, or the friendship between you will surely die.

4. <u>Friendship involves active daily communication</u>. Even though we have just looked at communication in the previous chapter, let's examine this issue more specifically in relation to friendship.

Real friends talk a lot together. Your best friend is the person you talk with the most. This is a natural fruit of friendship because friends enjoy being with each other and sharing all that happens to them. They can laugh or cry together and comfort one another. Friendship offers the opportunity to share your heart, and your friend shares back. This is how Jesus described friendship: *"No longer do I call you servants, for a servant does not know what his master is doing; but I have called you friends, for all things that I heard from My Father I have made known to you"* (John 15:15).

Jesus described His relationship with the disciples as more than the normal master-slave relationship. True, we are His servants, however we are also His friends. But notice why He called us His friends; because he has "made known all things" to us. All that He heard from His Father He has communicated to us. In other words, according to Jesus, a real friend is someone you could share your heart with. The more you talk with a person, the closer you become as friends.

The opposite is also true. The less you talk to a friend, the more distant you naturally grow toward him. Think of friends that you have had in the past that have moved away. If you fail to keep in contact with them, what happens? The distance in miles eventually translates into a distance in your relationship. However, if you work at writing and calling this friend on a regular basis, then the relationship continues.

Some have said to me, "Yes, Steve, my spouse tells me everything all right, but only those things I'm doing wrong. There is communication, but it is always negative." I remind people when this comment is made that Jesus also tells you things that are wrong in your life. The only difference is that He does it in love. He speaks the truth in love and so should you (Eph. 4:15). But remember, the truth also recognizes those behaviors that are good and beneficial.

Being able to speak to each other in love about the problems between you is vital for friendship. Friends must talk about conflicts in a respectful way and then resolve them. When two people resolve these conflicts, their friendship only grows deeper. Solomon said, "*Open rebuke is better than love carefully concealed. Faithful are the wounds of a friend, but the kisses of an enemy are deceitful*" (Prov. 28:5, 6). A caring friend will rebuke and correct you at times because he is your friend and doesn't want to see you hurt. If he sees you about to do something that could harm you, his love would naturally try to stop you. Sometimes this causes you some pain, but it's because your friend is faithful to you. Have you ever had a friend ask you, "Why didn't you tell me or warn me about this?" Friends expect you to rebuke them if you care.

Friendship means that you must be able to talk about all things, the good and the bad, encouraging and reproving each other as the need arises. You must grow in your ability to speak the truth in love and resolve the conflicts that come up as a result. This is how real friendship grows.

5. Friends don't try to control every detail of your life. You may be thinking, *Here is where your comparison between friendship with Jesus and friendship with my spouse breaks down*. Not so! Yes, Jesus does want to remake your life when sin and immorality are controlling it, but He doesn't try to change the nonmoral issues. He leaves those up to you to

decide. The best example of this freedom is revealed in the book of Romans. God inspired the apostle Paul to tell each individual that they had to decide for themselves where they stood on many nonmoral issues such as which days to worship or if they were to eat meat or only vegetables. He explained that these issues were not going to be dictated by God, nor should anyone else dictate them for the individual. He declared, *"Let each be fully convinced in his own mind"* (Rom. 14:5).

In your marriage relationship there are also a multitude of nonmoral issues that you must deal with every day. You probably have many differences with your spouse over your personal likes and dislikes that create conflicts. The problems come when you selfishly try to make your spouse into your own image or pressure your spouse to do everything just like you do. This is an unrealistic expectation and will destroy your friendship.

Think for a moment about your relationship with your best friend (other than your spouse). Would you get into your friend's car and start telling him which way to drive to his destination? Would you remark about his different type of clothing, or start berating his hair style? Never! If you did, you wouldn't be friends very long. You would never try to change every detail of your friend's life. You are very accepting of these details because you realize these decisions are personal and not your place to control. Besides, we are all different creatures, and the world would be a boring place if we were all alike.

Why then do you show a lack of acceptance for the personal decisions of your spouse? Are they any less your friend? It amazes me how we show such respect, courtesy, and acceptance for our friends, neighbors, and fellow workers, and then go home and act totally different. Why is this? It basically comes down to selfishness.

I am not saying that you shouldn't try to compromise over these nonmoral issues, especially if you know something is offensive to your spouse. But at some point you are going to have to accept the differences that exist between you. Your spouse will never be just like you nor like everything that you like. Your loved one will never act just the way you would act, and to expect it is simply unrealistic.

How Can You Build Romance?

Once you have established or reestablished friendship with your spouse, the ground is prepared to build romance. Let's look at some of the keys that will enable you to develop the intimacy of romance in your marriage.

1. <u>Romance is built by spending time together</u>. All the principles that inspire friendship require you to spend time together. There is no substitute for this activity. Friends always spend a lot of time together. This is how most relationships begin and why people fall in love and get married, because friendship naturally grows into romance.

As you read the Song of Solomon, it is quite obvious that there was a passionate romance between this husband and wife. There was also a close friendship between them as I have already explained. It is clear that a key ingredient to their friendship and romance was that they spent a lot of time together. "*Rise up, my love, my fair one, and come away...Let me see your countenance, let me hear your voice...I sought him...I called him...Come my beloved, let us go forth to the field: Let us lodge in the villages*" (Song of Solomon 2:10, 14; 5:6; 7:11).

How do you make time with your spouse a real priority? Notice that I didn't ask, when would you *like* to make it a priority. How do you make it a priority right now? We all have good-sounding excuses: "It has been so busy this month with business and the children, it will be better next month." No it won't! If you don't make time together a priority now, it will never happen. There will always be more things to do in one day than you have time to complete, and if you don't make time for your spouse, they will simply get squeezed out. I encourage you to say to your spouse today, "Come away with me for a walk in the park, or come away with me for lunch or dinner, or come away with me and sit on the porch and talk."

Do you still take the time to date each other? Is your mate's voice still sweet to your ears? If you want more romance in your marriage, then spend more time together and see what happens. If you don't, you are, in reality, killing the romance in your marriage.

2. <u>Romance is built by the words that you say to each other</u>. As you read the Song of Solomon you instantly realize that this couple was extremely verbal with each other. They were constantly declaring tender and loving words, and that explains why they were so in love. As I have already discussed in our chapter on communication, words can either build your mate up or cut like a razor to kill and destroy.

Notice the words that the Shulamite spoke to her husband. "*Behold, you are handsome, my beloved! Yes, pleasant...My beloved is white and ruddy, chief among ten thousand*" (Song of Solomon 1:16; 5:10). Solomon returned these words, "*Behold, you are fair, my love! Behold, you are fair! You have dove's eyes... Like a lily among thorns, so is my love among the daughters...You are all fair, my love, and there is no spot in you...How fair and how pleasant you are, O love, with your delights*" (Song of Solomon 1:15; 2:2; 4:7; 7:6).

Is it your habit to say such things to your spouse every day? When was the last time you told your wife that she is beautiful or that she is important to you? When was the last time you told your husband how handsome he is or how much you appreciate him going out to work every day? These are words that need to be said continually to each other. These are the words that romance is built upon. If you remember, these are the things you said to each other when you dated. Why don't you say them anymore? Either you don't love your spouse the way you did once, or you have simply become lazy in the expression of your love.

If the words you express are filled with criticism, anger, or sarcasm, you are killing the romance in your marriage. The conflicts that are causing these kinds of words must be resolved, and then the romance will return. In addition, if you are verbally unresponsive or inexpressive to your spouse, this also kills romance. If you are wondering why your mate is so unromantic, here are three good reasons. You need to spend more time speaking words that build up instead of words that tear down, then watch what happens. You might be surprised at how much romance has been hindered by these common problems.

Take the example that is given here in Scripture as to what enhances romance in a marriage. Apply this principle as soon as possible. When you get together at the end of the day, ask your mate to come away with you and then begin to communicate. Or, walk up and put your arms around your spouse and look directly at them and say, "I just wanted to tell you that I love you." This would be a good way to start a romantic evening together. But don't get upset if your husband or wife isn't immediately receptive. If you haven't been acting like this on a regular basis, it is going to take a while for your mate to become equally responsive. Your spouse will probably think you are just asking for sexual relations by your actions. You must communicate that what you really want is to spend time together to build your relationship. Once your partner gets the idea that you are interested in being together just because you care, the romance within your marriage will begin to grow.

3. <u>Romance is built by being unpredictable and spontaneous</u>. If there is anything that kills romance in a marriage, it is routine because it destroys the magic emotion of romance. It is much easier to fall into safe and predictable habits than it is to be romantic. Romance takes being creative, to plan some loving surprise. At other times it means being spontaneous, to jump in your car and get away together for a late night ice cream.

As you study the marriage of Solomon and his wife, you see anything but routine. He brings her gifts (1:11) and spontaneously invites her to take a walk to smell the spring flowers that are in bloom (2:10-13).

Similarly, she endeavors to make their lovemaking more exciting with a change of pace: *"Come, my beloved, let us go forth to the field; let us lodge in the villages. Let us get up early to the vineyards; let us see if the vine has budded, whether the grape blossoms are open, and the pomegranates are in bloom. There I will give you my love"* (7:11, 12).

What interesting, spontaneous, and creative examples are given here in Scripture. Unexpected gifts given, invitations to smell the flowers, and a wife approaching her husband to take a trip together to a very unexpected location for lovemaking. This is romance! When is the last time you brought a gift to your spouse when it was totally unexpected, or you went for a drive, just the two of you? Maybe you don't have a field nearby where you could go to smell the flowers, but you might try bringing some home from the florist. You also might not feel comfortable making love in a field some place, but why not schedule a romantic getaway at a hotel for the weekend? Remember, all of these examples are taken directly from Scripture, from a relationship that obviously had plenty of romance. If you take these actions, the same thing will result within your relationship.

4. <u>Romance is developed by physical expressions of love</u>. The expression of physical affection in marriage is very important and must not be neglected. Physical expressions of love are just as important to romance as any of the other issues we have covered in this chapter. We are verbal creatures, so God has ordained that we use words to express love to each other. We are social creatures, so God has ordained that we express love by spending time together. We are spiritual creatures, so God gave us the Holy Spirit to satisfy our longing for spiritual love. But we are physical creatures too, and so it stands to reason that we would need physical expressions of love.

One way you can express physical love to your spouse is by keeping yourself physically attractive. This would entail your overall appearance and personal hygiene. Often both husbands and wives tell me that their spouses have just let themselves go, physically. A man comes home and his wife hasn't taken a shower or fixed her hair from the time he left earlier that morning. Or, a wife tells me that her husband has gained fifty pounds or refuses to shave and shower when he comes home from work. These are the things that kill romance in a marriage.

When you read the Song of Solomon, you see a totally different picture. Solomon's wife did her hair so beautifully that he said he was captivated by it. *"The hair of your head is like purple; the king is held captive by its tresses"* (Song of Solomon 7:5). He remarks about the scent of her breath and how inviting it is to kiss her, *"The fragrance of your breath like apples...and the roof of your mouth like the best wine*" (Song of Solomon 7:8, 9). He was especially attracted to the smell of her perfumes. "*Your love is better than wine because of the fragrance of your good ointments...How fair is your love, my sister, my spouse! How much better than wine is your love, and the scent of your perfumes than all spices*" (Song of Solomon 1:2, 3; 4:10). The Shulamite also mentions Solomon's handsome physical appearance. *My beloved is...chief among ten thousand...His locks are wavy, and black as a raven. His eyes are like doves...Washed with milk...His lips are lilies, dripping liquid myrrh...his body is carved ivory...his mouth is most sweet, yes, he is altogether lovely*" (Song of Solomon 5:10-16). Obviously from these passages you can see how important your physical appearance and personal hygiene are to keeping the romance in your marriage.

Likewise, nonsexual physical touching is equally important for romance. Do you put your arm around each other when you sit together? When your spouse passes you in the hallway at home, do you spontaneously hold each other and kiss? When you go shopping together, do you reach out to hold your mate's hand? These are the things that keep the romance alive in your marriage.

These are the actions that should spontaneously be occurring in your marriage because this is what married people do when they are in love. Physical touching is what revealed the truth that Isaac and Rebekah were not brother and sister as he had told King Abimelech. The king looked out his window one day and saw Isaac "*showing endearment to Rebekah, his wife.*" The king called Isaac in and said, "*Quite obviously she is your wife*" (Gen. 26:8, 9). The manner in which he was touching Rebekah made it plain to the king that they were physically attracted to each other, and even intimate.

When I have tried to explain this principle, some have responded, "Do we have to touch all the time?" No, you don't *have* to, but I would hope that you would want to show your endearment toward your spouse in a physical way. I believe when you keep holding hands, rubbing backs, rubbing feet, hugging, kissing, and caressing each other as part of your time together, romance stays alive and will grow in your relationship. In addition, see Song of Solomon 1:2; 2:6.

Another physical expression of love is the sexual relationship itself. In the Song of Solomon, the sexual union is described in beautiful poetic terms such as "*I will give you my love*" (7:12), or in eating the fruits of "*my garden*" (4:16). It is important to note that Scripture describes sex as an expression of love between a man and his wife. In the New Testament, Paul wrote: "*Let the husband render to his wife the affection due her, and likewise also the wife to her husband"* (1 Cor. 7:3). The sexual union is one in which you are to give mutual affection. This concept is critical to keeping the romance in your marriage. If you see your sexual relationship as a duty that you must "grin and bear," there will be little romance experienced. Solomon is more explicit when he speaks of the sexual relationship in the proverbs. There, he encouraged his son not to be drawn away with immoral women, but to be faithful to the wife of his youth. *"Let her breasts satisfy you at all times; and always be enraptured with her love"* (Proverbs 5:19). The word *enraptured* in this passage means "to be intoxicated." This word clearly describes the excitement of romance that must be a part of the sexual relationship with your mate.

Scripture makes it clear that you need this romantic intoxication with your spouse in all seasons of your marriage. Therefore, whether you are a newlywed or you have been married many years, you should find true satisfaction in the physical expression of your love. In fact, this romantic intoxication with your spouse is what brings the greatest satisfaction in your sexual relationship. Don't miss it!

If there is little or no romance present in your marriage, it is simply because you have unresolved conflicts driving you apart, or you have failed to establish real friendship with your spouse. These issues can be remedied and the romance you had at the beginning restored. I know from personal experience that after twenty-five years of marriage I am more in love with my wife than ever before. I can hardly wait to get home at night to see and talk with my companion. Believe that God can do the same for you. Put these principles to work and watch the romance blossom.

Group Discussion Questions
1. How did romance begin in your relationship before you were married?
2. What are some things that have killed romance in your relationship?
3. What are some additional ways you can begin to build romance? Hint: Ask your spouse to write out a list of things they considers romantic.

✣ 18 ✣

BUILDING YOUR SEXUAL RELATIONSHIP

"Let the husband render to his wife the affection due her, and likewise also the wife to her husband" 1 Cor. 7:3

A good sexual relationship is a vital part of any good marriage. Even though the sexual act entails a very small amount of the overall time a couple spends together, it has a major effect upon your entire relationship. Let me give you a simple analogy to illustrate. The spark plug in your car plays a very small part of the overall working process of the engine, but without it your car is going nowhere. Even if the spark plug works, but is misfiring, it will make for a very uncomfortable ride, with power one minute and none the next. Obviously, it would affect the entire performance of your car.

This is equally true of your sexual relationship. For example, when there is a lack of sexual intimacy between you and your spouse, there is an immediate sense that something is "missing." You know there is a distance between you. Sometimes when this distance is prolonged, it becomes a wall, and you begin to wonder if your spouse still cares about you at all. With the affection, passion, and intimacy missing, the spark and excitement of your relationship will be wanting. You may go through the external motions of marriage, but the infatuation, the thrill, and the energy will be absent. If this distance continues, it creates tension, doubt, and conflict in other areas, and your marriage becomes very uncomfortable. Without the spark that sexual intimacy brings, your marriage cannot proceed smoothly down the road to maturity.

On the other hand, a struggling marriage will also affect your sexual relationship. When you have unresolved conflicts between you, they always seem to find their way into the bedroom. Unresolved conflicts cause you to pull away physically, emotionally, and spiritually from your spouse. As resentment builds in your relationship, the distance increases between you, and this in turn causes more tension in the bedroom. If you don't resolve these conflicts, you slowly move to a breaking point. Why? Because you can't separate your marital life and your sexual life. Therefore, it is essential that you see the powerful position the sexual relationship holds in your overall marriage.

Now, you may be thinking, *How can I change this destructive cycle and build a healthy sexual relationship?* The answer begins with a change in your thinking. You must start to think biblically about this area of your marriage and allow your ideas to be governed by the Word of God. I have found in counseling that most Christian couples have very little idea what the Bible teaches about sexual intimacy. Their concepts are governed by what they have learned from secular material, friends, or sometimes, by their experience as non-Christians. With little understanding of the Scriptures on the subject of sex, it is very difficult for people to actually obey God's commands and experience the blessings He promises. Truly, God has created the sexual relationship to be a blessing in your marriage, and not a hassle. He created the sexual union to draw you together and to establish and strengthen your relationship, not drive you apart. Only by understanding His plan will this be accomplished.

WHY DID GOD CREATE THE SEXUAL RELATIONSHIP?

God designed the sexual act with very specific purposes in mind. He had a clear plan and goal that He desired to accomplish that is revealed in His Word. How well do you understand the biblical purposes He has ordained? If you fail to understand the design and purpose of any man-made product, you will surely misuse it. For example, if you took one of your wife's best kitchen knives into the garage to cut wire, would it work very well when you brought it back? Or, if you took your kitchen mixer outside to cultivate the garden, how long would it work? Obviously, these products were made for an entirely different purpose. If you misunderstand these purposes, the appliance won't work very well.

The same thing is true with your sexual relationship. If you fail to understand the purpose for which God has ordained sex, it won't work very well either. If you try to force something that was never intended by the designer, it will be a struggle.

Is this what your sexual relationship is like? Is lovemaking something that you battle with every time you engage in it, or is it working well? Are you constantly forcing yourself to do your duty, or is it a special exchange of love? Consider with me God's wisdom in ordaining the sexual relationship within marriage.

1. <u>God designed sexual intimacy for the expression of love and affection</u>. God has designed many ways for you to express love to your spouse. In fact, isn't this why you got married? You went to the altar because you loved your spouse deeply and you vowed to express this love for the rest of your life. The sexual relationship is the most intimate way

two people reveal their love for each other.

Notice what Scripture teaches about God's design for your sexual relationship: *"Let the husband render to his wife the affection due her, and likewise also the wife to her husband"* (1 Cor. 7:3). Paul declared that sex is one of the primary means in which to express affection for your spouse. It is rendering the affection that is *due* your mate because you pledged and vowed your love for the rest of your life. You promised to meet your loved one's needs spiritually, emotionally, and physically.

Likewise, Solomon's wife describes her affection for her husband as the underlying cause for her sexual passion. *"By night on my bed I sought the one I love"* (Song of Solomon 3:1). Notice, it was love that motivated the Shulamite to approach her husband for sex. This passage also reveals that she did not believe it was ungodly or unladylike to approach one's husband in this manner. She was only seeking the one she loved.

Where love is lacking between two people, the sexual relationship will always be a struggle. If sexual intimacy is an obligation, a hassle, or a duty, love and the goal of expressing affection is the missing ingredient. If you are going through the motions and hating every minute of it, you know that something has got to change. But how? The change must first begin in your heart by asking God for the love to give yourself to your spouse. Ask God to change your perception of this sacred act, so you see it as an opportunity to express your love and affection toward your spouse. Don't you desire to do more than just go through the motions? You can return to the intimacy you once had if you will allow God to change your inner attitude. Love can only be satisfying as you give it away and express it to another person. Ask Him to renew your love today. Then choose to begin expressing it to your spouse again. This attitude will become the inner power and motivation that brings the magic to the external act.

2. God designed the sexual relationship to bring you into oneness with your spouse. God said, *"Therefore man shall leave his father and mother and be joined to his wife, and they shall become one flesh"* (Gen. 2:24). When you come together in sexual union, there is an obvious physical oneness that occurs because you are literally joined together. You have come face-to-face to verbally and physically express your love to each other. The sexual act draws you together in the most intimate oneness that is possible to man. This is God's design and purpose.

But there is more than just a physical oneness that occurs when you join with your spouse in sexual relations. There is an emotional union as well. You will never discover a more intimate way in which to communicate your emotional commitment and affection. Your tender words of desire and companionship would not be shared as often if there were no sexual union in marriage. God has designed this time you spend together to be an emotionally charged exchange of love.

Furthermore, you come into a *spiritual* oneness as you grow in your expression of love sexually. When you love your mate physically, it produces a spiritual unity within your relationship because you are following His commands to express your love in this manner. Paul said that all believers who walk in love are standing fast *"in one spirit, with one mind striving together for the faith of the gospel"* (Phil. 1:27). He goes on to say that if these believers loved each other, they would experience the *"fellowship of the Spirit"* (Phil 2:1). Because of their love and obedience to Him, they were becoming one spiritually, or as he describes, becoming *"of one accord"* (Phil. 2:2). If fellowship in the Spirit and being of one accord is the result of fellow believers loving one another, how much more does this occur when a husband and wife express their love together? This is the purpose the Father had in mind when He created the sexual union for married couples. He wanted them to come into oneness and to find a spiritual bond like no other.

Truly, sexual love produces a spiritual, emotional, and physical oneness that must be treasured and protected. This is why Paul warned about an adulterous relationship. *"Do you not know that your bodies are members of Christ? Shall I then take the members of Christ and make them members of a harlot? Certainly not! Or do you not know that he who is joined to a harlot is one body with her? For 'the two,' He says, 'shall become one flesh.' But he who is joined to the Lord is one spirit with Him. Flee sexual immorality...Or do you not know that your body is the temple of the Holy Spirit who is in you?...Therefore glorify God in your body and in your spirit which are God's"* (1 Cor. 6:15-20).

Paul clearly teaches that it does make a difference what you do with your body because your body is the temple of the Holy Spirit. When you are joined to the Lord, you become one spirit with Him. If you join your body with a harlot, you are likewise joining yourself spiritually to that person. Therefore, God warns you to keep yourself exclusively for your spouse. This is God's design for the sexual relationship and why He created it for marriage alone. His plan is to draw you to a physical, emotional, and spiritual bond with the one you love.

3. <u>God designed the sexual relationship so that you could give and receive pleasure</u>. This thought causes some Christians great trouble because many consider any kind of enjoyment as unspiritual or against the will of God. The concept that God would design the sexual union for pleasure is totally foreign to them. They read passages that describe people in the last days as being *"lovers of pleasures rather than lovers of God,"* and

they assume that all pleasure is evil (2 Tim. 3:4). Does this passage declare that all pleasure is evil or that it is forbidden in the marriage bed? Not at all. This passage is drawing a contrast between those who love pleasure *rather than* having a love for God. Scripture is clear; if a person lives for pleasure he is dead while he lives (1 Tim. 5:6). However, God desires for us to find a godly and lawful exchange of pleasure in the marriage bed.

Solomon describes the biblical plan for sexual pleasure in marriage. He says, *"Let your fountain be blessed, and rejoice in the wife of your youth. As a loving deer and a graceful doe, let her breasts satisfy you at all times; and always be enraptured with her love"* (Prov. 5:18, 19).

God desired the sexual relationship to be a pleasurable experience that would encourage couples to regularly come together to express their affection and oneness. If God hadn't created lovemaking to be a pleasurable experience between a man and wife, few would probably engage in it. The most important word in this text is *enraptured,* which means "to be intoxicated." The metaphor is a powerful one. The picture is of exhilaration and euphoria. Clearly, this is God's desire for your sexual relationship because His Word declares it.

We also see this same description of pleasure in the sexual union between Solomon and his wife. The Shulamite describes her sexual relationship with Solomon as her *"delight,"* that which *"sustained"* and *"refreshed"* her (Song of Solomon 2:3-5). Solomon speaks of their lovemaking in the same way. *"You have ravished my heart, my sister, my spouse; you have ravished my heart with one look of your eyes, with one link of your necklace. How fair is your love, my sister, my spouse! How much better than wine is your love..."* (4:9, 10). These two were intoxicated with the pleasure of each other. It was better than any effect that wine could render.

Scripture is clear on this issue, revealing God's heart and mind. There is nothing dirty, ungodly, or unholy about the enjoyment of the marriage bed. Even common sense dictates that God engineered your body for enjoyable intercourse within marriage. Do you think that God would create you with the physical construction to experience pleasure in your marriage bed, and then turn around and tell you that it was evil or dirty? That would be illogical. He is blessed when you enjoy each other.

4. <u>God designed the sexual relationship for marriage to bring forth children in the context of a loving relationship between two people</u>. There is a reason why I have left this point until last. It is because children are the natural fruit of this loving intimacy between a man and his wife.

Children are not the primary purpose for your sexual relationship, they are only the by-product. If children were the primary purpose of your sexual union, then children would result every time you came together. But children are not the fruit of every sexual experience, revealing that the primary purpose of your union is to allow you the opportunity to express your affection for each other. When you do produce a child from your "becoming one flesh," they are literally your own flesh and blood, twenty-three chromosomes from each parent.

That is how it was from the beginning. *"Now Adam knew Eve his wife, and she conceived and bore Cain..."* (Gen. 4:1). The fruit of your love is a child that becomes an additional loved one in your family. If this child comes into a home where the parents don't love each other or enjoy expressing their affection for each other, there is something missing. Love not only nurtures your relationship with your spouse, it also nurtures your relationship with your children. In other words, your children benefit directly from your love affair with your spouse. Don't make your children the primary focus. A harmonious marital relationship will create the best environment for your child's growth and maturity.

These are the principal reasons why God has created the sexual relationship for marriage. Good sex is a fundamental key to your overall relationship of oneness and the expression of love. If there are problems in your sexual relationship, don't let them go unresolved. These problems won't go away by themselves. Remember, attack the problem, not the person. God created sex and He can show you how to work through every problem you are having. Let's look at some of the common problem areas and how to deal with them.

Dealing With Common Sexual Problems

Sexual problems and adjustments are as common as any other problem in marriage. In fact, I can almost guarantee that you will have a conflict in your sexual relationship at some time in your marriage simply because you are two different people. However, most people don't like to talk about sexual problems until they are at the breaking point. This should not be the case, but it is. The fact is, the sexual problems that we experience are usually all very similar because we are all very much alike. Paul said, *"No temptation has overtaken you except such as is common to man; but God is faithful, who will not allow you to be tempted beyond what you are able, but with the temptation will also make the way of escape, that you may be able to bear it"* (1 Cor. 10:13). The problems you experience today will be experienced by your neighbor in the future. Yet many people think they are the only ones who are having problems, and this is simply not true.

Another important truth from this verse is that God is faithful and will enable you to find a solution or a way of escape. He wants you to find a way to deal with the problems you are having and to solve them. See if you can't find yourself in one or more of these dilemmas.

1. *"My spouse has little attraction or desire for me."* Why would this happen? There are many possible reasons. Let's look at the most common ones.

    A. There is little attraction or desire because of unresolved conflicts with your spouse. This is the most common reason for your spouse losing their sexual desire for you. When you are resentful and bitter toward your partner, it is very difficult, if not impossible, to give or receive love. If you have no desire for sexual contact with your spouse, or they have no desire for you, this is the first place to look for the cause. If you dislike sex it may simply be because you dislike your partner for the things they have done to you. You can't express sexual love toward someone to whom you are angry and resentful. Love and bitterness can't come out of the same fountain. James asked the question, *"Does a spring send forth fresh water and bitter from the same opening?"* (James 3:11). The answer to this question is no. You must resolve your conflicts, which will naturally translate into your sexual relationship as well.

    B. There is little attraction or desire because you have a problem with the quality of the relationship with your spouse. It's very difficult to be physically intimate with someone with whom you have no relationship. If there is a lack of good communication, little caring or touching, no real spiritual agreement or emotional support from your spouse, there will naturally be a lack of intimacy. This general void in the relationship will, of course, affect you in the bedroom as well. Remember how important friendship is in building this intimacy. You can't have intimacy with your spouse without real friendship. Remember what the Shulamite said attracted her to her husband? *"This is my beloved, and this is my friend..."* (Song of Solomon 5:16). Are you friends with your spouse? If not, begin to work at this aspect of your marriage and the physical intimacy will grow between you.

    C. There is little attraction or desire because of past hurtful experiences. Many men and women don't see the sexual union as a loving act but as a violent one because of past sexual abuse. If there has been sexual abuse as a child or as an adult, you must be sure you have fully resolved these issues before God. How can you be sure you have fully resolved them? Ask yourself, Do I have resentment toward God for this abuse? Do I still have resentment toward the person or persons that committed the offense? Do I feel guilty for anything in connection with this violence? If you answered yes to any of these questions, the issue is not yet fully resolved. Bitterness and guilt are two clear indicators that this is not a past issue and that it still holds you today. I would encourage you to get some biblical counseling from your pastor regarding how to fully forgive and put this issue behind you once and for all. Ask God to help you understand the biblical steps to a real solution. Without fully resolving these past painful experiences, your sexual relationship will be tainted and your perspective of sexual intimacy will be distorted.

Once you resolve the past, you will be able to build upon your present relationship. Your spouse didn't commit any violence against you, so don't make them pay the price. If you see the sexual relationship as unholy or dirty, let your thinking be transformed by what God says about sex. Don't let your past experience or the opinion of others taint your perception. God ordained the marriage bed to be a beautiful exchange between two people who love each other. When He finished creating man and woman, He told them to go forth and multiply. He looked at His work and said that it was very good (Gen. 1:26-31). It is very important not to call dirty or evil that which God calls good. You must ask God to change your thinking so that it might be in harmony with His. Correct thinking will translate into correct attitudes and ultimately into correct living.

D. Sometimes there is little desire because of selfishness. As I have said many times in this book, selfishness is the underlying problem in any conflict. Sexual problems in marriage almost always have some degree of selfishness as one of the elements that couples must battle. Selfishness is the opposite of love, and the expression of love is what makes your sexual relationship fulfilling. If you are the one with little desire for your spouse, stop and consider if this is the problem. Would you simply rather not be bothered by your spouse for sex? Would you rather be doing something else? Would you rather be sleeping or staying up late reading? Are your mate's sexual advances just an inconvenience to you? If so, this is selfishness. Your partner should never be an inconvenience to you. If that is the case, your love is very shallow. Sometimes I have seen selfishness revealed when one partner declares, "I don't care what all those verses of Scripture say. I don't like sex and I'm not going to do it." This is obviously a person with a very hard heart who is selfishly making a choice to reject God's Word in favor of their own will.

If any of these thoughts have gone through your head, my suggestion would be to renew your relationship with the Lord. When there is a lack of love toward your mate, this is always the place to start. As I have said over and over again, your love relationship with Christ will directly affect your love relationship with your spouse. The more distant you are from God, the more distant you will be from your spouse. You can't give what you don't have. If you are in love with the Lord, you will have plenty of love for your mate. John said it this way: *"He who loves God must love his brother also"* (1 John 4:21) As you fall in love with Christ, you will demonstrate love toward your spouse. As you renew your intimacy with Christ, it will help you to be intimate with your loved one.

E. Sometimes sexual desire fades because of medications you are taking. Recent scientific studies have confirmed that prescription and non-prescription medications can have a profound effect upon your sexual desire. If you are taking any medication on a regular basis, you should consult your doctor about the possible effects this medication may have on your sexual desire or potency.

F. Sometimes desires are different because of hormonal differences. Sexual development and drive in men and women are directly affected by the male hormone testosterone and the female hormone estrogen and the level of these hormones in your blood. There is not a lot you can do about differing levels within a marriage. However, knowing this fact can keep you from some fundamental misconceptions. One spouse may say, "All you want me for is sex." Or, on the other side of the fence, "Why don't you desire me? Do you even care?" Both of these statements reveal a possible misconception. Could the problem be simply the affect of a hormone raging inside your spouse, or the lack thereof? It may not have anything to do with how much your mate loves you or of seeing you as some sex object. The conflict may simply be caused by the amount of hormones flowing through your mate's blood stream.

This does not negate the fact that you or your spouse must still choose to love by initiating sex or restraining yourself. But having this knowledge of hormones will help to understand why there is such a difference in your sexual desires.

2. *"We argue constantly about how often to have sex."* Frequency of sex is another very common problem in which couples must find a loving compromise. Scripture does speak to this problem specifically and gives a very workable solution. To find this solution you must understand the biblical truths that will enable you to take the correct action.

    A. Understand that your body is not your own. Do you truly understand and believe this truth? When you got married, you gave up the sole right and authority over your body. This is what the Bible teaches. *"The wife does not have authority over her own body, but the husband does. And likewise the husband does not have authority over his own body, but the wife does"* (1 Cor. 7:4). When you made your marriage covenant before God, you agreed to give your spouse sexual access to your body. You gave up the right to refuse your spouse once and for all. This is another part of what it means to become one flesh with your spouse. Both husband and wife have equal access to the other's body.

    B. Understand that you can't deprive each other of sexual relations. Paul further explains, *"Do not deprive one another except with consent for a time, that you may give yourselves to fasting and prayer; and come together again so that Satan does not tempt you because of your lack of self-control"* (1 Cor. 7:5). Notice that this is the direct command of Scripture. Those who are refusing sexual relations to their spouse are disobeying the clear teaching of God's Word. Paul declares the only permissible way you may stop having sexual relations for a time is by agreement with your partner. When there is a question over frequency of sexual relations, the solution is found in finding a mutual agreement. The decision is not dictated by one partner, but by finding a loving agreement through compromise. This is the way all decision-making should take place in a marriage.

    C. Love is the solution. Love is the solution to any problem in your marriage, including problems relating to the frequency of sexual relations. Love should naturally motivate you to seek a solution and compromise with your spouse. I have counseled couples that are so different and far apart in their sexual drives that I have sometimes wondered why God would ever put two people like that together. When you meet a couple with one partner who wants to have sex every night and the other who couldn't care less if he or she ever had sex again, you can't help but wonder how could this ever work? How could these two ever find a compromise in which they can both live together in harmony in their sexual relationship? The answer is simple: God put two such diverse people together so they will learn how to love.

For those of you who have a very low sexual drive, love will always cause you to meet your partner's needs even when you don't have a lot of feeling or initial desire. Once you begin to lovingly give to your spouse sexually, just the love you are expressing will make it a satisfying time. This will be your compromise of love to give. For those of you who have a very high sexual drive, love will also enable you not to force your will on your spouse. You will learn to compromise by lovingly giving up your right because you care for your mate. Love will, at times, restrain your actions and desires, and at other times will motivate you to take actions that are contrary to your feelings and desires. I have seen this solution work in many marriages. People who are so different in their sexual desires learn how to love each other in this intimate area of their marriage. They learn how to give when it is against their feelings simply because they choose to love.

If you are struggling with the issue of how often to have relations, sit down and calmly discuss your needs with your mate. Find a mutual agreement about how often you will have relations together. Then ask God for the love to restrain your desires or the love to respond when you don't feel like it. It is equally difficult either way. Yet the Holy Spirit is very able to rule over you and motivate you to act lovingly if you will seek His help.

3. *"There is no passion in our lovemaking. It's just routine."* Routine is a part of life that you must deal with every day. It can be very helpful in order to accomplish a task that you want to repeat. However, when routine enters a personal relationship there can be certain problems. When we considered romance, we saw that routine can destroy the excitement very quickly between two people. This is also true in your sexual life. Let me give you an example of what I mean. Think of the most enjoyable meal you could ever have, including all your favorite foods. But if you had this same meal every night for the next month, wouldn't you get tired

of those foods and cry out for a little variety? Absolutely, because you know there are plenty of other foods in the market that you enjoy and would love to eat. Obviously, we would never get into such a rut as this in our eating habits. Why do people ever allow it to happen in their sexual life? Does this really happen? Yes it does! Boredom in the bedroom is one of the most common sexual problems I have heard over the years in counseling. Couples seem to fall easily into this trap, having sexual relations in the same way, in the same place, week after week and year after year. This kills the excitement and desire of your sexual relationship.

The Bible reveals another example in the Song of Solomon. As you read the description of the sexual relationship between Solomon and his wife, what do you find? It reveals that they were very spontaneous and didn't fall into this trap. They made love together in their bed chambers (1:4; 3:1). They made love on a trip to Lebanon (4:8-10). They went up to their vineyards and made love out in the field (7:11,12). Solomon also refers to their sexual encounter under an apple tree (8:5). Yet the most interesting revelation of their passion is revealed in Song of Solomon 6:13-7:10. It appears from this passage that the Shulamite does a sensual dance for her husband prior to their lovemaking. She called it *"the dance of the double camp."* As Solomon watches her dance, he describes her body in graphic detail. It is quite clear from the text that his wife has little or nothing on at the time of her dance. Her movements are implied by his description of the curves of her thighs and her quickness like a gazelle (7:1,3). This is in the Bible! All these behaviors surely must have kept this marriage from being routine.

Now you may not feel comfortable doing a sensual dance for your spouse or making love under the stars in some field, but my point is this: biblical example reveals that the sexual relationship between a man and his wife is to be anything but boring. You need to apply these ideas to your own marriage and become a more creative lover. Use your imagination. I'm sure you can think of something to get your sexual relationship out of the rut. If you do, be assured that the spark and excitement will come back into your love life.

4. *"My spouse just doesn't satisfy me."* This problem usually comes from two basic problems that are easily remedied if both parties are willing to work at them.

First, when your spouse tells you that you are not satisfying them, many times this stems from a lack of understanding of the practical mechanics of sex. The simple remedy is to read some of the great Christian books out on the subject of sexual intimacy. Many couples I have given these books to have come back and acknowledged that they had never understood the things they were now learning. They have confessed to me they needed the instruction in physiology and general insight into how their partner is aroused. If you are unsatisfied in your sexual relationship, consider getting one of the good books out on the market today and do some homework. Some suggestions: *The Act of Marriage* by Tim LaHaye (Zondervan) or *Intended for Pleasure* by Dr. Ed Wheat (Revell).

Second, if your spouse tells you that you are not satisfying them, this problem can also result from a simple lack of communication. Sex is a very sensitive issue. Many couples are reluctant to talk about the problems, especially if they are not being satisfied by their mate. However, without communication this problem cannot be solved. The solution is to tell your spouse what is pleasurable and what is not, even if you have to communicate this while you are actually having relations. This kind of freedom and communication is essential if you are to find the mutual satisfaction you desire. Your spouse would be only too willing to do what you ask, if they just knew what you were thinking. You must tell your mate if you want something to change. Why merely endure something that is not pleasurable to you? Yet I am amazed at how many couples don't talk about these things with each other. They just struggle day after day unhappy and unsatisfied. This ought never to happen in the marriage bed.

A satisfying sexual relationship takes lots of love, communication, understanding, and practice. Give your mate the understanding of what is pleasurable to you in your marriage bed. Remember, don't only be negative in your reproofs, "I don't like that." Rather, give positive encouragement such as "I like it when you _____." This gives your mate a specific action to take the next time you are together instead of just feeling put off. Remember that your requests must be mutually agreed upon. This is the biblical command.

God wants to bless your sexual relationship. Don't miss the joys of this vital area of your relationship. Study Scripture on the subject and allow the Lord to transform your thinking to be in harmony with His.

Group Discussion Questions
1. What differences can you observe between the biblical purpose of the sexual relationship and what the world teaches?
2. Why is it so difficult for husbands and wives to talk about this area of their relationship?

19

BUILDING SELF-DISCIPLINE

"I discipline my body and bring it into subjection,
lest, when I have preached to others,
I myself should become disqualified" 1 Cor. 9:27

Over the last eighteen chapters, I have discussed a multitude of issues with you that are essential to finding the oneness and companionship that God has ordained for your marriage. In some of these issues you needed only some simple encouragement, while in others you needed to make significant changes. However, right now I am concerned about those behaviors in which you need serious changes. What will bring about the changes needed in your life? What will enable you to keep the commitments and promises you've made to your spouse? What will cause you to leave a sinful behavior behind and press on to obey a righteous one? What enables you to achieve the lasting goal of change? The answer to these questions is *self-discipline.*

The lack of self-discipline is one of the hidden problems in most marriages because it is the fundamental problem in almost every person's life. Some individuals struggle more with it than others. But, I have come to believe that it is a major factor when I hear the anger and anguish of one spouse who calls me on the phone and says, "The counseling session was great last time, but my partner didn't do one thing that we agreed upon in your office." Often in subsequent visits when I ask if any action was taken over the problem, the response is, "Well, no I didn't have time," or some other excuse. After hearing these responses over and over again, I have come to the conclusion that lack of personal discipline is a major problem in seeing a marriage change for the better. One thing is clear, if your marriage is to change, then you must discipline yourself to change. Fixing any problem will never happen by itself. It will only occur when you take dramatic steps to discipline yourself to righteousness.

How about you? Is this your problem? Do you make commitments to your spouse and then fail to follow through on your promise? This could range from very simple problems such as keeping the house cleaner to staying within the financial budget or calling if you are going to be late coming home from work. The more complex and difficult issues include controlling your anger, spending the time to communicate, asking your spouse for prayer, or doing devotions with your children. In order to experience real and lasting change, each of these issues must be met with self-discipline and self-control. Being self-disciplined is what causes you to follow through with what you know is right or what you have promised to do. Discipline is the key to why you don't go back to the old sinful and selfish behavior, and why you continue to walk in new, godly behavior.

Some of you may think this is not a problem for you at all, specifically because you may be a very disciplined person in most areas of your life. You manage your time well. You can get things done in an orderly manner. You are focused and undistracted in reaching your goals. Yet, at the same time you may be completely undisciplined in other areas of your life such as failing to read your Bible or pray regularly, struggling with lust or anger, failing to bridle your critical tongue, or not controlling your thought life. If this is the case, you will appear on the outside to be very disciplined, but in reality, you are a person who struggles greatly with other issues. I believe all of us struggle with self-discipline in one way or another. The area where you need self-discipline is easy to find. Ask yourself where you are continually failing in your life. This will always be a self-control and self-discipline issue. The question is, do you really believe that this is an issue you should deal with right now, or will you wait until mounting conflicts force you to deal with it?

The Importance of Discipline

To effectively deal with the problem of discipline, it is essential that you understand the importance that the Bible places upon it. Without being convinced that this is an important issue, you will simply pass this chapter off as the ramblings of some legalist. However, God's Word declares that self-discipline and self-control are issues that are very important for your life. When you perceive the significance that God gives to this topic, you will realize that it is not something that you can put off until tomorrow. Let's look at some of these encouragements and see what Scripture reveals about this requirement for your life.

1. <u>Discipline is the goal and purpose of God's Word</u>. The apostle Paul wrote to Timothy concerning the many conflicts he was experiencing and gave him a plan to help overcome them. When Paul was finishing his encouragement to Timothy he declared this fundamental goal: *"All Scripture is given by inspiration of God, and is profitable for doctrine, for reproof, for correction, for instruction in righteousness, that the man of God may be complete, thoroughly equipped for every good work"* (2 Tim. 3:16, 17). The word *instruction* literally means "to train or discipline."

Paul was explaining how powerful the Word of God is in the work of changing people. The Word has the ability to convict and illuminate one's attitudes and motivations, effecting an inward as well as an outward correction. As a person responds to this inward conviction, outward change results. Each time the choice is made to obey this conviction and correction, we are being disciplined and trained in righteousness toward a profoundly new way of life. Ultimately, this change is what thoroughly equips a person for any work to which God has called him simply because he has disciplined himself to obey the conviction and correction of the Spirit of God.

Self-discipline is the ultimate goal and purpose of God's Word in your life. Paul reveals in this passage the means, the method, and the expectation that God has for you. His purpose is to totally transform you into a man or woman He can use for His glory. The lack of self-discipline is not some insignificant flaw that you need not worry about; it is a critical issue for every believer who desires to grow and mature in Christ. This is why Jesus called those who were serious about following Him *disciples*, meaning "one who is a disciplined learner."

Personal discipline is also a critical issue for your marriage because your relationship is fundamentally between two people who desire to live in harmony with each other. If you are undisciplined and out of control in any area of your personal life, it will affect your marriage as a whole.

2. Discipline is the only way to become a godly man or woman. In Paul's first letter to Timothy, he explained that discipline should be the priority of his life. Young Timothy had to deal with many false doctrines that were promoting ungodliness in the church. Paul warned him to reject these teachings and only accept the ones that would promoted true godliness. *"But reject profane and old wives' fables, and exercise yourself toward godliness. For bodily exercise profits a little, but godliness is profitable for all things, having promise of the life that now is and of that which is to come"* (1 Tim. 4:7, 8).

The word translated *exercise* literally means "to train or discipline oneself" as an athlete does for the Olympic Games. Paul employed a vivid analogy in order to illustrate precisely what discipline means and how it occurs. An athlete must train every day to strengthen his body for the ultimate test in the competition that lies ahead. He daily denies himself of many normal and lawful activities so that he might excel in his event. The comparison applies perfectly to our spiritual lives and specifically to our marriages. If a motivated individual would discipline himself this intently to succeed in an athletic event for worldly accolades, how much more should a believer train and discipline himself to excel in godliness and reap the benefits in his marriage? Godliness is profitable for all things and promises you God's very life and power to utilize in your lifestyle at home. This is what your marriage needs! It needs two self-disciplined and godly people who are filled with the power of the Holy Spirit, equipping them for every good work. Be assured, two godly and self-disciplined individuals will always enjoy a successful marriage.

3. <u>The lack of discipline can destroy your life</u>. I often speak to those who cannot comprehend why they have fallen into adultery, are given to substance abuse, or in some way have destroyed their lives. The fundamental key to each of these problems is the lack of self-discipline, which subtly, but very effectively, destroys lives. Paul valued discipline as a key in his own life to prevent himself from falling into sin. Using the image of an athlete again, he declares that *"everyone who competes for the prize is self-controlled in all things. Now they do it to obtain a perishable crown, but we for an imperishable crown."* Then he explains *how* to attain it. *"I discipline my body and bring it into subjection, lest, when I have preached to others, I myself should become disqualified"* (1 Cor. 9:25-27).

What insight this passage gives us into the secret of Paul's success! He knew the importance of controlling his bodily drives if he was to ever reach the victor's coronation. Do you believe that self-control is this important for your own life? If you do, then you must begin to deal with the areas in your life that are out of control. What are you doing with your undisciplined thought life, your spending habits, your lack of fellowship, your eating habits, the use of time, your harsh and critical tongue, and your explosive anger? Are you keeping commitments and promises to others? These are just some of the issues that will directly affect your spiritual health and marriage. Your battle in these and other areas of your life will always be one of discipline. It's a struggle to be self-controlled and to keep your drives and selfish desires under the control of the Holy Spirit. Paul brought his body under subjection, and without this action on your part as well, you will disqualify yourself and never reach the goals you are striving for in your life and marriage.

I talk to couples every month who are on the brink of divorce, and this is one of the key issues that plagues their marriages. You have, no doubt, observed the problems in your friends' lives that result from the lack of self-discipline. If you don't want to end up like one of them, discipline your body and your mind. Bring them into subjection. Paul explained how this could be done when he wrote to the church at Rome. *"If you live according to the flesh you will die; but if by the Spirit you put to death the deeds of the body, you will live"* (Rom. 8:13).

The answer lies in your surrender to the Spirit of God. Your drives are stronger than your will to resist them. You need a strength and power greater than yourself in order to overcome. As you invite God's Spirit to come and take full possession, you will discover the desire and the power to put your natural self to death. As you do, self's hold ceases to control you, only to be replaced by God's joy and peace. Will God really do this if you ask? Listen to the promise of Jesus: *"If you then, being evil, know how to give good gifts to your children, how much more will your heavenly Father give the Holy Spirit to those who ask Him"* (Luke 11:13). He *longs* to bless you with the victory of His Holy Spirit over your flesh. But you will never know how much until you ask! Ask Him right now to begin to put those old ways and old desires to death, and you will also begin to experience the life He promises.

4. <u>God wants to conform you into His image</u>. It is clear from even a superficial reading of Scripture that God has a *"determined counsel,"* a foreordained plan for the world that He intends to fulfill to completion (Acts 2:23). In a very structured and orderly manner, He brings every detail into line with His purposes and will. God's plan for man's salvation was highly disciplined, as is evidenced in Jesus' determined campaign against the works of the devil when He walked this earth. It is seen in His agony in the garden, in His silent and defenseless strategy before Pontius Pilate and the Roman guards, and in His bursting forth from the tomb as final victor. God's purpose and will to save all of mankind had been planned, predicted in the Scriptures, and then ultimately fulfilled in cooperation with the Son of God. You could say that God planned His work and then worked His plan. God declared the coming of the Messiah and then *"when the fullness of time had come, God sent forth His Son..."* (Gal. 4:4).

Why did He do this? Because God performs every word that He has promised, no matter what men do. Even if men rebel against Him, the Father will fulfill His sovereign plan apart from them. Concerning God's predictions for rebellious Babylon, Jeremiah declared that *"every purpose of the Lord shall be performed"* (Jer. 51:29). This prediction would, of course, include His judgment of their rebellion against His will for their lives. Ezekiel also declared God's purpose in fulfilling His Word: *"you shall know that I, the Lord, have spoken it and performed it..."* (Ez. 37:14). When God fulfills His Word regarding man, He is drawing our attention to His faithfulness. What He has spoken, He has performed. Faithfulness to His word is the best definition of His disciplined character.

God also wants to make you this kind of person. He wants to make you into a man or woman who, when speaking, promising, or making a commitment, will remain faithful to it. God would not declare His desire to bring you into a place of disciplined righteousness, and then not allow you to reach that goal. He wants to make you like himself in every aspect of your life, and He will accomplish it if you will acknowledge your need to change. Will you surrender to the teaching of God's Word over each issue you are struggling with right now? As you surrender each issue to the control of the Holy Spirit, He will empower you to walk in a disciplined manner.

WHAT KEEPS YOU LIVING AN UNDISCIPLINED LIFE?

Many people tell me they are aware of their undisciplined lifestyle and that it is destroying their marital relationship. However, they really don't understand why they continue to live that way. In order to deal directly with the causes of this behavior, you must know what they are, then you will be able to strike at the root of the problem. Merely attacking the symptoms only results in more failure and frustration. Don't simply snip the fruit off the branch; cut at the root of the tree. Therefore, what actually keeps you living in an undisciplined manner?

1. An undisciplined lifestyle is a choice to live selfishly by yielding to your sinful nature. Don't you realize that your human nature rebels at the very thought of restraint or discipline of any kind? Have you sensed that battle raging inside even as you have been reading this chapter? This is your sinful nature fighting against the law of God, which commands restraint and discipline. Every fiber of your being, every part of your sinful nature resists the control of God's law, which governs the new nature God has given you. Paul describes this struggle between the fleshly nature of man and the law of God in this way: *"The sinful mind is hostile to God. It does not submit to God's law, nor can it do so. Those controlled by the sinful nature cannot please God"* (Rom. 8:7, 8 NIV). This battle goes on inside every believer. It's a battle of who will control you, God the Holy Spirit or your sinful nature?

Paul explains further: *"For the sinful nature desires what is contrary to the Spirit, and the Spirit what is contrary to the sinful nature. They are in conflict with each other, so that you do not do what you want"* (Gal. 5:17, NIV). God makes it clear in this passage exactly what it is that keeps people from doing what they want and should do. When you yield to your sinful nature, you are not disciplining yourself to righteousness. The two are mutually exclusive. Your flesh will always attempt to drive you to excess and self-indulgence in one or more areas of your life. This was the problem with the Pharisees. Jesus observed that even though they outwardly appeared righteous before men, inside they were *"full of extortion and self-indulgence"* (Matt. 23:25). This happens simply because your sinful nature is stronger than your will to resist it (that is, without the power of the Holy Spirit). Even Paul revealed his personal struggle when he said, *"For to will is present with me, but how to perform what is good I do not find"* (Rom. 7:18). So, take heart, you are not alone, everyone experiences this battle.

This undisciplined lifestyle and battle with the sinful nature is also a key source of conflict in marriage. I hear people lament the same words of Paul every week in marriage counseling. When I encourage a wife who is struggling to keep the house organized, she will say, "Every day I try, but somehow it never gets done. I guess I just get distracted with other things." Or, when I ask a husband to make up a budget to control his spending, I often hear, "I don't want to be bound by a budget. It's too restricting." Anger, laziness, and living beyond our means are all indications that we are losing the battle between our sinful natures and the will of God. When you yield to your selfish desires, all self-discipline goes out the window. And all hope of ever changing these problems goes with it.

2. <u>An undisciplined lifestyle is choosing to obey your feelings over what you know is right</u>. This was the cause of the fall of man. When Adam and Eve were in the garden, God commanded them to eat from any of the trees of the garden with the exception of one. *"So when the woman saw that the tree was good for food, that it was pleasant to the eyes, and a tree desirable to make one wise, she took of its fruit and ate"* (Gen. 3:6). Eve chose to yield to what she considered pleasant and desirable, as opposed to disciplining herself to what she knew was right and what the law of God had commanded. What is pleasant and desirable is always what is the easiest and what feels good at the time. This, of course, was a fatal choice. Every time you yield to what is merely pleasant and feels good, disobeying God's commands, you, too, are making a fatal choice.

Do you make decisions based on the feelings of the moment because you are a feeling-oriented person? Do you battle with what you desire as opposed to what God commands? Do you choose to go with what is pleasant and easy rather than do something that is uncomfortable? Resisting your selfish desires will always be uncomfortable. However, the alternative is to grieve the Holy Spirit and surrender His joy and peace for constant failure. The Holy Spirit is drawing you, and your fleshly desires are drawing you. Which will you yield to? Will you live your life ruled by feelings or will you become a Spirit-oriented and commandment-oriented person? Remember, you actually find your life by losing it.

3. <u>An undisciplined lifestyle is choosing to allow circumstances to rule you</u>. Life is filled with all kinds of adverse circumstances, and no one is immune. There are financial trials, job trials, and children trials (just to name a few) that each require you to make choices. Will you do what is right, control yourself, yield to His Spirit, and obey God's commands, or will you choose to give in to the circumstances, exploding in anger and disobedience? If you are a person given to living by your feelings or acting selfishly, you will choose to allow the circumstances to control your emotions and decisions. You do this because it's just easier than battling your feelings and the difficult circumstances you are facing.

Solomon understood this tendency in man when he said, *"The slothful man says, 'There is a lion outside! I shall be slain in the streets!' "* (Prov. 22:13). In other words, the slothful man found a supposed circumstance to use as an excuse for not taking the correct action. He utilized the adverse circumstance (the lion in the street) as the reason he was looking for to free him from his commitment. It's just easier to stay home than to tackle the problem. In reality, it was his laziness that kept him from the right action. The circumstances were just a good excuse.

Is this the way you deal with your marriage problems? Do you use circumstances as an excuse to shirk responsibility toward your mate? If this is true, the change you desire in your marriage will never occur. Change will only result from disciplined and committed giving on the part of both partners.

Your spouse can usually see right through these excuses. As you continue to act in this manner, your spouse will lose respect for you and question your commitment to real change in the marriage. Eventually your mate will lose hope that any real change is possible.

4. <u>Don't blame others for your undisciplined lifestyle</u>. You cannot use your upbringing as a child, your friends, or your spouse as an excuse for why you are not a disciplined person. This is one of the most common things I hear in counseling. *If my friends wouldn't tempt me, then I would be able to do better. If my parents only would have raised me differently. If my wife would just do what she is supposed to do...* These are all circumstantial excuses in which you are shifting the blame to a situation or another person. This attitude only prolongs any solution to your problems. Yes, other people have affected and will influence you, but they cannot be blamed for your behavior today. You are ultimately responsible. Be honest with yourself. Other people cannot force you to live selfishly or righteously. Your choices are your own!

I have counseled with many people over the past twenty-seven years from all possible backgrounds and have found children from undisciplined homes grow up to be very godly, productive individuals. I have also seen the reverse. This teaches me one glaring fact. Each of these children have been blessed by the Creator with their own free will. The singular issue that determines the success or failure in a person's life will be the choices that are made today, not the influences of the past. The same is true for you in the context of marriage. You must accept personal responsibility for your attitudes and actions and make the right choices today.

In addition, God spoke many years ago about those who blame their parents for their personal sin. He used the prophet Ezekiel to inform the Jews that this was a wrong concept. The people had started using a proverb that captured this thinking: *"The fathers have eaten sour grapes, and the children's teeth are set on edge"* (Ez. 18:2). In other words, they believed that if fathers took an action that was wrong (eating sour grapes), their children would be punished (their teeth set on edge). However, God put His foot down concerning this false concept. *"As I live, says the Lord God, you shall no longer use this proverb in Israel"* (Ez. 18:3).

God further explained why He rejected this proverb: *"All souls are Mine; the soul of the father as well as the soul of the son is Mine; the soul who sins shall die"* (Ez. 18:4). God claims ownership over every human soul. Each person will stand before Him as an individual and each will bear his own responsibility for his own sin. Therefore, the Father will not allow you to blame your personal failures or defects of personality on your parents or anyone else. You must take responsibility.

You also see this truth illustrated when you follow the examples of parents and children given in Scripture. Children are free to choose their own path in life. For example, the godly King Jotham produced an ungodly son, Ahaz. Ahaz in turn had a godly son Hezekiah, who in turn had an ungodly son Manasseh. Then Manasseh's son, Amon, followed in his fathers footsteps and did evil in the sight of the Lord. But Amon's son Josiah turned from his father's evil and lived a righteous life. See: 2 Chronicles chapters 28-34.

Each of these examples proves one thing: no matter what your family background has been, you have the ultimate responsibility for your own actions. You are the one who chooses the path of your life. Therefore, don't blame your parents or anyone else for your undisciplined or ungodly lifestyle. God doesn't accept the excuse. He holds you responsible for your own actions and the person you have become. Yes, others have an influence upon your life, but that can never be used as an excuse for not making the right choices today. God declared through the prophet Isaiah that we are to *"choose what pleases Me,"* (Is. 56:4) because He wants us to experience life and freedom from self.

Will you make that choice now in your heart? Will you commit this part of your life to God and ask Him for His help to change your undisciplined life? No matter how long you have lived an undisciplined life, God can start right where you are today. All it takes is your willingness and invitation to begin the work. If you are willing, what steps should you take?

How Can You Make the Change?

Let me say right from the beginning that change from an undisciplined lifestyle will not be easy or comfortable. There is no easy road to a godly and disciplined life. If it was easy everyone would be living this way. But it is *easier* to live a disciplined and godly life than it is to live in rebellion and to experience the confusion and conflict that results. Be assured, the fruit of a disciplined life will result in harmony in your home.

It will also be much easier to walk with the Lord because you won't be battling His conviction all the time. When you rebel against God and His purposes, it is like swimming against the current in a stream. It is always much easier to swim with the current than against it. Self-discipline is like swimming with the current.

How can you begin to make the changes that are necessary for a disciplined life? If you follow these steps, it will change your life and your marriage forever!

1. <u>First, determine where you are specifically failing in the discipline department</u>. You can't change something if you don't know what you need to change. I encourage you to make a list of all the things you have promised to change, either to God or to your partner, and have failed to do so. Also list those areas in which your spouse has asked you to make changes and you have selfishly refused to do so. These issues will usually be the same things that you argue about constantly.

2. <u>Next, determine which area is the biggest issue on that list</u>. This is the one you want to deal with first. This area is where the greatest encouragement and help is needed in your marriage. Change in this area will cause your spouse to have the greatest hope that something is finally changing. This will also provoke your mate to begin to make changes in their own life.

3. <u>Study the Scriptures on this issue to determine what to do about it</u>. As you study the Word of God on this issue, you will first gain God's perspective on this problem and learn the specific action that should be taken. Without God's insight, you will be groping in the dark. You need God's perspective because your offensive behavior may not be immoral. You may simply be battling with your mate over issues that are your own personal choices, in which case only compromise is needed. The Bible must be the final authority on all these questions. As you obey God, you are choosing to please Him.

I would suggest purchasing a good concordance in order to search the whole Bible on a specific topic. If you have a computer, there are many good programs available. As you understand what the Bible declares, then you will be able to take the appropriate action.

4. <u>Ask God for the conviction of the Holy Spirit to actually take action</u>. Once you determine what God's Word says about your specific problem, His conviction is needed to begin the actual change. Conviction is where God begins to work on the inside of you, confirming that what you are doing is wrong. He causes you to take the correct action and sustain it. Conviction is that still, small voice inside that says, "Don't do that. Remember your spouse doesn't like that?"

Inner conviction is what keeps you from merely jumping through hoops to appease your spouse. External changes never last because you need an inner motivation to keep you moving in the right direction. People fail in the commitments they have made simply because they are trying to reform themselves externally instead of allowing God to transform them from the inside out. Ask God to give you no rest until you make these changes in your behavior.

5. <u>Ask God for the power of His Spirit to actually make the corrections necessary</u>. Once you have the conviction to do what is right, you need the power to do it. How many times have you sincerely wished to do what is right but lacked the wherewithal to pull it off? Remember, your selfish and sinful nature is more powerful than your will to resist it. If you yield to the Spirit, self-discipline results (Gal. 5:23). Your sinful nature is stronger than you are, but the Spirit of God is stronger still. As you surrender more and more to God's power in your life, the more you will sense His strength to obey Him.

6. <u>Daily choose to take action over this one issue no matter how you are feeling</u>. This is where the real discipline occurs. As I have already explained, living by your feelings is one of the main causes of an undisciplined life. You must begin to choose daily to forsake feelings for what

you know is right, what God commands. As you obey the inner correction of the Spirit of God, you will naturally live above your feelings.

Remember I gave you the biblical plan for change earlier in this chapter? *"All Scripture is given by inspiration of God, and is profitable for doctrine, for reproof, for correction, for instruction in righteousness, that the man of God may be complete, thoroughly equipped for every good work"* (2 Tim. 3:16, 17). Remember the word for *instruction* in this text literally means "discipline." Pay special attention to the method Paul reveals here. The Bible is profitable to teach, reprove, convict, and correct you. It is ultimately what disciplines you to righteousness and equips you for every good work. This is God's method of changing you and making you a disciplined individual. It starts with the Word of God, His tool to prick your heart for change, and it is sustained and perfected by His Word. As you make those choices daily to obey and take the correct action, you become disciplined. It can be done if you truly want it done in your life. It's never too late to start if you will take these steps today.

7. <u>Proceed to the next issue on your list</u>. Only continue after you have experienced victory over the biggest problem; then apply the same steps to the remaining issues. Remember, this is not a quick fix. Becoming a disciplined person will take your entire lifetime. God is not done with you yet. He still has plenty of work to do in and through you. It is critical to be patient with your spouse and with yourself. God is extremely patient as He is working to fully transform your life to be like His. Let Him do it!

The result of a disciplined life will be a godly life! A godly life is what causes you to walk in harmony with your spouse and results in a happy and fulfilling marriage. If you disregard this chapter, lasting change will not occur in your relationship, and you will never find the satisfaction that you desire. God wants to discipline you to righteousness. Let Him begin the work!

Group Discussion Questions

1. Why is self-discipline such a difficult problem for most people?
2. Can you identify any specific arguments that occur directly because of a lack of self-discipline?
3. In other areas of your life, what benefits have you seen from choosing to discipline yourself? Think of a problem that you have overcome in the past and share your insights.

20

LOVE REKINDLED

"Be kindly affectionate to one another" Rom. 12:10

God's intention for your marriage is to kindle a blazing fire of love in your heart toward your spouse and to keep it burning passionately throughout the years of your life together. My aim and the entire purpose of this book has been to bring you and your mate to this end. The methods and principles I have covered in the previous chapters are the specific instruction regarding how your love may be rekindled. What I want to do in this chapter is to give you a simple analogy that will help you remember how to keep the love strong.

LOVE AS A FIRE

Scripture reveals that love between a man and his wife is like a fire. This is how the Shulamite, in the Song of Solomon, described her love relationship with her husband: *"For love is as strong as death, jealousy as cruel as the grave; its flames are flames of fire, a most vehement flame. Many waters cannot quench love, nor can the floods drown it"* (Song of Solomon 8:6, 7). What an incredibly vivid analogy the Shulamite draws for us that we might sense the power and depth of her love. It is evident that her love for Solomon was like a passionate fire in her heart. She compared her love to the two strongest forces she knew: the power of death and the power of the flame. These two metaphors effectively describe the strength and passion of marital love.

First, consider the comparison of love to the strength of death. This is an illustration that we can all understand because death is so powerful and all-consuming. Death takes everyone sooner or later because it pursues every creature and never gives up. Love similarly pursues its object. The tenacity of love was demonstrated by Christ to the point of death. His strong love drove Him to sacrifice His life for all of mankind. His love has always been resolute and persistent toward you, and He is still pursuing you right now. At this moment, His eyes are looking to and fro throughout the whole earth to find willing and loyal hearts toward which He might show himself strong (2 Chron. 16:9). Is your heart willing to receive this kind of love that pursues, persists, and never gives up? God wants to give you His strong, persistent love for your spouse; a love that is totally committed and is as strong as death.

Consider the second illustration of love as a fire that blazes in the soul. Our salvation, or our love relationship with God, is described as a fire or "*a lamp that burns*" in a person's being (Is. 62:1). This fire that He plants in your heart is primarily a love that God kindles in your soul toward Him. The great commandment declares, "*You shall love the Lord your God with all your heart, with all your soul, and with all your mind*" (Matt. 22:37). Your heart becomes a lamp that burns with the fire of His love. If this love exists in your heart toward God, then it must also be seen in your relationship with your spouse (1 John 4:21).

The idea of love like a vehement flame can also work against you, however. If you do not return your spouse's love, or if you violate his or her trust, love then becomes a vehement flame of *jealousy as cruel as the grave*. When you reject your spouse's love, there can be powerful repercussions. You get to decide which fruit of love you will experience; the cruelties of jealous love or the strength of giving love.

The Shulamite observed that "*many waters cannot quench love nor can floods drown it*" (Song of Solomon 8:7). This is because marital love is a commitment and not some fragile emotion that is easily destroyed. This strength of love is what causes a spouse to hold on and not give up when the marriage goes through tough times. I have watched many marriage partners struggle for years, patiently working with an unwilling spouse and praying for God to work in their life. Why? Because of the strength of love. We looked at this truth earlier, but it bears repeating. Love "*suffers long...bears all things, believes all things, hopes all things, endures all things*" (1 Cor. 13:4, 7). This is the kind of love I have seen endure the floods of many waters that are trying to drown out the fire of a marriage. Solomon's wife is not saying that the fire of marital love cannot *ever* be put out, just that it is very difficult to do so.

But you are probably thinking, "*If love is not easily quenched, why then has the fire gone out in my marriage?*" This is a very important question. If you are ever to have your love rekindled, you must understand exactly what is killing your love relationship.

What Causes Love to Die?

Each of you has stood by a fire at one time or another, and you know very well what causes a fire to die out. It happens in only one of two ways.

The first is by inaction. If you fail to watch, stir, and stoke the fire with more wood, what happens? The fire slowly goes out. You don't have to do anything for this to happen, and it is the same in your marriage. Failure to love and neglect in attentiveness to your spouse will surely kill your love relationship in a hundred different ways. When you consistently do little to show your love, the natural conclusion is that you really don't care much anymore.

Therefore, if you want your love to die, just keep doing nothing. It won't be long before the warmth of love between you dies out and the fire that once burned turns cold. Let's face it. It's easy to fail in the maintenance required to keep the embers glowing. For example, do you consistently recognize your mate's labor and accomplishments at work or at home? Do you thank your spouse when they please you by remembering some request? Have you neglected to pray regularly with and for your partner? When is the last time you had a date together alone or you did something special for no reason? Each of these actions will stoke the fire of your love and make it burn hot and bright. If you're forgetting these things, the fire will slowly go out!

Each forgotten action of love is simply a sign of laziness in your relationship. Scripture encourages you to love in a different manner. Paul says, *"Be kindly affectionate to one another... not lagging in diligence, fervent in spirit, serving the Lord "* (Rom. 12:10,11). The term *fervent in spirit* means "to be hot or to boil." Love is depicted here as a blazing fire burning inside your heart to serve the Lord, in direct contrast to a lack of diligence or laziness.

If God is encouraging us to be diligent in our love for our brother, how much more fervent should we be toward our mate? Are you showing the kindness and affection toward your spouse that you should? If you are, the fire between you will never go out. It only burns hotter, brighter, and more intense with each passing day.

There is another way to put a fire out besides your inaction. Your deliberate actions will also cause the fire to go out. You can take the deliberate action of throwing water on a fire, and it will surely die. It may not be put out with the first bucket, but if you keep it up you will surely put the fire out. What pours water on your relationship? Are you verbally abusive? Do you criticize or mock your partner when you talk together? Are you physically abusive? Are you refusing sexual relations to punish your loved one for lack of attentiveness to you? Do you act harshly or rudely? Have you been seen flirting with someone else? Have you broken your vows by adultery? These actions will surely quench the fire of love.

Paul taught that doing evil to others is what quenches the Holy Spirit in our lives. He exhorts, *"See that no one renders evil for evil to*

anyone...do not quench the Holy Spirit...abstain from every form of evil."
Evil done to any person quenches the Holy Spirit in your life because it is
sin and grieves the heart of God. These actions grieve your spouse as well
and quench the love between you! Read the entire context of 1 Thess.
5:15-22.

Likewise, even the actions that are not evil or sinful in and of themselves can quench the love in your relationship. If you are doing something that you know is offensive to your spouse and you continue to do it,
as Paul says *"you are no longer walking in love"* (Rom. 14:15). Paul explains this principle in relation to the Christians in Rome and their habit
of eating foods in front of other believers who considered them to be
unclean. Paul agreed that there was *"nothing unclean of itself"* but that
"it is evil for the man who eats with offense" (Rom. 14:14, 20). The issue
was not what was done, but the offensive way in which it was done.

Therefore, you must consider all of your actions toward your mate.
Are they obviously evil or immoral? Or, are there things you do that are
inherently good, but simply done in an offensive manner? Things like
insensitive or harsh communication or the total disregard for your mate's
requests. The deliberate actions you take will make a big difference as to
whether you are stoking the fire of love between you or throwing a bucket
of water on it.

If you want to make a change in your relationship, don't wait any
longer. Begin today! Your love relationship can only take so much neglect. The flames of your love can only take so much dousing with water
before the fire goes out. Stir up the embers by taking the action God
requires.

It should not be a mystery why love dies within a marriage. It's as
simple as either failing to maintain the fire or continuing to dowse it.
When these conditions go unresolved in your relationship, you slowly
drift apart and the love dies.

What is really sad is that some couples do both. They do nothing to
stoke the fire of their love, and they are dumping water regularly on what's
left. Be assured, this relationship will not last! How do you stop this downward cycle? Read on!

WHAT REKINDLES LOVE BETWEEN YOU?

Many times couples ask me, "Is there any hope to ever renew the
love we once had?" They wonder if they could ever rekindle the matri-
monial fire. They think, *Too much has happened that can't be changed.
We've thrown too much water on the fire for the love to ever return again.*

Not so! When you start questioning the possibility of renewing your love, it only proves that you are on the right path and reveals the willingness to try and find a solution. Yes, there is something you can do! There is hope! What should you do?

Each of the principles I am about to give you is a summary of what this book has tried to communicate. The theme of the previous chapters has been to explain exactly how to restore and build your love and companionship. I have seen marriages healed over and over by applying these same principles. Therefore, I would like to end briefly, by reviewing the key issues that will rekindle the fire of your love, which, in essence, is a brief summary of the theme of this book.

1. <u>Return to your first love with Christ</u>. I have never seen a marriage that was in trouble where the two individuals involved weren't in need of spiritual renewal. Where there are unresolved conflicts, there will always be resentment. Where there is resentment, there is unforgiveness. Where there is unforgiveness, there is always a hardness of heart. With these attitudes inside, a person can't help but struggle in his relationship with God. You can't say you love God and hate your spouse at the same time (1 John 4:20). The hardness you have in your heart toward your mate will naturally bring a distance in your relationship with God, and this destroys any possibility for change. Jesus said, "*Without me you can do nothing*" (John 15:5). If you desire to rekindle your love relationship with your spouse, you need to return to your first love with Christ (Rev. 2:4, 5). You need Him! Remember, God *is* love (1 John 4:7, 8). He is the ultimate Source of all the love you need to rekindle your relationship. You can't give what you don't have, and that means you need Him to give you the love you lack in your relationship. First reconcile with Him those resentments you have in your heart. Ask His forgiveness for the hardness, unwillingness, and unforgiveness you've had toward your loved one. Ask Him to fill you with His love by being filled with His Holy Spirit. The fruit of His Spirit is love (Gal. 5:22)!

Once you've reconciled with Him, you will sense the power of His love working within you. You will then be able to take the action God requires of you. Herein is your strength, for "*it is God who works in you both to will and to do for His good pleasure*" (Phil. 2:13). You must be in right relationship with the Lord to have the power you need to have a right relationship with your spouse.

2. <u>Next, go to your spouse and begin to reconcile the conflicts that divide you</u>. How should you begin? Remember what I explained in chapter 9, start with yourself! Jesus said, "*First, remove the plank from your own eye, and then you will see clearly to remove the speck out of your brother's*

eye" (Matt. 7:5). He knew that this principle must be the priority for anyone to reconcile conflicts.

Once you determine your failures, go and specifically ask forgiveness for each of them. Don't start by pointing out your mate's faults, start
with your own (James 5:16). This action immediately softens the heart of
your spouse and usually creates a response in your partner to compile a
similar list. If this doesn't happen, gently encourage your spouse to consider their own faults and do some soul-searching as you have. Encourage your spouse that you want to change the direction of the relationship, and explain that only by reconciling these issues can the love return
between the two of you.

3. Begin to provoke your spouse to love by deliberate godly actions.
Paul said, *"Let us consider one another to provoke unto love and to good
works"* (Heb. 10:24 KJV). We usually provoke each other to wrath and
evil works; to provoke your spouse to love requires a loving action on
your part. This action requires the love of God reigning in your own
heart to subdue your selfishness and that sense of hopelessness.

Remember, love provokes others to love, which, incidentally, will
also take care of the problem of inaction I spoke of earlier. The word
provoke means "to stir up." Every action of love is like throwing another
log on the fire, which naturally stirs up the love between you. The more
you take these deliberate actions of love, the more the fire blazes. You
will naturally be attracted to the warmth of this kind of relationship, and
it will naturally draw you closer together. You will begin to look forward
to getting home to see your spouse because of the love that has been
rekindled between you!

4. Stop any of the deliberate sinful actions you are taking. If you
want the fire of love to begin to burn again, you have to stop throwing
water on the fire. This will show your spouse that you mean business!
When there is true repentance in the heart, it is always demonstrated by
reversing the direction of your life. If you are doing anything that is contrary to the Word of God, you must stop it. Where you are living selfishly,
reverse directions. Paul encouraged us to *"do works befitting repentance"*
(Acts 26:20).

This means that you must stop any verbal or physical abuse. Ask
God to control your explosive anger. Resume regular sexual relations. If
you are involved with another man or woman, cut the relationship off
today! This is what real repentance does. Only by taking these godly
actions will you ever have the chance to rekindle the fire of love between
you.

5. <u>Do preventive maintenance daily</u>. Often couples begin to work out their differences, and then one of the two will revert to the same old habits. This again quenches the love between them, and the whole destructive process starts all over again. You must guard against this with all your heart.

As you build a good fire by constant vigilance and attention, so you must be diligent to maintain your marriage by showing kindness and affection. This is a daily work. This is what love does; it works. Remember, Paul called it the *"labor of love"* (1 Thess. 1:3). If you love your spouse, you will put time and effort into building depth into your relationship. God loves you very much, and He has been at work for a long time to draw you to himself. The work of the Cross was His labor of love for you. His labor of love is a daily action as well; He daily loads you with benefits (Ps. 68:19). This is what He wants you to do with your spouse. Daily stoke the fire of your love together. Daily reconcile the conflicts that arise. Demonstrate your love today.

CONCLUSION

Beloved, if you will do the things I have discussed within the pages of this book, the marriage you desire will be yours. I believe with all my heart that the best God has for you is still yet to come. Why do I believe this? Because Scripture reveals that this is the heart of God. He longs to give to each of us more than we even dare to imagine. Remember, God is One who loves to give. We can't even fathom the riches of His grace that He has planned for us. Paul said of the Father's ability, *"Now to Him who is able to do exceedingly abundantly above all that we ask or think, according to the power that works in us"* (Eph 3:20). What have you been asking and hoping for in your life and marriage? He wants to do it and is able to do it abundantly above and beyond whatever you can dream. But the question is, do you believe this?

If you do, then you will seek the one who promises that He is able *"to keep you from stumbling and to present you faultless before the presence of His glory with exceeding joy"* (Jude 24). He is able to make all grace abound toward you that you might have all that you need to succeed in life and in this marriage (2 Cor. 9:8). Don't miss this incredible sufficiency that He is offering to you. Beloved, please don't let this be another marriage book that you put on your shelf and do nothing. Let God work His miracle work today in your life. Come to Him right now and allow Him to begin the work. Never forget, He is able! Trust Him to do the work.

Group Discussion Questions

1. What are some practical actions that quench the fire of love between you and your mate?
2. What are some practical actions that you could take to stir up the fire of love between you and your spouse?

 # Appendix A

WHAT IF YOUR SPOUSE REFUSES TO COOPERATE?

If you are reading this appendix first, I want to encourage you to stop now and begin at chapter 1. The reason is very simple. Until you have read and sought to fully implement the principles in this book, you are not giving your marriage the chance it needs. You will not have looked at yourself and the areas in which you need to change, nor at the godly actions you need to take to provoke your spouse to change. You also will not have given your spouse the needed time to make the changes before taking the action endorsed in this chapter. It is essential that you start at the beginning of the book and work through each principle one by one. This appendix merely offers help to those who have already done all that is required and have as yet seen no positive results. I understand that you may be frustrated with your mate, but it is due to issues in *both* of your lives. You must make a serious attempt to deal with your own life first. Then, if there is no response, the counsel here will be effective and helpful. Ultimately, my hope is that this appendix will be unnecessary for anyone. Therefore, begin with the first step, not the last one. Please, turn back to chapter 1 now.

Why have I entitled the appendix this way? Unfortunately, I have discovered that some individuals simply don't want to do anything to deepen their marriage relationships. Sometimes this is due to the fact that the unwilling partner is a non-Christian, yet, even Christians can take this position as well. Therefore, these issues must be addressed to help the willing partner to respond correctly.

There are two questions I am asked over and over again: "Why won't my spouse change?" and, "What should I do?"

WHY WON'T MY SPOUSE CHANGE?

This is a good question and deserves an answer. Why does a spouse refuse to make the changes required by Scripture? If you are able to determine the answer to this question, then you will have a much easier time knowing what to do. I believe there are several reasons why a spouse refuses to make the changes necessary for a successful marriage. Let's look at a few.

1. <u>Sometimes your spouse simply doesn't want to change</u>. That is why I started this book with the issue of willingness. Some people know what they should do but simply choose not to do it. These people like things the way they are and fully intend to continue living in a selfish manner. Nothing you will say or do is ever going to change these people because they enjoy living for self. Jesus said of the Pharisees, *"You are not willing to come to me that you may have life"* (John 5:40). The Pharisees wanted the status quo. They had no intention of denying themselves to follow Christ, even though the Son of God himself was in their very midst. He did miracles, He loved them, He always spoke the truth, and they still rejected Him. This reveals the hardness of men's hearts and the ability to reject even the most effective witness of all time, Jesus Christ.

This is one reason why your spouse may be unwilling to make any changes. They may have the same stubborn, proud, and rebellious heart. Be assured of this fact, even if Jesus came to your house and spoke to your spouse personally, there would be no change. In this case, there is very little you can say or do. This is not a pleasant thought, but it is reality. You need to accept the fact that your spouse must be willing to change.

2. <u>Sometimes *you* are the reason your spouse is not making the needed changes</u>. At this moment you must be brutally honest with yourself. Are you making the changes God requires of you, or are you continuing to live in the same manner as you have always lived and just expecting your spouse to make all of the changes? Have you ever considered that you might be the biggest hindrance to your mate changing for the better? Your life can either be an encouragement to your mate or a very real stumbling block. Scripture encourages us to *"provoke one another to love and good* works" (Heb. 10:24, KJV). To provoke your mate to love means that you must actively be loving first. If you are acting in a very resentful and hateful manner, it will only provoke your mate to be hateful too. If you are resistant to change yourself, it encourages your mate to be defiant in return. Your spouse may very possibly be using your unwillingness to change as just the excuse they need to remain stubborn and unbending. We know, however, that God does not accept this as an excuse.

I remember one unbelieving young man who sat in my office and confessed that he wanted nothing to do with Jesus Christ because of what he saw in his wife's behavior. He said, "If this is what a Christian is, I want no part of it." This statement crushed his wife, but much of what he said was true. She was angry with him most of the time for his lack of leadership in the marriage, would harshly criticize him, and then pressure him to go to church.

Therefore, look hard at your own life and consider how your life is affecting your mate. Your actions are either helping or hindering the process of change. This is why the apostle Peter encouraged the wives with unbelieving husbands to be very careful about their conduct. He said, *"Be submissive...even if some do not obey the word, that they, without a word, may be won by the conduct of their wives."* Furthermore, wives need to cultivate *"a gentle and quiet spirit, which is very precious in the sight of God"* (1 Peter 3:1-4). Would you say that you conduct yourself submissively and gently, or are you rebellious and harsh? Have you truly dealt with any bitterness or unforgiveness in your heart? Are you curbing the habits that offend your mate? Are you initiating the action necessary to build relationship, or are you waiting for your spouse to start? Your answer to these questions will determine if you are part of the reason why your mate refuses to change.

3. Sometimes there are still unresolved conflicts between you. Resentment or unforgiveness in your mate's heart over unresolved issues is often a great hindrance because no one desires to make changes while still possessing anger. Many times a spouse will refuse to change as punishment for some real or imagined sin that divides you. Your partner considers this a good way to pay you back for what you have done. Unforgiveness will always act as a wall to divide two people. Therefore, break down the wall and resolve those issues that prevent a willing attitude. Remember, you didn't want to make any changes in your life until you reconciled your sin before God. This principle is the same in any relationship. Reconciliation always precedes change. Christ came to *"make reconciliation for iniquity"* that He might *"bring in everlasting righteousness"* (Dan. 9:24). Therefore, reconciliation must always come before you will see any change of behavior.

Consequently, if you are not seeing the changes you desire, let me make one suggestion. Go back to your mate and ask them, "Is there anything that's unresolved between us?" Be sure of where your spouse stands on this issue. If there is no conflict that is still unresolved, you can take this possibility off your list. If there are still unresolved conflicts between you, get to work and resolve them using the principles in the earlier chapters as your guide.

4. Sometimes there is no change because your spouse is not fully surrendered to Christ. Without both partners in a marriage fully committed to Christ, you will never attain the kind of marriage you truly desire. Having a real relationship with God causes us to change daily. He is in the business of changing lives every day of the year. Before Jesus commanded you to love your neighbor as yourself He said, *"You shall love the*

Lord your God with all your heart, with all your soul, and with all your mind" (Matt. 22:37). As you love the Lord with all your heart, you can't help but begin to love others. As you fall in love with the Lord Jesus Christ, He fills you with His Spirit, who, in turn, fills you with His love (Rom. 5:5). Love is what makes both you and your spouse work at making changes.

No one can force change in another person's life. It must be motivated by an inner drive to give and serve another person. You and your spouse must hunger for it, cry out to God for it, knowing that only by His love captivating your heart will you ever be the man or woman God intends. If the changes aren't happening the way you want, this is the best place to begin.

What Can You Do?

Your reaction to an unresponsive spouse is very important. As I have already stated, you can either be a help or a hindrance to this process. How should you respond and what should you do? What would be a biblical response that would please God?

1. Patience. Yes, I know this sounds like a simplistic answer. It's very easy to tell someone to be patient. However, if you are walking with the Lord, you have the power of the Holy Spirit as your source of strength. You can be patient. Paul said, *"I can do all things through Christ who strengthens me"* (Phil. 4:13). You have the power of the Holy Spirit living within you, and the fruit of the Spirit is patience and longsuffering (Gal. 5:22). He will fill you with the patience you need if you will just ask Him.

Why should patience be your response? Because this is how God has dealt with you during those times when you were not willing to change some attitude or habit. Think for a moment about how many times you have been unresponsive to the Lord and His conviction. Did He kick you out of the kingdom? Absolutely not. He is long-suffering (2 Peter 3:9). He is probably waiting patiently right now in some area in your life. Therefore, bestow the same patience upon your mate that you have received. *"Now may the God of patience and comfort grant you to be like-minded toward one another, according to Christ Jesus"* (Rom. 15:5).

2. Prayer. Prayer is an essential aid in trying circumstances, especially when you are tempted to just give up. Jesus taught that *"men always ought to pray and not lose heart"* (Luke 18:1). Don't miss the blessing and the strength God wants to bestow upon you by failing to pray.

Prayer will first change you by encouraging you to not lose heart, and will bring the pressure of the Spirit to bear upon your spouse.

God wants you to come into fellowship with Him. He desires you to come to Him and rest. He commands: *"Come to Me, all you who labor and are heavy laden, and I will give you rest"* (Matt. 11:28). If you are heavy laden over your marriage, come to Him right now and let Him give you rest! When you have His rest in your heart, you will be able to handle all that comes your way no matter what your spouse does or doesn't do. Prayer provides the patience, comfort, and strength you need. Without prayer, you will forfeit any possibility of the inner strength and peace that you so desperately need at this time. *"Cast your burden on the Lord, and He shall sustain you"* (Ps. 55:22). David encouraged, *"Wait on the Lord; Be of good courage, and He shall strengthen your heart; Wait, I say, on the Lord"* (Ps. 27:14)!

Not only does prayer sustain and strengthen you, it also keeps you from the many temptations that naturally come from living with an unresponsive spouse. I am referring to temptations such as holding resentment in your heart, giving up in discouragement, or becoming attracted to another person that appears to be more loving and gracious than your mate. Jesus gave His solution for temptation when He said, *"Watch and pray, lest you enter into temptation. The spirit indeed is willing, but the flesh is weak"* (Matt. 26:41). Do you realize how weak you are at this moment? Enduring the trials of an unresponsive spouse puts you in a very vulnerable place. Prayer is the answer to this weakness of your flesh, and it will keep you on track. If you fail to pray, don't be surprised if you succumb to one of these temptations. Don't be like the apostle Peter who thought he would never give in to temptation. *"Let him who thinks he stands take heed lest he fall"* (1 Cor. 10:12).

Pray for wisdom. You need an incredible amount of wisdom with an unresponsive spouse. *"If any of you lacks wisdom, let him ask of God, who gives to all liberally and without reproach, and it will be given him"* (James 1:5). What should you do, and how? How should you talk to your mate, and what should you say? You must seek God's counsel and then ask Him to confirm His plan each step of the way. You need the guidance that only God can give you. Man's counsel is important, too, but you must take what men say and ask God's approval.

Finally, prayer is not just for you and your own strength. It is also for your loved one. Prayer is where you commit your spouse into God's hands. If Jesus told us to pray for those who persecute us, how much more should we pray for a spouse who is unresponsive. You must give them over to the

Father to allow Him to work in your mate's heart. This is the most power-ful pressure you can ever bring to bear upon your mate. In fact, prayer brings more pressure than all your yelling, arguing, and manipulating could ever do because God is working in the heart and mind. When you pray, God is doing an inner work of the Holy Spirit, that will be much more difficult for your spouse to resist. When you are saying nothing, the Lord continues to speak loud and clear to your mate's heart and mind. If your loved one will hear His voice and not harden his or her heart, God will do a good work (Heb. 3:7). Jesus said, *"My sheep hear My voice"* (John 10:27). As you pray, be confident that His voice is speaking to your spouse. Why should you be confident of this truth? Because He has prom-ised. Pray that your mate will choose to hear and yield to the Father.

3. You must continue to go forward in your Christian walk. Many times I have observed people struggling with an unresponsive mate only to watch them lose all patience and give up in their relationship with the Lord. Their spouses have refused to pray, attend church, or communi-cate, and they choose to continue in a totally selfish lifestyle. Therefore, the faithful spouse succumbs to the temptation to give up. Soon I don't see either of them at church. When I call to see what has happened, I am told, "God isn't doing anything. My spouse isn't changing. Why should I seek the Lord?" This individual has simply given up, not understanding that God won't force the unresponsive spouse. God has given us all a free will and will not violate it. He waits for an individual to respond to His invitation to come. Don't blame God for what is clearly the willful rebel-lion of your spouse.

In addition, if you give up and choose to forsake your Christian walk, you will be the loser. You will not only forfeit any possibility of the marital relationship you long for, but you will also be forsaking the only one who loves you and is committed to helping you through all that is ahead. You need His strength and wisdom, but this will only be found in a growing and intimate relationship with Christ. Remember God's prom-ise: *"Those who wait on the Lord shall renew their strength; they shall mount up with wings like eagles, they shall run and not be weary, they shall walk and not faint"* (Is. 40:31). Ask for His renewing strength today.

I have also seen situations where a spouse has labored, waited, and prayed for years, but then gives up. Then the unresponsive spouse turns around and wants to work on the marriage, but now the roles are re-versed. Now the one who has struggled all those years becomes the unre-sponsive one in the marriage. I am sad to say that this happens more times than you would think. All this could have been avoided if the spouse who had patiently waited would have kept their heart willing and responsive to God.

I am happy to say that I have also seen a spouse who patiently prays and perseveres and finally sees their mate yield to the pressure of the Spirit. What a joy this is to see. Yes, it does happen! I know it is tough, but if you wait and persevere in faith, you have the best hope of seeing the lasting change you desire.

4. <u>Guard your tongue</u>. As you give yourself to prayer, this does not mean you cannot speak to your spouse about their unresponsiveness. However, you must be very careful about what you say and how you say it. You must choose your words carefully without nagging. Pressuring someone is usually very unproductive. Can you think of how you have felt when someone has tried to coerce you into something that you didn't want to do? Didn't it make you want to dig your heels in and resist all the more? Sure it did! This is exactly what your spouse will feel like as well. Remember, your words will either drive your mate away from you or be an invitation to change.

Guard your words and keep yourself from becoming critical and cutting. Be especially attentive to your attitude when you speak because our words reveal the true intent of our hearts. If you will pray about your tongue on a regular basis, it will be possible to speak the truth in love to your spouse (Eph. 4:15). Speaking in this manner will prove to your mate that you care more about the relationship than only winning an argument. Your life and love are a powerful testimony and will provide the most favorable atmosphere in which to see change.

In addition, speaking the truth means that you must lovingly tell your spouse the frustration you are experiencing. This is the truth. Explain to your partner exactly how you feel. Express the emptiness and distance you are feeling inside because of these unresolved issues. You must be specific by giving examples and circumstances where commitments and promises were not kept. Also, be sure to pick the right time for this conversation. Don't discuss these issues when your mate is tired after a long day or late at night. Wait until you are both rested and in a good mood.

5. <u>Ask your spouse if they will go to counseling</u>. Especially with long-term issues, it is very important to get your pastor involved so that he may give both of you some specific and impartial counseling. *"Where there is no counsel, the people fall"* (Prov. 11:14). I have seen many a marriage partner miserably fall because they chose to keep the marriage problems a secret and refused to come in for counseling. I hope this will not be your mistake.

Why do you need your pastor to get involved at this time? Because what you have been doing is not working, and you need some outside input as an encouragement to get things moving. Do you know of any better person to get involved in your marriage than an individual who knows the Word of God and cares about you? Sometimes people resist going to their pastor because they believe the counseling will destroy their friendship. People have said to me, "I've hesitated to come with these problems because I didn't want to jeopardize our friendship by bringing up all this dirt in our marriage." However, the opposite happens when I counsel couples. There are no people that I grow closer to than the people I spend time ministering to. When you spend hours loving, encouraging, laughing, and crying with people, you can't help but grow closer to them. Therefore, forget the excuses and go for counseling.

What happens if you ask your spouse, and they refuse to go for counseling. Should you forget the whole thing and just live with the problems? No.

6. You make the call. First, however, wait until you have another conflict and ask your spouse to go for counseling again. Explain to your mate that it is obvious that things are the same, and you are not working the problems out. If you wait for the next conflict to arise to make this comment, it makes it extremely difficult for your spouse to rationalize the need away. Your spouse cannot say that everything is fine. Yet, your mate may say, "Oh, it's not that bad. We can work this out." Just wait until the next conflict and again gently bring the issue of counseling up once more.

If your spouse continues to refuse counseling, you make the call to your pastor. Even if your mate refuses to see their need for counseling, you still need it. This book cannot answer all of the questions for all of the varied circumstances that may arise in a marriage. This is why you need your own pastor to sit down with you in order to give the specific counsel that is appropriate to your situation.

What should you do if your mate tells you that you shouldn't call your pastor or personally go for counseling? Should you still go? Yes, absolutely! What if your spouse gets angry because you are going to reveal personal information that will make them look bad? Is it right to speak to your pastor when your husband or wife is opposed to you going? Yes! Here is the biblical basis for doing so.

Jesus said, *"If your brother sins against you, go and tell him his fault between you and him alone. If he hears you, you have gained your brother. But if he will not hear, take with you one or two more, that 'by the mouth of two or three witnesses every word may be established'"* (Mat 18:15, 16). Your husband or wife has a fault of unresponsiveness in your marriage relationship and probably many other faults as well. It is your responsibility to first go to your mate and try and resolve this conflict on your own, *between you and him alone*. If this problem is not resolved between you, Jesus is the one who gives you the freedom and the command to get someone else involved.

Therefore, do not let your spouse keep your problems in the darkness of secrecy. Let the light of truth, honesty, and the counsel of the Word of God shine into your marriage. The encouragement of Jesus in the above passage makes it clear that there are some conflicts that require outside help in order to resolve them completely. After you have counseled with your pastor, take the next step.

7. Ask your pastor to approach your spouse. I have approached many unresponsive mates at the direct request of the men and women I have counseled. I have called believing and unbelieving mates; it makes no difference. Many of the non-Christian mates will ultimately come to Christ after sitting down to talk over their marriage problems. This is one of the most rewarding opportunities a pastor can have in his ministry. Even if a husband or wife doesn't ask or suggest my calling the unresponsive spouse, I will usually take the initiative and ask if I can approach the other partner. Usually I get a very favorable response when I call, and the unresponsive spouse will come in for counseling. Many times this has been the first step to a wonderful reconciliation. There are times when a spouse will come in for counseling only to appease me and ultimately continues to be unresponsive. Then one or both will say to me, "Well, this was a waste of time." I have to disagree. At least everything that could be done, was done, even if it was unproductive. Even when an unresponsive mate initially refuses my invitation for counseling, they will often have a change of mind later. This occurs because they have seen that I am not on anyone's side and that I only want to help them resolve their conflicts. This gives people a little spark of hope inside that germinates and ultimately sparks the desire to try again.

How do you know what will happen until you try? Will you take the action required by Scripture to seek outside help? If you will, no matter what the outcome, you will know that you have done everything you could to reconcile your relationship.

You may ask, "What do I do if my church doesn't offer marriage counseling, or my pastor refuses to call my spouse, declaring he doesn't want to get involved?" Let me say this as tactfully as I can: If this is the case, you need to find a church that *does* offer marriage counseling and a pastor who *does* want to get involved. For any pastor to refuse to counsel you or to refuse to reach out to your spouse is a denial of the direct command of God for a shepherd of the flock of God. A minister should have a heart to feed and tend the flock of God (Acts 20:28). If all Christians have been given *"the ministry of reconciliation"* and *"the word of reconciliation,"* how much more should a leader of the church fulfill this call (2 Cor. 5:18, 19)? All Christians are called to restore their brethren when they see them overtaken in a fault and fulfill the ministry of a peacemaker when there is a conflict (Gal. 6:1; Matt. 5:9). Each of us has this responsibility to our fellow Christians, but this is the special call of a minister of the flock of God. Paul told Timothy that the Scriptures were able to make him *"wise to salvation...that the man of God may be complete, thoroughly equipped for every good work"* (2 Tim. 3:15, 17).

However, in very large churches a senior pastor will not always be able to help everyone that is having marital difficulties. In such cases, seek out an associate pastor, marriage minister, or elder who can help you and meet your needs for biblical counsel. These individuals are equally able and qualified to reach out to you and your spouse.

8. <u>Take the action that is appropriate to the response of your mate</u>. This will be different in every case. Sometimes more patience is required, sometimes more action. At other times, more counseling is needed. Your pastor is the best one to give you this counsel. Remember, if you take the biblical action required in Scripture, it will yield the best opportunity for real and lasting change.

9. <u>As much as lies within you, live at peace with your spouse</u>. This is a principle that is essential when you are dealing with any difficult relationship. Paul said, *"Repay no one evil for evil...If it is possible, as much as depends on you, live peaceably with all men"* (Rom. 12:17, 18). When your spouse is unresponsive and unwilling to make any change in your marriage, it can become a very deep wound of rejection to your heart and soul. It is a very natural thing in the flesh to want to render evil to anyone that hurts or rejects you. God wants to give you a supernatural response of love to this offense and rejection. From your side *as much as depends on you*, God desires that you seek peace with your mate. This, again, is only possible when you are continuing to surrender to the Lord.

"I beseech you...present your bodies a living sacrifice...And do not be conformed to this world, but be transformed by the renewing of your mind..." (Rom. 12:1, 2). The only way to live peaceably with your spouse is to present yourself to God. Don't be conformed to this world. Be renewed and transformed daily inside by the power of the Holy Spirit. By first surrendering yourself to God, you will be able to seek a compromise and find solutions to the differences that are between you. All Paul is encouraging here is that *as much as depends on you*, don't be the one creating the conflicts.

Notice the phrase *if it is possible* in verse 18. This implies that sometimes there are going to be circumstances in which it is not possible to live at peace with your spouse. There are, at times, extreme situations where your spouse refuses to live at peace with you. They are simply pushing you into a corner where it is not possible to live in harmony with this person. I am referring to an intolerable living situation in which a spouse is physically abusive, inappropriately spending the household money because they are controlled by drugs or alcohol, or continually committing adultery. You can't do anything about these actions. All you can do is take care of your attitude and take the actions required by Scripture. I will discuss further how to respond to some of these extreme circumstances in Appendix B.

As much as depends on you, do all that you can to resolve the issues that divide you. Then commit yourself and your spouse to the Lord. Ask Him to do whatever work is needed as you surrender to Him.

✣ Appendix B ✣

WHAT IF YOUR SPOUSE IS OUT OF CONTROL?

M
any times an individual will come up to me, usually after a church service, and ask to talk to me. This in itself is not unusual, but the stories I hear many times are unusual and sometimes quite bizarre. A wife describes her husband who is physically abusive, or is dealing drugs out of their home, or perhaps recounts stories of nightly drunken screaming matches. In other cases, it's not the husband, but the wife who is out of control. A husband tells me of his wife who is committing adultery, abusing the kids, or using drugs or alcohol during the day while he is at work. Then the question always comes, "What should I do? Should I leave? Should I submit? Should I turn my spouse in to the police? What does the Bible say I should do?"

If you are in one of these trying circumstances right now, I know and understand that this is a very difficult situation, and that you desperately need good counsel to make the decisions in your specific situation. What I will attempt to do in this appendix is to give you some biblical principles to help you to make a wise decision. What I will *not* do is try to tell you specifically what to do. There are too many variables and specifics that are special to your situation that must be taken into account. You must take the biblical principles I will share here and apply them to your personal situation, tempering them with the counsel of your pastor or an elder of your church. Let me encourage you right at the beginning that you need the counsel of a trusted spiritual leader who is close at hand and can help you to weigh each decision with God's Word.

What are the biblical principles that relate to the extreme circumstances I've referred to above?

1. You must first choose to please and obey God, even if your spouse will not. This must be the primary motivation of your heart and will enable you to take all of the actions needed and commanded in God's Word. Your spouse is obviously not doing what is right before God, but you must! If you will honor God first in your life, the best that can possibly happen will occur. This doesn't mean that everything will work out so that everyone lives happily ever after; that is not promised anywhere in the Bible. Jesus promised that in this life we would have plenty of tribulation, but He said, *"In Me you may have peace"* (John 16:33). Everyone

has hardships in life, but only the one who honors and obeys God will experience the help and the peace that He gives. Long ago God promised, *"those who honor Me, I will honor..."* (1 Sam. 2:30). This is a glorious promise that I hope will grip your heart. God wants to bless you and your life. No matter what your spouse does, God wants to honor you, if you will but honor Him and put Him first in your life. He will strengthen and provide for all that you need in your life. He *will* guide you in this most difficult time! This is what Jesus promised when He said to His disciples, *"Seek first the kingdom of God and His righteousness, and all these things shall be added to you"* (Matt. 6:33). Seek Him first, seek to please Him and obey Him, and He will add all that you need. This is His promise!

Jesus declared that to honor and please the Father was his highest priority in life. He said, *"I always do those things that please Him"* (John 8:29). In the same manner He said, *"I honor My Father"* (John 8:49). Aren't you glad Jesus honored God? That is why He took the actions He did, what motivated Him to suffer and sacrifice His life for you. This motivation to honor and please the Father is also what will enable you to sacrificially take the correct action needed for your marriage. No matter what you feel like or how hard the steps will be for you ahead, your desire to honor God in all that you do will keep you on the right track.

Will you choose to put the Father first in your life right now? Will you begin to seek His will and guidance for your life and marriage? Will you choose to obey Him when He reveals what He wants you to do? If you will, you have the best chance of saving your marriage. In these extreme situations, if you please yourself or go on trying to please your spouse, the marriage will surely continue to deteriorate. Only by putting Christ first and obeying His Word is there hope for change.

For your marriage's sake, for your own sake, for your children's sake, for your testimony as a Christian, and for God's sake, tell the Lord in prayer that you want to honor Him in these difficult circumstances. Begin to ask God what He would have you to do.

2. Don't hide the sin of your spouse. Most of the time when one partner comes to tell me of the disaster that is occurring in the home, it has been a well-kept secret for a long time. This sinful behavior has been hidden from everyone, but now the circumstances have become intolerable. Sometimes I am even asked to continue to keep the secret. The husband or wife says to me, "I need you to keep this confidential, pastor." Obviously, confidentiality is important and it would be inappropriate for me to reveal this problem to others in the general church body, but hiding this sinful behavior is not the answer either. This activity must be

dealt with lovingly, directly, and personally with the offending spouse or the marriage is over.

You may be thinking that it is wrong for a spouse to disclose certain secrets to me. You may remember the Scripture that says, *"Debate your case with your neighbor himself, and do not disclose the secret to another"* (Prov. 25:9). This verse of Scripture teaches us the *first step* of dealing with a conflict. You should first speak to your neighbor or your spouse personally about the problem. In this first stage of attempting to reconcile, you are not to reveal the problem to anyone else. Jesus taught the same thing when He said, *"If your brother sins against you, go and tell him his fault between you and him alone. If he hears you, you have gained your brother"* (Matt. 18:15). Notice what Jesus goes on to say you should do if your brother does not receive your reproof. *"But if he will not hear you, take with you one or two more, that by the mouth of two or three witnesses every word may be established. And if he refuses to hear them, tell it to the church. But if he refuses even to hear the church, let him be to your like a heathen and a tax collector"* (Matt. 18:16, 17).

This text of Scripture is critical for you to follow. If your spouse hears your reproof, then you should *not* say a word to anyone else. If your mate actually turns from a sinful behavior, then you have solved the problem. I would still encourage you to ask your spouse to seek further counseling and help from your pastor. Sinful behaviors do not die easily in anyone's life and require specific counsel as to the causes and long-term solutions.

If your spouse denies that they have a problem and rejects your counsel, you must reveal the secret to someone else. This is the only way you can obey the teaching of Jesus, to bring one or two additional witnesses with you. I would encourage you in these extreme situations to immediately call the pastor of your church. A phone call from the pastor is an extremely powerful encouragement for your mate to deal with their problems. If your spouse continues to reject even your pastor's call to repentance, Jesus said to count this person as a heathen or an unbeliever. This means you must now consider your mate a non-Christian. Why? Because this man or woman is consistently rejecting the counsel and messengers of the Lord Jesus Christ and is willfully practicing sinful behavior. This refusal to turn from sin is simply a refusal to follow and obey Christ. Jesus said, *"If you love Me, keep my commandments...If anyone loves Me, he will keep My word...He who does not love Me does not keep My words"* (John 14:15, 23, 24) Then what?

From that point on you need to begin to evangelize your mate. Why? Because your spouse is in full rebellion against God and against His Word.

You should not hate your spouse, but recognize what the real need is by continuing to share the message of Christ, who is seeking their restoration. By encouraging your partner to return to faith and obedience to Christ, you are attacking the real problem and not just the symptom.

It is important that you don't hide these major moral issues that are destroying your life and your children's. God does not intend for you to try to handle this by yourself or to attempt to hide the evil that is occurring in your home. Even in the Old Testament, when the people were offering their children up to the god Molech, God told the people not to *"hide their eyes from the man"* (Lev. 20:1-5). God considered anyone who did as guilty of the same punishment. He also told the Jews not to *"conceal him"* (Deut. 13:8). Clearly God's intention was that major moral issues like this were not to be covered up and hidden. Solomon also taught this same truth when he said, *"He who covers his sins will not prosper, but whoever confesses and forsakes them will have mercy"* (Prov. 28:13). If you have been concealing your spouse's sinful behavior, you need to first confess it to God and ask His forgiveness. Then call your pastor.

3. <u>Don't deal with the problem alone</u>. There are many reasons why you need other trusted people involved in your dilemma. The serious family problems that are occurring in your home bring with them a confusion of thoughts and feelings. Many times a husband or wife will come to me and say, "I'm worn out, Steve. I don't know if talking to you is even right. My husband (or wife) would be so mad if he (or she) knew I was here talking to you. But I'm at the end of my rope. I don't know if my spouse is sincere or not in the professed attempt to change. I don't know if I love him (or her) or hate him (or her). Help me!"

No one should deal with this confusion alone. What is first needed is the objective counsel of a third party who will minister the Word of God. His Word brings light into the darkness that seems to surround, control, and overcome families with such problems. His truth will destroy the lies that are being heard in the mind and brings the hope that God does have answers to the confusion. This is what the counsel of a godly friend or a pastor can do. Solomon said, *"Plans fail for lack of counsel, but with many advisers they succeed"* (Prov. 15:22, NIV). *"Every purpose is established by counsel"* (Prov. 20:18). If you want to succeed in the midst of this turmoil, then be sure you get wise and godly counsel. It will establish your heart and keep you from failing in the midst of probably the greatest trial of your life.

Don't underestimate the help and encouragement you can receive from the counsel of another person. Many people in these circumstances go on and on for months and years trying to hide the problems, trying to work it all out themselves. Jesus never intended for you to do this! Again, remember the counsel Jesus gave in Matthew 18:15-17.

4. <u>You must take action no matter what your mate does</u>. You may ask, "Why must I do anything? Why can't I just wait and see if things will change by themselves?" This, again, is what many individuals do, hoping that somehow their spouse will pull out of their sinful action all by themselves. I am not saying that this never happens, but when it does, it is definitely the exception and not the rule. Usually it takes the direct action of the spouse, with the help of others to bring repentance and change to a marriage in such dire circumstances.

Why is this the case? Because when a person is caught in any sinful activity, he is controlled by his own sinful nature and bound by lies that captivate and hold him in a steady downward course. The Scripture teaches that when a brother is *"overtaken in any trespass, you who are spiritual restore such a one in the spirit of gentleness, considering yourself lest you also be tempted. Bear one another's burdens, and so fulfill the law of Christ"* (Gal. 6:1, 2). Your spouse is overtaken and controlled in a sinful behavior and needs the help of other spiritual individuals to be restored. This passage teaches that others must take action no matter what this sinning brother is doing. This is the law of Christ. Christ himself took this same initiative and action when each of us was dead in our sins. He came to rescue and redeem us from the bondage of our sin.

If you are glad that Jesus took this action for you, should you not do the same? Your spouse is bound by sin, and they need your help. Begin the restoration process today.

5. <u>If there is no repentance by your spouse, the problem will only get worse</u>. How can I make this statement? Because of the testimony of God's Word and my experience of dealing with many couples over the years in these circumstances.

The testimony of God's Word is the most powerful. Paul said the direction of evil men in the last days would be *"worse and worse"* (2 Tim. 3:13). Paul knew what the Scriptures taught about the corruption and the depravity of man's nature. If human nature is uncontrolled, it will naturally lead men to a greater and greater distance from God and will ultimately drive a person to greater and greater evil. Isaiah described this downward force of man's sinful nature with a metaphor that all would understand. He said, *"Wickedness burns as the fire, it devours the briers and thorns"* (Is. 9:18).

The wickedness of man's sin is depicted here as a fire that devours all in its path. Each of us understands that a fire is never satisfied until it consumes all it touches. It must be resisted and put out or it will consume everything. Proverbs declares that this is the nature of a fire; it is never satisfied. *"There are three things that are never satisfied. Four things never say, 'It is enough': The grave, the barren womb, the earth that is not satisfied with water, and the fire that never says, 'It is enough' "* (Prov. 30:15, 16).

I use this metaphor as an illustration of how sin in your mate's life can get way out of control and consume their entire life. At the beginning of any sinful behavior, your spouse thinks they can handle what is being indulged in, not knowing that sin is a progressive power that constantly wants to control more and more. Sin is never satisfied with the status quo. Whatever your spouse wants that is forbidden will never be enough; they will always crave more.

Sin is progressive, possessive, and deceitful! It makes you think, *I can handle this.* At the same time, you are subtly losing control to its progressive and possessive power every day. This is what Paul called the *"deceitfulness of sin"* (Heb. 3:13). The word *deceitfulness* actually means "delusion." Sin itself has deluded us into thinking that we can violate God's laws and still get away with it. The delusion of sin convinces us that there are no consequences and we are stronger than the power of our own sinful nature that rages inside of us. This is a deceitful lie and a delusion!

In reality, the longer a person yields to sin, the harder it is to resist yielding. It becomes easier to rationalize the behavior and to continue the slow process toward bondage. This is the reason why Paul said to the Ephesian Church, *"Put off, concerning your former conduct, the old man which grows corrupt according to the deceitful lusts, and be renewed in the spirit of your mind, and that you put on the new man..."* (Eph. 4:22-24). Notice what Paul said about the sinful nature or the old man. He said it *"grows corrupt according to deceitful lusts."* The verb is in the present tense in the Greek, which describes a continuous process of growing corrupt. You either put off this old man or it will grow more corrupt every day.

Therefore, knowing these things about what the Scripture teaches regarding sin and its deceitful progression into bondage, you must act. Your spouse must also act to put off this behavior that is destroying their life and your marriage. The church you attend and your pastor must help you to act. Be assured that the longer you wait, the worse it will get.

6. If you fail to take action, your spouse will only lose respect for you. You may be afraid to take action against your spouse because they may get angry, throw you out of the house, beat you again, go on another

binge, or some other major consequence. This may be true. However, the alternative of doing nothing is simply unacceptable. Yes, there may be a temporary consequence for taking biblical action, but the long-term situation will definitely improve. In fact, your mate will secretly respect you for taking action, even though they may never say this to you. I've seen it happen.

Most of us respect a person for taking a stand based on conviction. We also see inaction and compromise of a person's convictions as weakness. Your spouse knows that what he or she is doing is wrong and detrimental to your marriage, but this person is caught in the grip and power of sin. Many people have told me later that they were inwardly hoping that someone would confront them and help them out of their dilemma. When your mate sees you doing nothing, they perceive it as weakness. Your spouse will lose respect for you, and your relationship will only deteriorate further.

In Scripture, respect is the direct result of loving correction. The writer to the Hebrews noted this fact when he reminded them that *"we have had human fathers who corrected us, and we paid them respect"* (Heb. 12:9). Why did we respect our parents? Because we saw them as correcting us for what were obvious errors in our behavior. We considered this correction as right. They loved us enough to hold us to a moral standard and did not compromise their values. We counted that correction as proof that our parents really cared. If they had never corrected us, we would have considered it as weakness on their part and a demonstration that they had no moral standards worth standing up for.

If you will take the appropriate biblical action to deal with your spouse's problem, you have the best chance of seeing your marriage healed and restored. Your mate will understand that in the long run, you care about them and your marriage enough to stand up for your convictions. Your spouse will respect you for caring enough to attempt saving the relationship. Remember, biblical action will always be your best option. Don't compromise here!

7. Your personal safety and that of your children are of the utmost importance. There are some situations where your mate's sinful behavior will become a direct threat to your personal safety and that of your children. I am referring to situations such as drug dealing going on in your home, physical abuse to you or your children, or when your mate drives you or your children around in the car while drinking. This cannot be allowed to continue.

God cares about your safety and that of your children. There are many passages of Scripture that clearly reveal this fact. When the children of Israel were about to pass over the Jordan River into the Promised Land, Moses revealed God's intentions for them. He declared that God wanted them to *"dwell in safety"* (Deut. 12:10). Likewise, the Lord wants you to dwell in safety too. He doesn't want you or your children subjected to threats of harm or actual beatings. This is the practice of evil by another human being and He wants to protect you from this.

King David also saw the Lord as a God who cared for and protected the oppressed and needy. David declared, *"For the oppression of the poor, for the sighing of the needy, 'Now I will arise,' says the Lord; 'I will set him in the safety for which he yearns' "* (Ps. 12:5). Believe that this is what God wants for you and your children too. He wants your safety as much as you do. He knows that you yearn for that safe place, and He will provide it if you will just obey Him. You can always call your pastor and ask for help.

God's wisdom in these circumstances will cause you to take actions that will bring you to safety. This means you must listen to Him. God promises, *"Whoever listens to me will dwell safely, and will be secure, without fear of evil"* (Prov. 1:33). If you are living in fear of what will happen next, something is very wrong. This is not what God envisions for your home. Don't accept anything less.

8. <u>What will it take to motivate you to do something</u>? Sometimes people are extremely reluctant to do anything until disaster occurs. If this is the way you are, let me ask you this question. What does your spouse have to do before you will take the appropriate action? Where is your line in the sand? How much is too much? Please do something before disaster strikes. Do something before you are beaten again. Do something before your children are abused again. Take action before your house is taken from you because there is no money left.

Sometimes asking and pleading will not stop your mate's behavior. Sometimes, under these radical circumstances, your only solution is to leave. Let me give you a biblical example. In the Old Testament a man named Lot lived in the city of Sodom. This was an extremely evil city and God purposed to destroy it completely. God sent two angels to the city to warn Lot and his family to get out before the destruction came. When the angels came to the home of Lot, the homosexual men of that city came and began to beat on his door so that he would send the angels out that they might abuse them. Lot pleaded with the men, *"Please, my brethren, do not do so wickedly,"* but to no avail. The angels ultimately struck the men with blindness, and then because *"he lingered,"* the angels took Lot, his wife, and daughters by *"the hands...being merciful to him, and they brought him out and set him outside the city"* (Gen. 19:1-16).

If you have pleaded and your pastor has pleaded to no avail, do not linger. God is being merciful to you by sending those to you who are trying to lead you out of this situation. Take the hand of the "angels" that He has sent to you and leave.

9. <u>When you should submit and when you should not</u>. This is a question asked most often by wives: "Should I submit to physical abuse by my husband? Should I submit to him when I know he is committing adultery regularly? Should I submit to him when he asks me to do things that are contrary to God's Word?" The answer to these questions is *absolutely not!* God has not called you to ever submit to sinful acts or abuse of this kind.

Submission is never portrayed in Scripture as an act that is unconditional in all circumstances. God has placed limits and many qualifying statements on the command to submit. These must be understood and obeyed if you are to fully please God in situations that are out of control. Let's look at a few of these principles.

The command to submit, given to wives by the apostle Paul, is qualified by the word *fitting*. "*Wives, submit to your own husbands, as is fitting in the Lord*" (Col. 3:18). What does this phrase mean? The word *fitting* means "to take the proper action that is due another individual." A proper and appropriate action would always be the right or biblical one. This would refer to any action that is in accordance with the commands of Scripture. Obviously, this would bar all requests for you to do what is evil or violates the Word of God in anyway.

This action is further qualified by the phrase "*in the Lord.*" The submission referred to would be appropriate and in harmony with any submission you would give the Lord himself. Now take this definition and make a simple comparison. If the husband-wife relationship is a picture of the love and submission between Christ and His church, merely ask yourself what Christ would ask you to submit to. What is fitting to submit to must always be taken in the context of Christ and the church. Would Christ beat you and then ask you to submit to this action? Would He ask you to do something that would contradict His Word and then ask you to obey? Absolutely not! Christ would never commit evil or ask you to do any such thing. This action would not be fitting, nor would your submission be fitting in these circumstances. Let me give you another example that illustrates this point.

In the Book of Acts we have an example of the apostles refusing to submit. One day they were commanded by the Jewish council not to speak or teach anymore in the name of Jesus. What was their response? They declared, "*Whether it is right in the sight of God to listen to you more than to God, you judge. For we cannot but speak the things which we have seen and heard"* (Acts 4:19, 20). And they continued to preach Christ everywhere they went, refusing to submit to this edict. When the council realized that the apostles had not submitted to their commands, they brought them back again and asked them why they had not obeyed. They replied, *"We ought to obey God rather than men"* (Acts 5:29).

Here is a perfect example of men who knew what was fitting submission in the Lord. The apostles knew that it was not fitting for these rulers to contradict the very command of Christ, and so it was not fitting for them to obey their command. They knew that they should obey the laws of the land and be obedient to their rulers, but only when these laws did not contradict the commands and laws of Christ. They knew they must please and obey Christ first. This was fitting in the Lord.

When anyone requires you to take an action that is contrary to the Word or the command of Christ, you must obey God rather than man. When you are asked to submit to or allow anything that is unbiblical, unethical, or ungodly, you have the right and the responsibility before God to resist. This is the only action that is fitting before God.

Another reason why you should not submit in these circumstances is that your spouse is not following Christ. Paul said, *"Follow my example, as I follow the example of Christ"* (1 Cor. 11:1, NIV). This is basically the same principle as described above. Don't follow your spouse if he is not following Christ. You are personally responsible to God for your own actions, therefore you must obey Christ. To follow Christ instead of the command of a disobedient spouse is fitting in the Lord.

Scripture is absolutely clear that when you are in a relationship in which one partner is out of control, disobedient, or abusive, you should flee if they refuse to change. Let me give you some other examples from the Word that illustrate this principle. When King Saul was out of control and ready to kill David, what did David do? He fled from his presence. He didn't stay there as a submissive subject to Saul (1 Sam. 19:10). David used common sense and fled from this unsafe situation. In the same manner, if your mate is seeking to harm you, common sense would tell you to flee. David's example gives you plenty of biblical proof that fleeing would be perfectly acceptable to God.

Take Joseph for another example. When Potiphar's wife pressured him to have sexual relations with her, he resisted vigorously. Day after day she pressured him, and day after day he resisted. Finally she tried to physically force him to sleep with her. What did Joseph do? Did he submit to a woman who had authority over him? No. He fled from her presence, leaving his coat in her hands (Gen. 39:1-12). This is an excellent example of an individual in authority over another who was demanding disobedience to God's Word. Joseph's conscience could allow no such thing. He would not submit, but removed himself from the situation. Likewise, if your spouse is requiring you or forcing you to do anything contrary to God's Word, you must, for conscience' sake, resist, and if need be, flee.

10. <u>What are your options?</u> This is a very difficult question to answer due to the multitude of potential circumstances. There are no easy answers to this question, but here is a summary of your best options.

A. First, get some good counsel from your pastor or an elder in your church. You need an objective third party outside of friends and other family members to counsel you.

B. Next, confront your spouse according to the principles of Matthew 18:15-17. I have seen this method work countless times, and it is the best way to see real results. If you love your spouse and want to gain the relationship back again, don't sell this method short.

C. As much as possible, stay together. Usually people are too quick to want to leave and separate. I would not encourage this unless there is an unsafe or physically abusive situation occurring. Then, by all means, separation is an essential step. But if there is no physical abuse or a threat to your safety, then stay there because you are just a little closer to the situation and have that much more opportunity to minister to your spouse. Paul encouraged believing mates to stay with their partner for a very specific purpose. *"For how do your know, O wife, whether you will save your husband? Or how do you know, O husband, whether you will save your wife"* (1 Cor. 7:16)? Staying within the home also gives you the best opportunity to see if real changes are actually occurring once there is repentance. It is much more difficult to do this if you are separated.

D. If someone has to leave, let it be the offending spouse. It is important to ask your pastor or an elder to be with you if you have to ask your mate to leave the house. Again, don't try and handle this by yourself. You need help and the encouragement of others. This is the reasoning of Matthew 18:15-17. You may also have to get a restraining order from the court to give some muscle to your request for your spouse to leave, especially if your spouse is physically abusive. There is nothing unbiblical about getting a restraining order. When Paul the apostle believed he was in danger of losing his life unjustly, he appealed to Caesar (Acts

25:1-12). The legal system has been put in place by God and ordained to help you in situations just like this (Rom. 13:1-4). Remember, if separation must occur, continue to govern your decisions from that day forward with the goal of seeking reconciliation as taught in 1 Corinthians 7:10, 11. Do this until it is obvious there is no remedy.

E. Establish clear standards for reconciliation and the return of your spouse. Sit down with your pastor and establish clearly in your mind what biblical steps your spouse must take before they can come home. Example: If your spouse is committing adultery. You should require:

1) the adulterous relationship be terminated immediately
2) acknowledgment from your spouse that this action was sin as well as a request for forgiveness
3) agreement that your spouse will go for personal counseling
4) marital counseling

One of the biggest mistakes I have seen people make is allowing their mate to come home too quickly after some tears and convincing words of repentance.

Many times the same situation occurs within a week and the whole process begins again because the spouse that has been out of control has not had any time to really deal with his or her personal problems in counseling, and therefore has no idea of how to change or to maintain that change.

11. <u>Don't believe anything but sustained action</u>. This is the bottom line for any reconciliation in these extreme cases. In your own life, think of the times that you have promised to take some action and then failed to fulfill your commitment. Words can be easy to say but are difficult to live. The same thing is true for every other human being on this planet, including your spouse. When a spouse is out of the house and wanting to return as quickly as possible, they may say or do anything in order to come home. Words alone cannot produce the lasting changes that are necessary.

My encouragement to you who are struggling with these very difficult circumstances is to look for and believe only sustained action. This is where the best hope for lasting change will be found. Actions speak louder than words. This is a true and biblical statement.

With regard to salvation, Jesus said, "*Not everyone who <u>says</u> to Me, Lord, Lord, shall enter the kingdom of heaven, but he who <u>does</u> the will of My Father in heaven*" (Matt. 7:21, underline added). This passage reveals that God is not fooled by religious words and clever clichés. He wants to see action, not just hear words. Jesus declared that the only means of entrance into His house is doing what's right, not saying what's right. This important concept will enable you to always discern what a false profession looks like.

The apostle James also believed that it was easy to make a profession of faith in Christ. He taught that *"faith without works is dead"* (James 2:19). Therefore, if anyone professes faith, you must see action to prove it. James put it another way when he said that men must be *"doers of the word, and not hearers only, deceiving yourselves"* (James 1:22). It is easy to deceive ourselves in this manner. It means nothing that your mate hears the correct counsel if you can't see it being demonstrated in their life. Let your mate put feet on their faith and walk their profession for a while. Then have your spouse go to counseling with you and see if there is real honesty and repentance expressed there. Remember, real change must be seen in attitudes, words, and actions. This is what is required by God of all who come to Him.

When Paul preached to the Gentiles, he told them *"that they should repent, turn to God, and do works befitting repentance"* (Acts 26:20). In other words, if there is true repentance, then there must be works and action that prove it. The word *befitting* means "to take an action that corresponds to the profession that has been made." Action is the only thing you can believe. As Solomon said, a man speaks with his feet (Prov. 6:13, KJV).

Jesus taught this same principle in relation to himself. When the Lord asked people to believe in Him, He encouraged them to examine two things. *"Do you not believe that I am in the Father, and the Father in Me? The words that I speak to you I do not speak on My own authority; but the Father who dwells in Me does the works. Believe Me that I am in the Father and the Father in Me, or else believe Me for the sake of the works themselves"* (John 14:10, 11, underline added). It's very interesting that Christ himself didn't want people to believe just *His words.* He wanted the people to look at *His works* to see if the two agreed. Were His works in harmony with His words? Were His works in harmony with the prophetic Scriptures? Jesus believed that an examination of His life on the basis of these two criteria would reveal the truth.

Therefore, do not listen so much to what your spouse says in the reconciliation process, but more to the action they take after the talking is done. Is the behavior in harmony with the words? Is it in harmony with God's Word? If you do this test, it will keep you from listening to fair speeches, only to be let down again and again. If you require your mate to take concrete action, you have the best possibility for seeing a lasting change.

May God give you the grace to discern the truth regarding your partner's willingness to walk a biblical path, effecting true reconciliation. Once your marriage is reconciled, labor to build real relationship with your mate using the latter chapters of this book as your guide. My prayers are with you!

Covenant Keepers

A Marriage Ministry For Your Church
"She is your companion and your wife by covenant" Mal. 2:14

Covenant Keepers, a ministry of Pastor Steve Carr, is a quarterly publication dedicated to strengthening marriages through the teaching of Biblical principles alone. Each article addresses a specific area within the martial relationship and brings powerful and practical solutions to the problems couples face.

This publication is presently used by hundreds of churches as bulletin inserts, additional reading material for couples engaged in counseling, or as a study guide for married couples' fellowships.

Covenant Keepers is only dispersed to churches who in turn reproduce the material for use within their church body. If your church would like to be added to the Covenant Keepers mailing list, please have your pastor request such in writing to Covenant Keepers, 1133 Maple Street, Arroyo Grande, Ca 93420. Because the churches do their own reproducing, there is no charge for these publications. Back issues are available upon request.

Couples and counselors who would
like additional marriage resources
by Pastor Steve Carr may visit:
http://www.covenantkeepers.org

Order Form

Postal orders:
Pastor Steve Carr, PO Box 463, Arroyo Grande, CA 93421

Telephone orders: (805) 489-9088
Have your VISA or MasterCard ready.

E-mail orders: Send all mailing and credit card information to:
scarrck@lightspeed.net

Please send *Married And How To Stay That Way* **to:**

Name: _____

Address: _____

City: _____ State: _____ Zip: _____

Telephone: (_____) _____

Book Price: $12.99 in U.S. dollars.

Sales Tax: Please add 7.75% for books shipped to California addresses.

Shipping: $4.00 for the first three books and $1.00 for each additional book to cover shipping and handling within US, Canada, and Mexico. International orders add $10.00 for the first book and $2.00 for each additional book.

Payment:
❑ **Check**
❑ **Credit card:** ❑ **VISA** ❑ **MasterCard**
Card number:

_____

Name on card: _____ Exp. Date: ___ / _____

Signature _____

Quantity Discounts Available · Please call for information
(805) 489-9088